Build the Ultimate Custom PC

Build the Ultimate Custom PC

Adrian W. Kingsley-Hughes
Kathie Kingsley-Hughes

WILEY

Wiley Publishing, Inc.

For Bruce and Joyce — thanks to for letting us spread computer parts all over your house while we took the photos for this book. Oh, and thanks for all the cups of tea!

For our kids — you really are the best!

Build the Ultimate Custom PC

Published by
Wiley Publishing, Inc.
10475 Crosspoint Boulevard
Indianapolis, IN 46256
www.wiley.com

Copyright © 2006 by Wiley Publishing, Inc., Indianapolis, Indiana

Published simultaneously in Canada

ISBN-13: 978-0-471-76099-3
ISBN-10: 0-471-76099-4

Manufactured in the United States of America

10 9 8 7 6 5 4 3 2 1

1B/RW/RR/QV/IN

For general information on our other products and services or to obtain technical support, please contact our Customer Care Department within the U.S. at (800) 762-2974, outside the U.S. at (317) 572-3993 or fax (317) 572-4002.

Wiley also publishes its books in a variety of electronic formats. Some content that appears in print may not be available in electronic books.

Library of Congress Cataloging-in-Publication Data

Kingsley-Hughes, Adrian.
 Build the ultimate custom PC / Adrian W. Kingsley-Hughes, Kathie Kingsley-Hughes.
  p. cm.
 Includes index.
 ISBN-13: 978-0-471-76099-3 (paper/website)
 ISBN-10: 0-471-76099-4 (paper/website)
 1. Microcomputers—Design and construction—Amateurs' manuals. I. Kingsley-Hughes, Kathie. II. Title.
 TK9969.K56 2006
 621.39'16—dc22

                    2005026412

About the Authors

Adrian Kingsley-Hughes and **Kathie Kingsley-Hughes** have written several successful technical/PC books on a variety of computer and IT-related topics. They have also developed numerous successful training manuals and Internet-based courses over nearly a decade.

Along with their day-to-day work, Adrian and Kathie also currently teach online courses for several training providers. Adrian also teaches several highly successful online courses for Barnes & Noble University. Together, they have produced courses and materials that have been used extensively by many Fortune 500 companies and leading universities.

PCs are something that Adrian and Kathie are surrounded by, and when they're working they're either in front of their PCs or tinkering with them and taking them apart.

Put simply, they're both geeks!

Credits

Acquisitions Editor
Katie Mohr

Development Editor
Jennifer Eberhardt

Technical Editor
Jason Cross

Production Editor
Felicia Robinson

Copy Editor
Foxxe Editorial Services

Editorial Manager
Mary Beth Wakefield

Production Manager
Tim Tate

Vice President and Executive Group Publisher
Richard Swadley

Vice President and Executive Publisher
Joseph B. Wikert

Project Coordinator
Ryan Steffen

Graphics and Production Specialists
Denny Hager
Jennifer Heleine
Stephanie D. Jumper
Barbara Moore

Quality Control Technicians
John Greenough
Brian H. Walls

Proofreading and Indexing
TECHBOOKS Production Services

Contents at a Glance

Contents

Part III: Starting and Testing Your PC   275

Chapter 19: Everything You Need to Know about Warranties and Beyond

Part IV: Appendices

Acknowledgments

A book like this is never the work of just the authors. It comes about as a result of a lot of hard work and the collaboration of dozens of people. The names on the cover represent just a small part of the equation. As authors, we feel that we are standing on the shoulders of a great many people who don't get their names on the cover.

Knowing where to start thanking people can be difficult, but with this book it's not. First and foremost, our thanks and appreciation go out to Katie Mohr, our tireless, hard-working acquisitions editor, and Wiley who first approached us with the opportunity to write this book. The amount of work and effort you put into this book Katie was just amazing, and the final product is infinitely better thanks to your input into the project.

Thanks also go to Chris Webb for his input in the early stages. Thanks for putting up with what must have been dozens of different "versions" of the book proposal in the early stages and for working through them and providing good, solid feedback.

Our thanks also go to our excellent development editor, Jennifer Eberhardt, who suggested a number of improvements and changes. Your feedback was very valuable and it was a real pleasure to work with you!

Many thanks go to Jason Cross at ExtremeTech for his excellent technical review skills. We really appreciate that you found the time to work through the manuscripts and suggested some important changes! Thanks Jason!

There are a whole bunch of folks over at Wiley who we haven't mentioned — people who have worked anonymously in the background laying out the book, indexing, proofreading, advertising, signing checks — we appreciate your valuable contribution to this title.

A book like this also gets a lot of help from the outside, and we'd like to give special thanks to a few people who really helped. Special thanks go to Gemma McAllister and Gill Smith at Crucial Technology, Shelby Koontz at Waggener Edstrom, which handles Microsoft PR and Erin Hartin at Maxtor.

No electrons were harmed in the making of this book, but some did have to work extra hard in order to meet deadlines. Also, a power supply was found to be "dead on arrival," which was disposed of decently.

Introduction

Welcome to *Build the Ultimate Custom PC*! If you're reading this, then chances are that you're either looking at this book in a book store or you've bought the book and you've started reading it (the third option might be that you're waiting for parts to build your PC, you're a little bored and decided to read the introduction!). If you've already bought this book, then congratulations on making a good choice! If you're reading this in a bookstore, then feel free to keep on reading!

There are literally millions of PCs in use all around the world right now, but the sad fact is that most people put up with a PC that they've bought either from a store or by mail order, from a catalog or more likely nowadays over the net. These companies assemble computers by the millions, box them, and ship them with the ultimate goal of making as much profit as possible for each PC shipped. Corners are cut in terms of product quality and accessories (such as system discs and drivers), and there's little room for customization. Most companies offer technical support and a warranty, but if you check out the net, you'll find thousands of people who are totally dissatisfied with the PC they ended up with and have nowhere to turn for help.

So, what's the solution? Build your own PC of course! That way you take control over your PC right from the start and get the parts you want, not the cheapest parts the PC manufacturer chooses. You also get a decent warranty because each part you buy comes with a separate warranty (and usually technical support), so you don't have to settle for the generic tech support you'd otherwise get from the people who assembled the PC.

And building your own PC isn't hard! In fact, it's surprisingly easy! We'll introduce you to all the parts, explain what they do, guide you through which parts you need, and then show you how to put them all together to make a working PC.

Who This Book Is For

This book is basically for anyone who wants to build a PC for him- or herself. If you can handle a screwdriver, then you can build a PC!

If you've never built a PC before or even taken the case off your existing PC, then we've written this book especially with you in mind. We'll guide you through what you need and what each part does. You will learn how to assemble the parts and then how to test and troubleshoot problems, should the need arise.

Those of you with a little more PC tinkering experience are also welcome to follow this book. Building a PC from the ground up is different from upgrading a PC, and we'll show you in detail where to start building your own PC, what parts you need, and in what order to assemble them.

One of the biggest hurdles faced when building a PC is the worry that you are going to spend money on the wrong parts and be stuck with a pile of components that don't fit together. Don't worry about this because we'll make sure that you only get what you need and what works! Likewise, if you're worried about damaging components by handling them, then fret no more — we'll show you the right way to handle PC parts!

Just a note — if you're a hardware specialist or you've built so many PCs that you can now assemble them blindfolded with one hand tied behind your back (not recommended!), then this book isn't written for you. You might, however, find some of the test procedures interesting, and it might help you to clarify the differences between particular technologies, but on the whole, we've not written this book with you in mind — sorry!

What You'll Find in This Book

Put simply, this book covers everything you need to know to build a PC. We'll start by looking at all the components that go into a PC. We'll cover all the essential components that are core to a PC and examine their relationship to one another and how the parts come together to create a PC.

This book is about building a PC, a normal, regular PC. Whether you end up with a budget PC or a super-PC is up to you and how much you're willing to spend. A PC is a PC, and we leave it up to you to decide what kind of PC you want that to be.

There's a lot of jargon in the PC world, and we will lift the veil on the jargon surrounding the components so that you can make the right choices when buying the parts for your own custom PC.

Buying parts can be quite an experience, and there's scope for things to go wrong. We'll show you how to make the right choices and what you should do if you have a problem.

We'll show you how to take care of your components and how to assemble them properly so that there's no risk of damage — to you or the parts!

In this book, we're only going to be building one PC and chances are that your PC is going to be quite different from ours. However, there's no need to worry about this because the parts you have and the parts that we use are going to be similar enough that it doesn't matter.

After you've assembled your PC, the next step will be to bring it to life. Chances are that it will come to life without any problems, but just in case you do run into problems, we'll look at the most likely causes of trouble after the build and give you step-by-step instructions on how to solve the problem and get your system up and running quickly!

After the Build

Most people get such a real jazz out of building a PC that they feel that they want to share the experience with others. This is perfectly normal. Given the number of PCs in existence nowadays only a tiny fraction of these have been built by their owners, so building your own PC is still something special. You might want to document your PC building experience and share with others what you learned during the building and testing process — a good way to do this is to start a website or blog about it. If you've got a digital camera, so much the better, you can show everyone what you did and the PC you ended up with!

After you've built your PC, we'd love to hear from you! When you get the chance visit us at `www.kingsley-hughes.com/build-it` or `www.pcdoctor-guide.com` and drop us a note — we'd love to hear from you! If you have a website, blog or photos on the web, send us a link. We'd love to see how you take the instructions in this book and customize them to your needs!

How This Book Is Structured

As we mentioned, we're going to walk you through everything you need to know to be able to build a PC.

In Chapter 1, "Staying Safe," you will get all the information you need to keep yourself and all the parts that you are going to buy and handle safe. This is vital reading for anyone planning to build a PC!

In Chapter 2, "Choosing the Tools You Need," you will discover what you need to be able to build a PC (it's probably a lot less than you imagine!).

In Chapter 3, "Choosing a Suitable Case and Power Supply," you will look at the important considerations to bear in mind when choosing a case and power supply for your PC.

In Chapter 4, "Choosing a CPU and Motherboard," you will get all the information that you need to make the right choices when it comes to buying the motherboard and CPU for your PC — the two most crucial parts of the build.

Chapter 5, "Choosing the Right RAM," goes on to look at what kind of RAM you need for your PC and how much, and gives you information about making the right choices that will allow you to get the best performance out of your system.

In Chapter 6, "Choosing Hard Drives and Floppy Drives," you will look at the storage needs of your new PC.

A modern PC isn't complete without an optical drive, and in Chapter 7, "Choosing CD/DVD Drives," we look at what optical drives are, what choices there are available, and how to choose the right kind of drive.

In Chapter 8, "Choosing Video Adapters and Monitors," we demystify video adaptor cards and look at what you need to know when buying a video adaptor card for your PC. We also examine the pros and cons of using a video adaptor that might be built onto your motherboard.

Chapter 9, "Choosing Sound Capability," looks at what you need to bear in mind when adding a sound system to your PC, and also examines the pros and cons of using a sound card integrated onto a motherboard.

No PC is complete without a raft of fittings and cables to hold it together and hook up components with. In Chapter 10, "A Tour of Cables and Fittings," you will take a tour of the variety of cables and fittings inside a modern PC.

By Chapter 11, "Checking and Testing Components," we are assuming that you've bought all the parts that you need and that you're now ready to begin building your PC. However, before you start it's important to check and test the parts in case of defects or failures. This chapter shows you how!

Chapter 12, "Top 10 Things You Don't Want to Forget," is, just as the title says, a list of the common things that people forget when building a PC.

Now the chapter you've been waiting for! In Chapter 13, "Assembling the Case and Fitting the PSU," you begin the PC building process, carry out any assembly needed on the case and fit the power supply unit.

Chapter 14, "Fitting the Basic Parts," cranks up the building several notches when you add the motherboard, CPU, CPU cooler, RAM, and video card into the PC. We show you how to do this in simple steps.

In Chapter 15, "Adding Storage," you will add a hard drive and a floppy drive to your system. We show you how to fit and wire-in the devices.

In Chapter 16, "Fire Up and Burn In" you will bring your PC to life and check that what you've done so far works. This will be an exciting phase in the build process, and it's where all your research and hard work pay off! Just in case things go wrong, in Chapter 16 we also cover troubleshooting and what to do if your system doesn't actually come on!

In Chapter 17, "Final Tweaks and Installing Windows XP," we'll show you how to load Microsoft Windows XP onto your new system!

Chapter 18, "Check and Test, Check and Test Again!" is all about testing and checking, and things to do before you button up the case.

Chapter 19, "Everything You Need to Know about Warranties" tells you everything you need to know about warranties and what to do if your PC goes wrong.

What You Need to Use This Book

You don't need much to build your own PC. The two most important things that you will need are a screwdriver and a sense of adventure. Another thing that you will need is some spare time to read the book, do some research, shop for parts and actually build the PC.

Some other things that can come in handy are a grounding strap to protect your parts from electrostatic discharge (don't worry if you don't know what this is yet, by the end of Chapter 1 you will!) and a place to store your parts and build the PC.

A place with a dedicated workbench is handy, but people have built PCs in their living rooms, bedrooms, kitchens, greenhouses, garden sheds, attics; you can build a PC pretty much any-where, including the outdoors if the weather is nice and there's not much dust — in fact, about the only place we'd recommend you not try to build a PC is in the bathroom! For those still reading in a book shop, they probably won't let you build a PC in there either. . . .

We hope that you enjoy building your PC! Remember, take your time, enjoy the process and have fun!

Choosing Components for Your PC

part

Staying Safe

Whenever we poll people who want to build a PC for the reasons why they haven't gone ahead and researched the topic more or even taken the plunge and actually built a PC, the top response is always "Safety."

This is not without good reason.

PCs run on electricity, and most of us learn from an early age that electricity is dangerous. Carelessness with electricity can kill, maim, injure, and cause a great deal of property damage. That alone might seem like a good reason why PC building should be left to the professionals. Truth is, though, that it is possible to make building a PC as safe as, if not safer than, changing a light bulb or using an extension cord.

Before looking at the tools and techniques involved in building your own PC, it is important to spend a little time looking at safety. Building your own PC is fun, and a big part of having fun is being able to carry out the build knowing that your working practices are safe.

 Please read through this chapter before attempting to build a PC of your own. Okay, you're eager to get going and a chapter all about safety doesn't sound all that compelling, but your safety — and the safety of those around you — are of paramount importance. We don't want to lose any of you in mid-build!

Also of great importance is the safety of the PC components you have bought. A millisecond's carelessness can cost you hundreds of dollars.

In this chapter, you will look at the dangers that face you and the PC components you will be handling. Also, you will learn how you can avoid the dangers and build a PC safely.

A Breakdown of the Dangers

The key to safety is knowledge. Knowing what the dangers are in the first place. It's easy to understand why some people are really jazzed about the idea of building a PC but worry about the dangers (maybe you reading this right now are one of these people).

If you already are a PC owner, you probably have noticed that the back of the unit came with a few warning stickers that make proclamations of death and destruction. If you've ever gone as far as cracking open the case on your PC and taken a look inside (perhaps to carry out some repairs or maybe an upgrade), then you will more than likely have noticed a few more warnings with a similar theme.

 Note   You will typically find warning stickers on the PC's power supply unit, the most dangerous part inside a PC.

These warnings are there for good reason. A PC that's plugged into the electrical supply can, without doubt, be a dangerous environment. But the main thing to realize when building a PC is that for 95% of the time, the PC being built won't be plugged into the power supply anyway, making it safe to work inside.

But what about the other 5% of the time?

Don't worry! This book shows you how, with care, you can make it safe to have the system plugged in and running while the case isn't all buttoned up.

You can break down the dangers associated with building a PC into two categories:

- The dangers to you and those around you
- The dangers to the components that you are assembling into a PC

Let's begin by looking at the most important of these — the dangers to you!

Personal Safety

Inside a PC is a whole host of dangers awaiting you. The four big, most serious dangers are:

- High-voltage things
- Hot things
- Sharp things
- Spinning things

There are also some other miscellaneous dangers that face you too, but before we come to them let's take a closer look at the big four.

High-Voltage Things

Without a doubt the biggest danger that you face when inside a PC is from high voltage. PCs are designed to take in voltage ranging from 110 volts to 250 volts, which is then converted into lower voltages that will be used by the motherboard, hard drives, optical drives (CD or DVD drives), and other devices, such as fans, that all live and work inside the PC.

It's no joke or exaggeration to say that high voltage can kill. An electric shock in real life isn't like it's depicted in the movies where someone touches a live wire, is thrown 30 feet away and then gets up, face black, clothes smoldering but otherwise OK. According to the National Institutes of Health, some 1,000 people die in the United States each year because of electrocution. Electricity kills by stopping the heart and breathing, and it can kill instantly. If you are lucky enough to survive contact with electricity, then you are likely to suffer from burns and nerve, muscle, and tissue damage.

We're not telling you this to scare you; on the contrary, we're giving you the dangers straight so that you understand them and are able to know what is safe to do and what is not. Everything that we show or tell you in this book is 100% tried, tested, and safe. Follow the instructions and you'll be OK.

If you are ever in any doubt, pause and reread the instructions.

The best way to protect yourself from electrocution is to limit your exposure to electricity. Most of the time when you are working on your PC you don't need it plugged into the electrical supply. That way, no power is going into the PC and the dangers of electrocution are eliminated.

There may be times when you will want to run your PC without having the case all buttoned up. For example, you might want to check out whether all the fans inside the case are spinning properly. The best advice here is to keep your hands, head, and all hand tools out of the case. If you want to look at something, do so from a distance and use a flashlight to get a better view.

Whenever a PC is plugged into the electrical supply without having the case buttoned up, remember the old adage of "look but don't touch."

The biggest danger from electrocution comes after a PC has been plugged into the electrical supply and is then switched off. It's very easy to forget that it's been on and still connected and then set about to work inside. A visual marker that the PC is connected to the power outlet can be very handy. Here are two good techniques:

- **Tape a fluorescent bit of plastic, paper, or fabric to the power connector.** You'll find the power connector at the back of the PC. By taping something to the power connector, you have a handy visual reminder that your PC is still plugged in and live. Unplug the power socket from the back of the PC, and you make it safe again.

- **Equip your workplace with a hanger for the PC power cable.** For this, a bent over bit of wire will do just fine. Make this a visible spot, and remember to hang the power cord on the hanger when working inside the PC (the fluorescent plastic, paper, or fabric tag makes it even easier to spot when the PC is safe!).

The following list includes additional safety tips:

- **Let others know what you are doing.** It always helps if everyone else is clear about what you are doing. This way those around you will be appreciative of the risks that you are taking and hopefully ease off any practical jokes (those "pretend" electric shock gags get real old, real fast, anyway). Also, this way you get other people to keep an eye on you while you are working just in case anything does go wrong.

- **Keep liquids away from the PC work area.** Spilling water or other liquids into a PC can cause short circuits and electrocution, as can working in a wet or damp environment. Wet rags, tools, and work surfaces can also conduct electricity. Keep liquids away from the work area, and keep the area clean and dry.

- **Use insulated electrical tools.** These tools are the types that have a rubber or plastic handle that can't conduct electricity. No matter how careful you are, accidents can happen. These tools can offer you protection against accidents but shouldn't be used as a substitute for taking the proper safety steps.

Not all plastic or rubber handled tools offer protection from electricity. If you want to buy safety tools then make sure that the handle clearly states that the tool is insulated and also what the rating is (usually "electricians" tools protect the user from up to 1,000 or 10,000 volts, depending on the quality of the tool). Chapter 2, "Choosing the Tools You Need," takes a more detailed look at the tools you should be using to build your PC.

Hot Things

Where there's electricity, there's usually heat. A PC that's been switched on for a few minutes can generate a lot of heat, especially from the power supply, hard drives, and CPU, and this heat can be enough to give you a nasty burn. Getting a burn on the back of your hand while trying to do something can be bad enough, but it can also mean that you drop things or knock against things and cause further damage to your hand or your PC.

As a general rule of thumb, if a PC has been switched on for more than 5 minutes, then it's a good idea to wait 5 minutes before setting to work inside it, and if it's been on for an hour or more, then wait at least 10 minutes. Taking the side panels off the case will help it to cool down quicker.

If you want to test for hot components, then a good trick is to use the back of your hand. By moving the back of your hand close to the metal surfaces, you have a good, safe way to judge how hot components are. This method is far better than using your fingertips, which you don't want to burn because you'll be needing them later, and it's hard to work with a bandage on!

Sharp Things

The inside of even the best PC case contains a number of sharp metal edges and corners all waiting to catch you. There are some things that you can do to help reduce the number of sharps that are present (check out Chapters 3, "Choosing a Suitable Case and Power Supply," and 13, "Assembling the Case and Fitting the PSU"), but no matter how carefully you choose a case and how much you try to remove edges, some will still remain (the edges and corners of hard drives are particularly nasty!).

The best advice for working with sharp things? Take care and take your time. Working on a cool PC makes accidents from sharps less likely, too. Snatching your hand away from something hot is the number one cause of PC-related cuts, so it's another good reason to give the system a cool-down period before setting to work on it.

Spinning Things

Many people are surprised by the number of exposed "spinning" things that are inside a PC. These are fans of one sort of another, and most are quite unlike other fans that you have in your home because many, if not all, have no wire guard to keep your fingers away from them.

However, there is little danger to fingers from the fans that live and work inside a PC. All of them will have blades made of light plastic, and while some might be big and spin quite fast (up to a rate of several thousand revolutions per minute), they have little power behind them. You would hardly be able to feel the blades hit you, let alone have them cause you any damage.

In reality, the biggest danger from fans is getting your hair or clothing caught up in them. Keep your hair and clothing tidy, and keep them away from fans when they are in operation.

Creating a Safe Working Area

Another key to safety is a having a good working environment. There's no need for you to dedicate a whole room or garage to building a PC, but having a good workspace makes the job of building a PC safer and easier. Figure 1-1 shows the wrong environment for building a PC, and Figure 1-2 shows the right one.

FIGURE 1-1: The wrong PC-building environment.

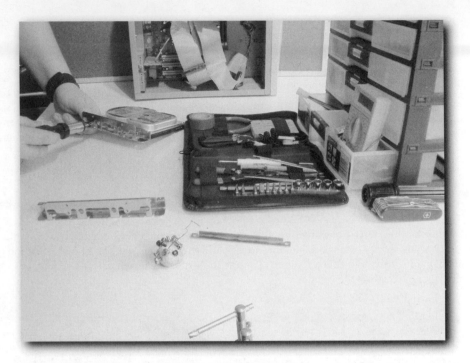

FIGURE 1-2: **An example of a good PC-building environment.**

Here are the top requirements of a good, safe working area:

- **Have an assigned work space and work area.** Pick out the spot where you are going to work. Your *work area* is the place you're going to be working in (corner of the living room, kitchen counter, bench in the garage), while the *work space* is the area you are going to be moving about in when working in the work area.

- **Find a large enough work area.** The smallest work area we recommend is 3 ft by 2 ft. A table or bench is ideal. Ideally, you should be able to leave things on the bench or table for several hours of days until you are finished. If this isn't possible, then make sure you have a space that you can pack everything away into when you're done for the day.

 Throw a dust sheet over the project when you're not working on it to keep contamination to a minimum.

- **Do not eat or drink around the PC as it is being built.** A spilled soda or a poorly placed peanut butter and jelly sandwich can cause a major setback, not to mention damage.

- **Set up a bright and well lit work area.** Natural lighting is best because it is diffuse and doesn't cast harsh, dark shadows, but artificial lighting will do if you can't work near a bright window. Augment what lighting you have present with a good flashlight.

- **Be sure to have a power outlet nearby.** Ideally, it should have a good grounding point nearby too (such as a water pipe or radiator).

- **Avoid working on carpeted surfaces, if possible.** A carpeted work area increases the static electricity that you generate when walking about. However, if you can't avoid this, don't worry, we'll show you how you can deal with static charge build-up in the section "Electrostatic Discharge (ESD)" later in this chapter.

- **Cover the work area with white paper.** This makes it easier to see things like little screws when you drop them. Also, the white encourages you to be tidy and others to keep away!

- **Keep children and pets out of the work space.** We agree that pets in the work space are a bad idea for a variety of reasons, but kids might be interested in what's going on, and both you and your child might find the PC-building process interesting and educational. If so, then a good idea is to set up an observation area where they can watch what's going on in safety and without getting in the way, messing about with things, or stepping on expensive electronics.

- **Keep all the tools and equipment you will need close at hand in the work area.** The less you walk about, the less likely you are to knock stuff over or trip. Building a PC involves having cables and boxes in and around the work area. Be careful that these aren't in places where you can trip over them.

- **Keep the work area tidy and clean and free from liquids.** Liquids are especially nasty, as a small amount of liquid can go very far indeed!

- **Keep a small first aid kit and fire extinguisher nearby — just in case!** Outfit your first aid kit to deal with small cuts, and make sure that you have plenty of bandages in the kit!

Dressing for Safety

Just as important as the work space is how you dress when you are working on a PC. Don't worry, you won't need to invest in a new wardrobe just so that you can build a PC. Just follow these simple tips:

- **Wear cotton clothing and rubber-soled shoes (such as sneakers).** These are best because they reduce the build-up of static charge.

- **Avoid loose clothing.** Sleeves, collars, scarves, and ties are a bad idea, because they can catch on the edges of the equipment. The absolute best clothing for PC building is a boiler suit!

- **Be careful if you wear glasses.** You don't want your glasses falling into the workings of the PC. You can get an elasticized band, such as a sports band, that fits around them to hold them in place if they are a little loose and you're worried about them falling off.

- **Remove all jewelry if at all possible.** Jewelry such as rings, necklaces, bracelets, and pendants can cause short circuits that can damage delicate components. If you have rings that you can't or don't want to remove, then cover them with insulating or surgical tape.

- **Put long hair in a ponytail or use hair clips.** You don't want that hair caught in anything!

- **Use thin cotton gloves.** Cotton gloves come in handy if you are worried about touching something hot or with a sharp edge. Make sure that the gloves are cotton and not synthetic (the last thing you want is hot, melted nylon or polyester on your hands!).

- **Wear a barrier cream.** A PC, no matter how short a period it has been switched on for, tends to gather dust and dirt quickly. This dust can be quite an effective skin irritant, so if you have sensitive skin, you might want to invest in a special barrier cream (a special cream available from hardware stores that you rub into your skin, which protects it from dust and chemicals, that you wash out when finished) to rub into your hands. Wash your hands after you've been working on a PC.

Component Safety

By now you should know how to keep yourself, your family, and your pets from being electrocuted, prevent your hair getting caught in the fans in your PC, and eliminate the risks of strangulation from neckties and scarves. But it's not just your safety that you have to be worried about — you also have to care for the safety of the components that you are going to be handling and that are going to become integral parts of your PC.

Dangers You Can See

Here are some general common-sense rules that you can follow to avoid component troubles:

- Don't drop components. This is the number one cause of component damage.

- Don't bend or flex components. No matter how sturdy a circuit board looks, it takes very little pressure to crack it or pop off an important component.

- Don't put components down on top of one another or on metal surfaces.

- Keep components clean and dry.

The easiest way to accomplish all of the above is to store components in their original packaging until needed. This packaging is designed to protect the components on their trip from the factory where they were made to the store selling them, and it's usually so good that it can protect the contents from the biggest test of all — snail mail delivery!

Tip

There is a very good chance that you will be buying at least some of the parts for your PC via mail order. Mail order is by far the cheapest way to buy components unless you are really lucky and live nearby to a very good supplier. However, component damage in transit is a real problem.

Check all items you receive carefully. What you are looking for are components that arrive well packaged and in an undamaged state. Look for signs of damage, both at the packing stage (improperly packaged items, items packed loose) and for damage in transit (ripped, torn, or crushed packaging, items repackaged by the carrier or foot/tire prints on the package — yes, we've seen it all!).

If anything looks damaged then either refuse to sign for it, or, if you have to sign for it write "NOT EXAMINED" clearly next to your name/signature and get in touch with the seller.

If, during the build, you think that you may have damaged a component through dropping it or handling it badly, then make a note of this. Damage caused can be difficult, if not impossible to spot, so if you have problems later on, having information on components that might have been damaged can save you a lot of time and energy in tracking down the fault.

Unseen Dangers

If you go about dropping components and flexing components to test their strength, then it's pretty obvious that you're asking for trouble. However, there are a number of unseen dangers that can quickly and silently damage your new PC components. Specifically, these dangers stem from:

- Magnetic fields
- Electrostatic discharge (ESD)

Magnetic Fields

Back in the days when floppy disks were popular, people were much better about keeping magnets away from the PCs because they knew that even a weak magnet could damage or completely erase the disk. Now that most of us have shifted from magnetic media to optical media (such as CDs or DVDs), we're far less careful about such things.

It's true that taking a magnet near a working PC won't cause massive damage to it. A magnet might make the screen display go funny, and you might have to switch the monitor off and back on again a few times to dissipate the magnetic field by a process called *degaussing*, which occurs every time you switch on a monitor (tube-based monitors, not the newer flat panels), but it's not likely to cause any long-term damage or data loss. In fact, a PC has a number of magnets inside it, ranging from small ones inside fans to bigger ones in speakers and massive and powerful ones inside the hard drives. However, it's still a good idea to keep magnets away from the build area for these reasons.

- The magnetic field might damage something. It's not worth taking a risk.
- Magnets (especially strong magnets) can magnetize other metallic items. This can cause them to attract one another and come flying together at high speed. These can be damaging high-speed collisions.

Note The reasoning behind not having magnetized screwdrivers is similar—the magnetic field of a screwdriver tip is going to be pretty small, but magnetic screwdriver tips can be attracted toward other metallic objects at quite high speed, damaging delicate components along the way.

Electrostatic Discharge (ESD)

Electrostatic discharge, otherwise known as ESD, is a real danger to electronic devices. It is a swift, silent killer.

Here's why.

As you walk about, you rub your feet against the floor, and your clothing rubs against itself. This rubbing generates static electricity. The process is similar to how a balloon rubbed against a T-shirt will stick to a ceiling or how a Van der Graaf generator works by having a roller that rubs against brushes that both generate and collect the charge.

The human body is a pretty good insulator and can generate thousands of volts of static electricity. You've probably experienced it — you walk along a carpeted floor and go to open a door and ZAP! It might just seem like fun (or an annoyance) to you but that single "ZAP!" is at least 3,000 volts (below 3,000 volts you don't get a spark), and probably a lot more.

Note The human body can carry around with it 25,000 volts of static charge easily. How are 25,000 volts of power typically lethal when 25,000 volts of static build-up aren't? The reason is that the power the current-producing capability of an ESD is less than a thousandth of an amp. This is why at 120 volts AC, 1 amp of current is lethal, but for ESD 25,000 volts DC, the microamps of current produced are not.

So, why is static electricity so damaging? Let's stop and think about it for a moment. The typical PC component runs at between 3 and 12 volts, but they can be damaged by anything between 10 and 30 volts of static discharge. Remember, you don't see anything or feel anything until the charge build-up is somewhere near 3,000 volts! To make matters worse, it's not just a simple case of "ZAP!" and a component is dead. At least if it were, people would probably learn from their mistakes sooner. No, ESD, while it can kill a component, is more likely to damage it and significantly shorten its expected lifespan.

Other Sources of Static Charge

It's not just us humans walking and shuffling about that creates static charge. Pretty much anything that moves creates ESD. Electrical motors are a huge source of static charge and can cause build-up in excess of 100,000 volts. This is why it's a bad idea to go sticking the nozzle of a running vacuum cleaner into a PC. Brushing components is also a dangerous activity unless you have a special antistatic brush. If you want to clean dust from components, the quickest and safest way is to use canned compressed air.

Other causes of build-up of static charge include:

- **Poorly shielded cabling.** Replace damaged cables rather than repairing them with tape.

- **Large curtains.** Avoid working too near to large curtains as they can store a lot of static charge. Washing them with fabric softener dramatically reduces the risk of ESD.

- **Polystyrene.** Avoid storing components in polystyrene boxes, and don't place components on top of polystyrene of drag components over the top of a sheet of the stuff.

The Weather Makes a Difference

The funny thing about ESD is that it is a dry air phenomenon. If the air has more that 50% humidity then static charge cannot accumulate, whereas below 50% humidity it can, and ESDs become likely. Air conditioning can help to reduce or even eliminate the risk of ESD.

Air temperature is also a key factor — the warmer the air, the greater the risk of ESD.

So, to summarize:

- Warm, dry air = Bad!
- Cool, moist air = Good!

Caution Don't try to artificially "alter" the humidity of the air in your work space by using sprayers or humidifiers. These can cause the air to become saturated with water and then the water will condense out onto components, causing short circuits.

ESD Precautions

Okay, cool, moist air helps to reduce or even eliminate ESD but unless you have devices to measure the humidity of the air this information is pretty useless. Also, what if you live in a hot, dry location? What are you supposed to do if you want to build a PC? Move?

Also, moving about is bad because that's how the human body generates most of the static charge in the first place. You could sit still for the whole time you are building the PC.

The solution? Antistatic wrist straps and ESD bags.

Antistatic Wrist Straps

Although it's important to know what ESD is and how it is bought about, prevention in this case isn't better than cure. What we need to have is a way of discharging the static build-up in a safe and controlled way. Fortunately, all you need is a cheap antistatic wrist strap, available at any good PC parts outlet.

An antistatic wrist strap, as shown in Figure 1-3, is a strap that the PC builder wears around the wrist. Different types of strap use different materials. (The cheaper ones are plastic, while more expansive ones are made of a synthetic conductive weave.) At the other end of the wrist strap is usually a clip, which is attached to a good grounding point such as some bare metal on a radiator or water pipe. Connecting the wrist strap and the clip is usually a length of coiled wire.

Tip You can buy grounding clips for metal water pipes from most hardware suppliers. It's recommended that you attach one to a convenient pipe in your workspace.

No convenient water pipe? No problem. You can connect to the electrical grounding system (you can get special plugs that allow you to do this safely) or you can take a copper or iron stake and drive it into the ground outside (minimum 12 inches) and connect to that. If you have to resort to the stake method and you live in a particularly dry location, you might need to treat the ground surrounding the stake with up to anything between 4 and 20 pounds of regular salt or Epsom salts (hydrated magnesium sulfate salts) mixed with water (this treatment needs to be repeated every few years).

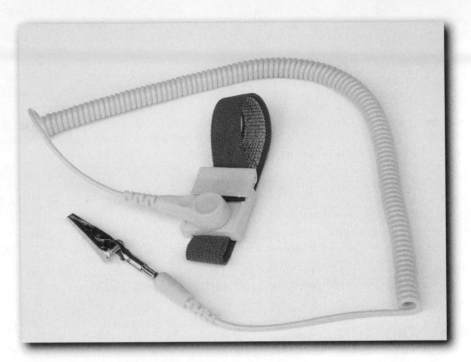

FIGURE 1-3: Antistatic wrist straps discharge static build-up.

If a wrist strap is just something that grounds you to an earth point, why not just make one yourself? This isn't recommended because most good antistatic wrist straps hide a simple but effective safety measure. If you are wearing a strap that grounds you to discharge static charge, then that ground can work both ways — and help ground electricity as well as static charge. So, if you accidentally touched something live when working on a PC (which you shouldn't be able to because it's disconnected, right?), the grounding strap will also ground this power straight through you in the middle. An electric shock has the potential to be far more lethal if the person receiving the shock is well grounded.

How do good ESD straps avoid this? They have a resistor built in (usually a 1 million ohm resistor, called 1 megaohm) that allows static charge to be dissipated but which offers the wearer some protection against grounding a lethal charge (don't let this make you sloppy with checking that the juice to the device is off before working on it though!).

When buying an ESD strap look for mention of a 1-megaohm resistor. There are plenty of good straps available for a few dollars so get a good one — it could save your life one day!

ESD Bags

Remember earlier that we said that it is a good idea to keep components in their packaging until they are needed because this offers them the best protection. Well, one thing that you might have noticed about most components is that most are shipped in an odd semi-silvered bag, sometimes with black grid lines on the outside (see Figure 1-4). This bag isn't just designed to look cool and futuristic; it serves a purpose. This bag is designed to protect the contents from ESD by directing the charge around the outside of the bag rather than through the components.

FIGURE 1-4: ESD bags protect your components from static discharge.

Note ESD bags come with a variety of names ranging from the obvious "ESD bag" to the more techie-sounding names like "isolation bag" or "Faraday bag" (after the scientist Michael Faraday).

Using these bags is easy—you just pop the component inside the bag. You can, if you want, fold the end over and even add a staple to it for extra security (it doesn't affect the ESD properties of the bag at all).

Summary

In this chapter, you've looked at one of the most important aspects of building your PC — staying alive so that you can enjoy using it later on! We've also looked at how you can make sure that your actions don't result in the early demise of a vital (and possibly expensive) component.

Make sure that you read (and reread) this chapter and follow the advice given. We'll also be reminding you to work safely as you progress with hints, tips, and cautions along the way, starting with Chapter 2, where you learn more about the tools you need to build a PC.

Take Action

Before you move on to the next chapter, be sure that you're prepared:

- Find a suitable work space.
- Create a suitable work area for yourself.
- Buy a good quality (1-megaohm) antistatic wrist strap.
- Find a good grounding point near to the work area.
- Keep any components in their original packaging until you are ready to use them.

Choosing the Tools You Need

I n this chapter, you're going to take a look at the various tools that you can use during your PC building adventures. Some of these tools you will definitely use; others are optional. And chances are that you already have most of the tools that you'll need.

Don't worry, though, if you are the kind of person who doesn't have any tools around the house. You won't need to invest in one of those big red rolling toolboxes, and you won't have to turn your working space into an Indy 500 pit stop! If you keep things basic and simple, then you will only need a small number of cheap, easy-to-use tools, and these are more than likely to cost you less than $10. Even if you choose to buy a more comprehensive toolkit, you should still be able to manage this for well under $50.

Note Although a basic toolkit is cheap enough to get, if you go for the best possible tools for your toolkit, you can expect to splash out much more than $50.

The Tools

Let's introduce you to the tools that you need, in order of importance. We'll draw attention to the important ones and also point out the ones that you might not want to get in the early stages.

If you are the type of person who is going to be building more than just the one PC, then over time you are likely to build up quite a toolkit (you'll probably be surprised, but it's amazing how family and friends, unhappy with the system that they bought from a "big-name" maker, will turn to you for advice or even come right out and ask you to build a system for them when they find out that you broke away from the herd and built your own system!).

Tip Don't complicate matters! If you're not a "tool" person then just get the basics for now. If you need anything else along the way, you can always run out to the hardware store and get it!

Note A quick tool reference is also presented in Appendix B, "Checklist."

Let's begin by looking at the most useful tool a PC builder can have.

The Screwdriver

The screwdriver is the single most useful tool you can have. Without a screwdriver or two, you're not likely to get very far with your PC building. You will need screwdrivers to attach the power supply unit, fit hard drives and CD/DVD drives to the system, hold expansion cards in place, and possibly even to put the actual case together (although today many cases have gone to using plastic catches that are quicker and more convenient to use but generally not as robust). In this section, you'll learn about the types of screwdrivers you need and how to care for them.

Warning Never, ever, ever use any kind of powered screwdriver on any PC components. Even poor-quality powered screwdrivers (such as the cheap battery-operated ones you can find advertised on TV or for sale for next to nothing in hardware stores) have enough power to chew up the screw head or strip the thread off the screw (or worse still, the screw hole in, say, a hard drive).

Types of Screwdrivers

There are two basic types of screwdrivers (see Figure 2-1):

- The Phillips head screwdriver (sometimes, incorrectly called a crosspoint screwdriver)
- The straight-edged (or flat head or sometimes it's even called a blade) screwdriver

Tip Use the right screwdriver for the screw you are working with. Don't try to force or bash an unsuitable screwdriver into shape! Since we are looking at building a new PC here, most if not all of the fasteners that you will be using will be new ones, so you're unlikely to have any problems—but take care not to damage the screws because one day you might be the one who has to try to reopen it!

First, let's talk about the Phillips head screwdriver.

The Phillips Head Screwdrivers

Whenever anyone mentions Phillips head screwdrivers, there's generally confusion. This confusion generally arises from the fact that the Phillips head screwdriver (and for that matter the Phillips screw) is but one type of screwdriver (or screw) that has a cross-shaped slot in the head.

The Phillips head screwdriver and screw were invented by Henry F. Phillips, an Oregon businessman between 1934 and 1936. He invented and patented these screws as a way of speeding up mass production systems such as car assembly lines. One of the great features of the Phillips design was that is was almost impossible to overscrew (or overtighten) the screw because the screwdriver slips out (or cams out) of the slot rather than allow overtightening. Problem is, this cam out can make screws that have tightened over time or with age and corrosion hard to remove. This cam out action also makes it easy for the screwdriver to chew the heads of the screws, making removal tricky.

Why Are Phillips Screws Used If They "Cam Out"?

Good question! It all dates back to the birth of the early IBM PC and IBM AT systems. Somewhere there probably exists some dull and dusty document that specifies that an "IBM compatible" PC had to use Phillips screws. This specification was probably handed down and over time it's just become an accepted part of PC building.

In Chapters 10, 13, and 14 when we come to look at the screws that hold a PC together, you'll find that there is a lot more to this story!

FIGURE 2-1: You will need both a Phillips head screwdriver (left) and a straight-edged screwdriver (right).

Because of this cam out, over the years a number of other screws and screwdriver that make use of a cross-shaped slot have been patented. These are marketed under names such as POZIDRIV and SUPADRIV (see Figure 2-2). We only need to concern ourselves with the Phillips head screwdrivers, since all standard cross-slotted screws in a PC are of the Phillips style.

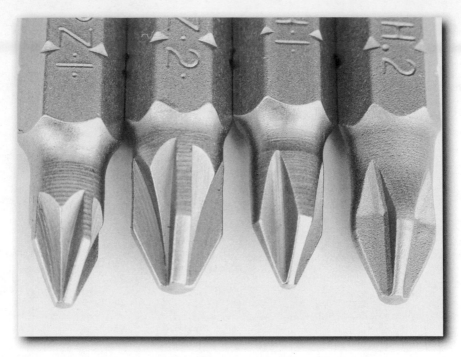

FIGURE 2-2: Phillips head screwdriver heads and POZIDRIV heads (left to right POZIDRIV No. 1 and No. 2, Phillips No. 1 and No. 2.).

Tip

It is possible to tell the difference between a Phillips head screwdriver, a POZIDRIV screwdriver and a SUPADRIV screwdriver because the Phillips head screwdriver has a cone angle at the tip of 26 degrees and is the most pointy of the three. POZIDRIV and SUPADRIV screwdrivers have a similar cone angle of 26.5 degrees and 22.5 degrees, respectively, but both have a blunt, squared-off, tip. While the screwdrivers for each of the screw designs look similar, they aren't, and using the wrong screwdriver can cause damage to the screw head, making its fitting or later removal tricky.

Okay, you know you are now looking for Phillips head screwdrivers, but if you go to a hardware store or look online, the next thing you are going to notice is that they come in different sizes. Let's cut to the chase here and say that you are looking to buy two:

- Phillips No. 1
- Phillips No. 2

Take a closer look at these and two you'll notice that the Phillips No. 2 is larger than the No. 1 (the Figure 2-2 shows this quite well).

The Straight-Edged Screwdrivers

Next are the straight-edged screwdrivers. These are simpler than the Phillips head screwdrivers because a straight-edged slot is just a straight-edged slot, and no one has yet come across a way of making these any more complicated.

You generally don't come across many straight-edged slot screws in a PC, but increasingly we're noticing that some screws designed to secure hard drives and CD-ROM drives are using a Phillips-style head that also incorporates a slot in it for a straight-edged screwdriver so it's worthwhile having a few close to hand.

Straight-edged screwdrivers also come in a variety of sizes. There are two units of measure for straight-edged screwdrivers:

- Length of the screwdriver
- Width of the slotted end of the blade

Length isn't all that important, but a length somewhere in the region of 4 inches (about 100 mm) is ideal. If your budget allows, try to get two straight-edged screwdrivers:

- 3/16 inch (4.5 mm)
- 1/8 inch (3 mm)

Screwdriver Care

Screwdrivers are like any other good tool — they need looking after and are designed to do particular job — in this case, do up and undo screws.

To help screwdrivers to do their job well, follow these simple rules:

- **Don't overtighten screws.** Gentle hand tight is all that's needed. If you have a strong grip, then do the screw up only as tight as you can manage with a thumb and forefinger.

- **Get the right-sized screwdriver for the screw in question.** You'll know by the solid feel of the screwdriver in the screw slot when you are using the right size. Don't use a screwdriver that's too small because all that will do is damage the screw. Similarly, don't use one that is too big either (don't, whatever you do, try to bash the screwdriver into the slot!).

- **Do not use a screwdriver as a substitute for a pry bar.** Or paint can opener, lever, scribe, center punch, a probe, a hole borer, or anything else not associated with the doing up or undoing of screws!

- **Check your screwdriver tip for damage before each use.** You're looking for blade damage or bits that are missing (this is especially important with Phillips head screwdrivers).

Tip

A good way to check the tip of the screwdriver is by running your fingers along it — you'll feel the rough edges of damage easier than you'll see it.

TORX Drivers—Don't Bother!

Many PC repair toolkits that you'll see on the market come with special screwdrivers designed for TORX® fasteners (licensed by Textron Fastening Systems). These fasteners have star-shaped slots in the heads, as shown in Figure 2-3, and are designed to overcome the limitations of Phillips screws.

FIGURE 2-3: TORX drivers are rarely used when building PCs.

These are great fasteners and are often used as a way of making items tamper-proof (although the proliferation of TORX drivers among hardware stores has made this somewhat a moot point). You might come across these on items such as laptops, but you shouldn't need them for anything that we are going to be covering here.

Tweezers

You're probably surprised by the fact that the humble tweezers are number two on the tools list. You were probably expecting something fancy like a sonic screwdriver or tricorder! But tweezers, while not being an essential item, are one of the most useful bits of equipment you can have.

When you are working on a PC, one thing that you will see a lot of are small bits — screws, washers, jumpers, and so on. These can be really hard to pick up by hand (especially if you have stubby fingers), and a pair of tweezers comes in really handy. They can also be handy for picking up a single screw or washer from a packet without having to spill the contents all over the place to do it!

There are two general types of tweezers:

- **Straight tweezers.** These are ones whose gripping blades are straight.
- **Curved tweezers.** These have a curved end (obvious really!).

Again, while stressing that they aren't essential, these will make life easier. Particularly handy are the style of tweezers that open when you squeeze the handle and close when you release it (see Figure 2-4). These are much easier to control than regular tweezers where you have to squeeze the handle to keep the pressure on to hold whatever is being gripped.

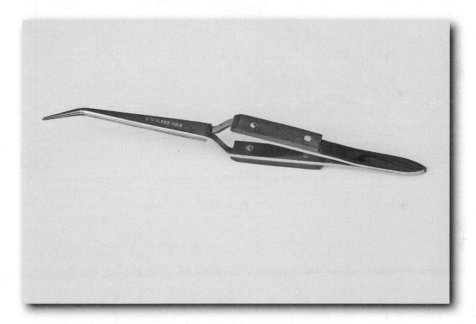

FIGURE 2-4: Curved tweezers help you pick up small components.

Most tweezers are metal, but you might be able to find plastic ones (see Figure 2-5). Plastic ones are normally a lot weaker than metal ones, but this can be an advantage — plastic ones are unlikely to damage delicate components.

You can also get special antistatic tweezers that reduce the risk of electrostatic discharge too. These are usually quite cheap (under a $1, although some places seem to charge a premium for them) and are usually of high quality. However, since you are mostly going to be picking up small items (usually stuff you've dropped somewhere hard to get at) quality doesn't matter that much.

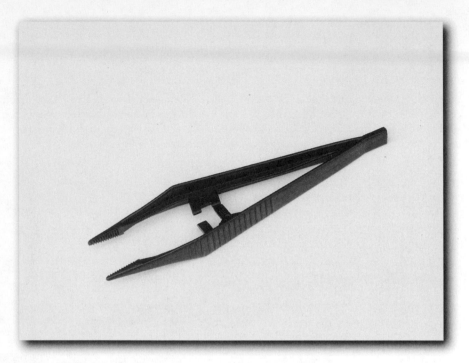

FIGURE 2-5: Plastic tweezers can be easier on delicate components.

Tip

If you are prodding around inside a PC with tweezers, it's a very good idea to wear an antistatic wrist strap when using any kind of tweezers because the tips are a good starting point for ESD.

Forget about those unwieldy "magnets on a telescopic stick" type screw retrievers. These are just going to swing around wildly and cause damage inside the PC case.

Flashlight

The flashlight is another item that's on the optional list but still highly recommended (see Figure 2-6). Why? Well, a PC case, as all boxes do, has dark corners that make things hard to see. Such working conditions don't help and so it's a good idea to have a way to cast some light into the shadows.

FIGURE 2-6: Plastic flashlights are lighter and easier to hold.

Some flashlights are better suited to the job of building a PC than others. Here are some criteria that should help you find a good flashlight for the job:

- **Small.** A flashlight that has the capacity for 2 AA batteries is ideal.
- **Lightweight.** Nothing too heavy that can cause damage.
- **Plastic construction.** Makes things lighter to prevent damage.
- **LED-powered.** These emit a more diffuse, pleasing light that doesn't cast harsh shadows. The light they give off is also cold (compared to the heat of a bulb) and the LEDs will last for years. You also get very good battery life, which means that they are cheap to run.

Tip Avoid the big, metal, police-style flashlights. These may be cool but they are not suited to PC work. They are too big and heavy and will certainly cause a lot of damage if you drop one inside the PC.

You might want to augment a hand-held flashlight with one of those head-mounted lights that are now popular among hikers. These are the kind that are mounted onto an elasticized strap and fit around the head. Same rules apply as to a hand-held flashlight — keep it small, light, and plastic!

Magnifier

A magnifier may seem like another frivolous item (and it's certainly not an essential item), but when you've been spending time looking at little screws, wires, connector blocks, and jumpers, you might get to the point where you can truly appreciate a little "bionic" vision.

The best kind of magnifier we've found is the type that you can mount on your head and bring down when you need to se a little better. A good, well-made magnifier is the OptiVISOR® by the Donegan Optical Company (see Figure 2-7). You can wear the OptiVISOR on your head comfortably for extended periods — and it can be used if you wear glasses.

An OptiVISOR can be bought from a variety on online retailers for about $30.

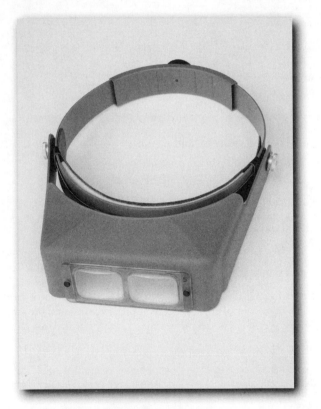

FIGURE 2-7: The OptiVISOR is a precision, head-mounted magnifier.

Canned Compressed Air

Canned compressed air is a really handy tool. No matter how careful you are, dirt and dust will make it into your system before you even switch on for the first time. In order to give things the best start possible, it's a good idea to remove it.

Canned compressed air comes in two varieties:

- Aerosol-style
- CO_2 bulb-style dust guns

Both have advantages and disadvantages. The aerosol-style can of compressed air is a disposable can (you use it until it runs out) whereas the CO_2 bulb-style dust gun is refillable using disposable seltzer bottle CO_2 cartridges. Dust guns are also smaller and more powerful than aerosol canned air. Although they are more expensive to buy initially, in the long run the refills are cheaper than continually buying the aerosol cans.

Multitool

You've seen multitools — you might even have one. These tools are designed to be carried in a belt pouch (they're generally too big to carry in a pocket) and have been popular with outdoor types and engineers alike for a number of years now. They come under a variety of names (we'll just call them generically "multitools") and are manufactured by countless different companies and range in quality from cheap junk to high quality.

We've used a number of these, and the best out there are made by the Leatherman® Tool Group.(See Figure 2-8.) By far these have the best quality pliers and screwdrivers of all that we've looked at and used and can act as a credible "portable" toolkit.

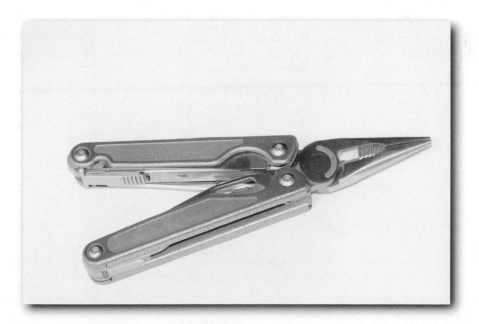

FIGURE 2-8: The Leatherman Charge multitool.

Here are the things to look for in a quality multitool:

- Small needle-nosed pliers — you don't want anything too chunky!

- Reasonably lightweight

- A medium-sized Phillips head screwdriver that will fit many of the screws and fasteners on a PC

- A straight-edged screwdriver

- Comfortable handles

Tip

For most screws the diameter of the actual shaft of the screwdriver doesn't matter, but there are times when you might want to get at a screw that's sunken in or recessed (case screws are sometimes hidden away in a recess). These kinds of screws can pose a problem for many of the Phillips head screwdrivers present on a multitool, so make sure that you have a standard screwdriver as a backup.

Final point on multitools — good ones aren't cheap. Expect to spend anywhere between $50 and $100 or more for a good-quality one. Bear in mind that combining the excellent build quality and exceptional warranties that good multitools have, it's likely that it will last for many years (or until you lose it!).

Multimeter

Next we come to the multimeter (see Figure 2-9). This is a tool that all budding electricians will have. A multimeter is a usually a small box that has a dial and a display (nowadays usually a digital display but older ones may have an analog "needle" type display). Multimeters are designed to take a number of different electrical readings.

Basic multimeter functions include the capability to test:

- Voltage (both AC and DC)

- DC current

- Ohms (a measure of resistance that can also be used to check continuity of cables)

- Diode polarity

- Fuses

- Batteries

More expensive multimeters incorporate functions such as temperature displaying and also the capability to show information in the form of graphs rather than numbers on the display.

We'll be covering basic multimeter use in the course of building the PC. Whether you buy one or not is entirely up to you, but there's no doubt that it's a very handy tool that goes a long way to making the job easier. A good hobbyist digital multimeter can be bought for around $15.

FIGURE 2-9: A digital multimeter is a necessity when working with electricity.

Miscellaneous Items

Here is a short list of other items you might find useful to have:

- **Plastic film container.** Very handy for storing small items (screws and so on). These are getting rarer nowadays as digital takes over from film, but any photo-processing place will be able to give you more than you will ever need!

- **Pencil and paper.** You will want to take notes along the way.

- **Sticky labels.** Labeling cables and connectors is a simple way to avoid getting confused about what goes where.

- **Lump of modeling clay.** This is a great — and safer — alternative to using a magnet to keep small parts like screws and washers from rolling around! Just stick them in the clay! Don't go sticking electrical components into the clay, though!

- **Plastic ties.** Ties are great for tying loose cabling and keeping things tidy inside the case. Use the all-plastic cable ties and not ones with wire inside.

- **Dust sheets.** Use these for throwing over unfinished projects to keep the dust off.

Tool Storage

You'll want something to store all your tools in. Big metal toolboxes aren't recommended. You're not going to have much in the way to tools anyway, so you're not going to need a lot of space. A small plastic toolbox is a good idea, but even these can be a bit big unless you can find a particularly small one. If you do take the plastic toolbox approach, then try to get one with little compartments to store small items in (such as screws, washers, jumpers, and bits of cable).

Here are some other options for storing your tools:

- **Tool roll.** A roll of plastic or leather into which tools can be placed in a pouch.

- **A zip-up folder.** These are common among "PC toolkits." Again, these are quite effective, but generally the range of tools you can store in it are quite limited and there is little room for your own additions. Also, these premade kits tend to be much more expensive than buying the parts individually.

- **Plastic container.** A cheap alternative is to store all your tools in a plastic container with a snap-on lid. For a free alternative, you might be able to recycle any suitably sized plastic tub you can find.

Summary

This chapter has all been about the tools you need (or might need) when you undertake your PC build. You're probably quite surprised by the fact that you can, if you want to be minimalist, probably get away with nothing more than a No. 1 and No. 2 Phillips screwdriver and an antistatic wrist strap (which you should have bought after reading Chapter 1). But minimal isn't the easiest route. With the addition of a few simple and inexpensive items, such as a flashlight and tweezers, the job at hand becomes much easier.

The most expensive item we've covered here (apart from the multitool, which is more of a luxury!) is the multimeter. These can be very useful for troubleshooting, fault-finding, and making sure that items such as power supply units are working properly.

In the next chapter, you will look at choosing a case and power supply for your PC.

Take Action

Before you move on to the next chapter, be sure you're prepared:

- Get a basic toolkit (consisting of at least a Phillips No. 1 and No. 2 screwdriver).
- Decide on what optional tools or items you may want.
- Buy a small box or tool roll, or devise some other way of storing your tools.

Choosing a Suitable Case and Power Supply

L et's begin our tour of the parts you'll need to buy and handle during your PC build project. The first item you need? A case and power supply for your PC.

A PC's case might seem like one of its most unimportant elements, and it is by far the most overlooked, underestimated PC component (and yes it is a component, just as much as the CPU is or a hard drive). When most people think of a PC case, they think only of the box that holds all the other parts of the PC together in one convenient unit.

"What's special about a box? A case is just a case, right?"

Wrong! While a case doesn't give you more speed or performance like choosing the right CPU or buying a lot of RAM will, and true, it's not as important as having a nice, clear monitor on the system, a well-chosen case is vitally important for a number of reasons. Get a good case and you'll be making your life easier. Choose badly and you'll be cursing it within hours of starting the build.

Along with looking at what makes or breaks a PC case, this chapter also covers the power supply unit. These two items are covered together because nowadays most cases come fitted with a power supply unit. The power supply unit is another PC component that often gets little or no attention but, once again, choosing that vital piece can make the difference between a good PC and a poor one.

The PC Case

If you go back in PC history, for a very long time indeed PCs were packaged into small metal — usually beige — boxes. PCs all looked pretty much the same, apart for the maker's badge and perhaps a model number badge discreetly stuck to the front. The only other difference was the case style. Basically (as you'll see in a moment) there were two basic types of case: desktops and towers. However, all were metal, pretty much all of them beige and all very basic.

First Rule of PC Building

Nothing is ever as simple as a single term makes it seem to be. Going into a PC store or online and trying to buy a "desktop" or "tower" case is a bit like going into a Starbuck's and asking for "coffee." There are countless variations on the "desktop" and "tower" theme.

Fortunately things are now very different — there are a multitude of different types of PC cases. The two basic types of cases still exist but the beige metal box of the late eighties and nineties has now been replaced by plastic (or at least the outside is plastic) and thankfully comes in many different colors and shapes. Style is now a very important consideration. Once the PC started to escape the office, infiltrating the home and actually coming into the living room, this change was inevitable.

One of the first items you should buy when building a PC is the case. Why? Simple, it's a place for you to put all the other parts safely as you work with them!

As already stated, cases come in two basic styles. These are:

- Desktop
- Tower

The following sections describe the two types and examine the pros and cons of each style. This should give you an opportunity to choose the style that best suits your needs.

Desktop Cases

The desktop case was the first, and up until the mid-nineties the most popular type of, PC case. In simple terms, the desktop case is a flat, box case that sits on the desk flat side down. The floppy disk drive and CD drives are at the front of the case, along with the on/off and reset buttons.

Why were these cases so popular in the late eighties and early nineties? Well, a lot of that popularity had to do with desk space. Many companies were replacing typewriters with PCs, and the desktop case had a similar footprint to a typewriter. Also, the desktop case was a handy monitor stand. Place the desktop case on the desk, pop a 14-inch monitor on top (which was the norm those days), and the monitor is at an almost perfect viewing height! Nowadays monitors are much bigger, and this arrangement doesn't work at all.

Tip

Desktops, as you can tell by the name, are designed for on-desk use and are virtually useless when placed on the floor — they take up a lot of space, are easily kicked and tripped over (their low profile makes them hard to spot), and it's hard to reach the drives and buttons when seated.

Another reason why desktops have fallen out of popularity is that people want their systems crammed with hardware — hard drives, CD drives, DVD drives, extra expansion cards. All this takes up room, room that is simply not present inside most desktop cases, which are more compact than towers.

In fact, size plays a big factor with desktop cases, and there were two basic designs:

- The standard desktop case
- The smaller slimline desktop case

The slimline desktop is rarely seen in the home and is mainly reserved for corporate workstations. See Table 3-1 below for average case sizes.

Table 3-1   Average Desktop Case Size

Case style	Average Width	Average Height	Average Depth
Desktop	17 inch 43 cm	6 inch 15.5 cm	16.5 inch 42.5 cm
Slimline desktop	13 inch 33 cm	4 inch 10 cm	16.5 inch 42.5 cm

Advantages of Desktop Cases

Here is a quick rundown of the pros of desktop cases:

- Small size, which is useful if you don't have much space
- Low-profile makes them suited for use as a media center PC system (they fit well into an existing audio/video stack)

Disadvantages of Desktop Cases

Here is a quick rundown of the cons of desktop cases:

- They're not suitable for floor use.
- The cramped interior limits system specification (that is, it's hard to have four hard drives or two hard drives/two optical drives, limited number of expansion card slots).
- The cramped interior makes working inside the case difficult.
- The small size makes upgrading tricky.
- Modern monitors aren't suited for placement on top of the desktop case.
- The cases are notoriously difficult to open (although modern ones are much better).
- There is a limited range of choices because they are less popular than towers.

Tower Cases

Nowadays the tower style case is by far the most popular. Most PCs you see for sale will have a tower case. The reason they have become popular is a combination of versatility and upgradeability. A tower case is equally happy being on a desk as on the floor, and the internal size provides greater space for components and more scope for upgrades.

There are three different types of tower cases:

- Mini-towers
- Midsized towers
- Full-sized towers

The main difference between the different types of cases is size. Table 3-2 lists the average sizes of the three styles of cases.

Table 3-2   Average Tower Case Size

Case style	Average Width	Average Height	Average Depth
Mini-tower	7.5 inch 19 cm	14 inch 35.5 cm	14 inch 35.5 cm
Midsized tower	7.5 inch 19 cm	18 inch 46 cm	17.5 inch 4.5 cm
Full-sized tower	8 inch 20.5 cm	20 inch 51 cm	18.5 inch 47 cm

Of the three, the midsized tower is the most popular type of case because it offers the best compromise between size and space for components. See Figure 3-1.

The bigger the case the more room there is inside for components. However, full-sized tower cases can be very expensive and are generally reserved for specific applications (for example, a stand-alone server).

Advantages of Tower Cases

Here is a quick rundown of the pros of tower cases:

- Most popular case style (the midsized tower is the most popular tower choice)
- Plenty of choices
- Ideal for both on-the-floor and on-desktop use
- Big enough to allow for a good selection of components and offer good upgrade possibilities in the future
- Easy access to front controls of the PC

Disadvantages of Tower Cases

Here is a quick rundown of the cons of tower cases:

- Small mini-towers quickly fill up and offer less scope for upgrading.
- Larger full-sized towers cannot be placed underneath a desk.
- Larger tower cases are expensive.

FIGURE 3-1: The midsized tower is the case that is used for the project in this book.

Buying a Case

So you want a tower case for your PC (let's assume for simplicity that it's a midsized tower). How do you go about buying a case? What do you look for? How can you tell a good case from a poor one?

Note From here on we're going to assume that you are going to use a tower case for your build project (we're convinced that at least 99% of readers will prefer this style of case). The size of the case makes little difference in how the PC will be built—a smaller case is trickier to work with (unless you have small or dexterous hands), and using one gives you fewer options, but you'll still be able to do everything that we're going to cover here.

If you choose to build a PC using a desktop case, then, apart from layout differences, the procedure for building one is exactly the same. However, given how cramped the inside is going to be, building a PC inside a desktop case is not recommended for the beginner.

First things first, in order to really judge the quality of a case you need to see it and handle it. Now we all know that mail order and buying online is much cheaper and less hassle than going to a store, but a case is something we'd recommend you go and take a good look at and examine before you buy. It's very hard for pictures or even a detailed description to compete with actually seeing and handling a prospective case.

Tip

We know it's not possible for everyone to go to a store to buy PC components—you may have limited choice in your local area and mail order might be your only real option. Just make sure that wherever you buy from allows you to return a case if you're not happy with it and that their delivery charges aren't too high. As with everything else, shop around to get the best deals, and this includes the best deal on delivery charges.

Take your time when buying a case. Don't rush. Get the best case for the price. Don't feel rushed by the sales assistants. If they get too pushy and you feel a hard sell coming on, or if they are pressuring you to buy one particular type of case, leave and find a store where they're actually willing to be helpful.

Let's take a look at what you need to be looking for when buying a case.

The Right Case for the Motherboard

When you are looking for cases, you'll see mention of motherboard style. (The motherboard is the main circuit board inside a PC. For more information see Chapter 4, "Choosing a CPU and Motherboard.") We'll look at motherboards in greater detail in the next chapter, but let's just clear up one thing that links in with cases. Cases are specific to motherboard types. We don't mean that there are different cases for different types of motherboards, but instead cases are specific to the style of motherboard (this in known as the form factor of the motherboard). Specifically, the differences come down to size, placement of various items, and screw-mounting holes.

On some cases, you might come across the abbreviation "ATX," such as "ATX midsized tower." This refers to the case's support for the motherboard. Most readers will be building a PC based upon an ATX motherboard, and you'll have no problem finding a case to suit. You might also find that some cases support several different types of motherboards, for example AT, ATX, and Micro-AT boards. Figure 3-2 shows how the motherboard fits into the case.

Note

In case you're wondering, ATX stands for Advanced Technology Extended.

Qualities of a Good Case

So, how do you tell a good PC case from a not-so-good case? As already mentioned, this is something best done in person at the store where you intend to buy. People can and do buy cases via mail order all the time but unless you really know what you are doing, have a good idea of what you want, trust the vendor, and they have a fair return policy, buying the case for your first build-it-yourself project sight unseen is probably a recipe for a bad start to the project.

First Rule of PC Building—Strikes Again!

Remember "nothing is ever as simple as a single term makes it seem to be"? This is also true for case support for motherboards. While a case might describe itself as "ATX compatible" there are rare occasions when they're just not compatible enough! For example, the BIT BX6 board is an ATX motherboard, but there are ATX cases for sale that simply won't hold this board.

Don't let this worry you right now—these incompatibilities are rare, and we mention them only so that you don't feel alone if you happen to be extremely unlucky and encounter this type of problem. If you do find yourself in this situation, return the case and get a different one.

FIGURE 3-2: Screw threads hold the motherboard in place. This shows the relationship between the case and the motherboard.

So, you're in the store looking at a selection of PC cases. What do you look for? What are the signs of a good case, and what are the warning signs of a bad one?

The elements to look for can be broken down into:

- Size
- Looks
- Features
- Stability
- Ease of opening
- Ease of closing
- Interior

Size

Take a look at the outside of the case you are interested in. How big is it? Remember, you're going to have to put that case somewhere. Ideally, your finished PC should be placed somewhere where it will have at least 6 inches (15 cm) of air space all around the case for optimum cooling. That massive tower PC might look great in the store, but it's not going to look so great when you discover you have nowhere to put it. Measure the area where you plan for the finished PC to live, and take these measurements with you.

Looks

Now onto cosmetics. Do you like how the PC case looks? Some cases will be very plain and utilitarian, whereas others can be quite dramatic looking, with neon lights, LED decoration, clear and panel windows to see the inside of the PC. Still others are molded into fancy sculptures.

Although how your final PC will look might seem like a small consideration compared to, say, power or performance, it's still an important and sometimes overlooked consideration. Think carefully about the PC and where it will go. A case that's packed with glowing neon tubes and blinking LEDs can look great in the store, but will it look great when you get it home? If the PC is going to be in a shared work space, will the others that inhabit that work space enjoy the neon/LED light show? Will that "alien head" molding on the front of the PC fit in with the surroundings? Does it matter? Give this some thought, and work this into your thinking when buying a case.

All this might seem like very minor considerations but they are important and can make the difference between a final PC that you're proud of and one you're not. If you are uncertain about a nonstandard PC case design, then err on the side of restraint and get a "standard" case — you can always change the case later anyway.

Tip   Please don't let looks alone be the deciding factor for a case! There are plenty of other, more serious considerations to bear in mind.

Features

Many cases have a lot of bonus features on them, such as CPU and hard disk temperature displays, front-mounted USB and FireWire ports, and audio connectors. Bear in mind though that these will need motherboard support.

Stability

Stability of the case is important. Simple test — place the prospective case on a flat surface and check that it sits solidly without any wobbling. If not, reject it immediately. A good PC case will have four rubber feet that mold to the minute surface irregularities of your desk (see Figure 3-3). Cheaper cases have hard plastic feet, which aren't as good and can result in more noise due to vibration.

FIGURE 3-3: Rubber feet on case reduce noise and mold more easily to irregular desk surfaces.

Opening the Case

Happy with the outside of the case? Good! Now it's time to take a look inside. Before you pop the case open, however, read through the following list of questions. You will need to pay close attention to these items as you open the case. Ease of access to the inside of the case is an extremely important factor when building a PC.

As you open the PC case, ask and answer the following questions:

- **Does the case rattle?** The absolute last thing you want is a case that rattles because this will drive you nuts in no time. The fans and vibration from the hard drives will amplify this vibration to the point of making the PC unbearable to use. The two reasons cases can rattle or otherwise make a noise include something not fitted right (which you can fix) or a problem with the case (something that you're going to have to live with or try to repair).

- **What holds the case shut?** Some cases will use screws, while others will make use of a screwless design, using press-in thumb tabs instead.

- **Was getting into the case easy?** How robust are the thumb tabs? How much pressure did it take to press open the tabs (some can be murder on the thumbs!)?

Which type you choose here is a personal one, but we strongly recommend against any case that has more than a couple of easy-to-use thumb screws holding the case together because they simply become a pain to open (see Figure 3-4). At all costs, avoid cases held together by dozens of screws that require a screwdriver. These become a major pain to open, and the screws are prone to loss.

FIGURE 3-4: Thumb screws that secure the cover can be difficult to open.

- **Was it easy to open the case, overall?** Remember, as a PC builder you will be opening and closing the case a lot more than the ordinary PC user.

- **What are the catches that hold the side onto the main body of the case made of?** These catches need to be metal, as shown in Figure 3-5. Plastic is a nonstarter because, sooner or later, it will break off.

FIGURE 3-5: Metal catches that hold the case together are sturdier than plastic.

- Does the side access panel on the PC come off or just hinge? (See Figure 3-6.) The left-hand side panel as you face the front of the case will be the main access panel, but remember that with towers you should be able to access both sides. A case with just a hinging side panel needs acres of space to fully open and is best avoided. Ideally, you want a case you can open and close when it's in that 6 inches of space where it's eventually going to live. If you need to clear your desk or, worse still, move furniture every time you want to get inside your PC, you're going to regret your choice of case pretty quickly.

FIGURE 3-6: Side-opening cases make for easy access.

Closing the Case

Just as important as opening the case is closing the case. Here are some questions to ask as you test closing the case:

- **Is it easy or is there a struggle involved?** A case that's tricky to shut when new is unlikely to get much better with use (no matter what the salesperson might tell you!).

- **Does it snap into place easily and satisfyingly?** Or is it hard to align the side with the case?

- **Does it seal perfectly or are there gaps?** Reject any cases that don't close properly.

- **How easy is it to fit the thumb screw?** (If the case is not a screwless design.) One that's tricky will eventually get left off and lost.

Finally, open the case again. Easy or not?

Inside the Case

Now we come to another important aspect of PC case design — the inside. Until you've built a few PCs, it's hard to know exactly what makes a good case because a lot depends on what kind of PC you intend to build. It's possible to buy a case that's far too big and too high-spec for the PC you intend to build, but in the early stages a good, well-designed, spacious case makes the build process much easier and eliminates unnecessary frustration. After you've fitted RAM modules or a hard drive a few times, you might eventually find yourself being able to do it by feel alone and not really need to have a roomy case. But for a first PC, why make things hard for yourself?

First thing — check the metal edges inside the case (see Figure 3-7). Do this VERY CARE-FULLY because some cases have sharp edges that will give you a nasty cut. (You really don't want to have to get a tetanus shot every time you venture inside the case.) We're continually horrified by the number of cases filled with rough metal, pointed splinters, or, worse still, razor-sharp edges. It's possible to get some very deep and painful cuts from a badly made PC case. Take this threat seriously, and examine prospective cases very carefully, bearing in mind the serious concern that if there's a risk you can cut yourself on a bit of ragged metal, someone else might have done so already! While the health risks are small, they surely exist. Visually examine all the metal edges of the case carefully. If not, you may regret it later on during the build stages!

FIGURE 3-7: Nice, safe, rolled edges prevent cuts!

Tip Run your thumb across potentially sharp edges, not along them. This way you can feel for sharp edges without actually cutting yourself on them.

Once you've checked for sharp edges, next check out the quality of the metal. It is strong or weak and aluminum-foil-like? Dismiss any cases that are made of inferior metal because these cases will be structurally weak and prone to breakage. We've seen cases where there is a considerable amount of flexing and twisting displayed by the case, which can result in a number of problems, such as cracking the motherboard and causing expansion cards to pop out.

Next, have a general look inside the case (see Figure 3-8). Be on the lookout for clutter—some cases, even when empty, are cluttered and have strengthening bars across the opening on the left-hand side of the case (when you are facing the front of the case). Reject these types of PC cases—any bar or strengthener across the opening is going to get in your way when you're building. You want a roomy case with easy, unhindered access to the interior.

FIGURE 3-8: Clutter-free interiors give you more space for your components.

Tip

You might find that even the best case has a sharp corner or sharp edge — if you later come across some of these, you can always cover them with a little tape or fold them over with pliers. Never file them — the metal particles can go everywhere and cause short circuits!

Fans

Cooling the interior of your PC is going to be vitally important. A PC case is an effective heat trap, and you can have a temperature difference of many degrees between the air inside a PC case and the air in the room that the PC is situated in. You will want a way to remove that excess heat, and fans are the best way of doing this, by bringing cooler air into the PC using one fan and exhausting hot air with another.

Note

Some big, full-sized towers might have louvers on the side of the case to allow cool air to enter — these are normally not required on smaller cases.

Make sure that any case you choose comes equipped with two fans (excluding the fan on the power supply unit): one of the front, one at the back. If fans aren't included, then make sure that there are places to fit fans yourself.

Some cases have removable air filters to clean the incoming and expelled air. These are unnecessary and generally ineffective, clogging up quickly.

Port Accessibility

You're going to want to connect stuff to your PC. Most modern PC cases have front-mounted audio, USB and/or FireWire ports (see Figure 3-9). These allow you to plug devices such as headphones, microphones, USB flash memory, card readers, video cameras, digital cameras, MP3 players, and so on into ports that are conveniently located. While not essential, they do make life a lot easier — climbing round the back of the system unit each time you want to connect something can become very tedious.

Note

If the case you've chosen doesn't have front-mounted USB ports, don't worry, you can always add these on later. Many add-on kits exist to bring USB, FireWire, and even digital camera memory readers to the front of the unit.

Expansion Possibilities

There's a good chance that after building your PC you are going to become the kind of person who adds and changes components regularly, adding new components, upgrading others.

Plan ahead for this expansion and for future upgrades. For the initial build, you might only want the case to contain two drive bays (one for a hard drive and one for an optical drive), but soon you might find yourself wanting to add more — so make sure that you take this into account now, and you'll save yourself the cost and headache of having to swap cases later.

FIGURE 3-9: Front-mounted audio and USB ports on cases make it easier to access peripherals.

Power Supply Units

We've bundled power supply units (also known as PSUs) in with our discussion of PC cases because most PC cases come equipped with a PSU, and many readers will get their PSU bundled in with the case they have chosen.

The PSU is attached to the case by using a small number of screws. The PSU (shown in Figure 3-10) is fitted to the top of a tower at the rear. For a desktop case, the PSU will be situated at the back of the case, on the right. (Chapter 13 covers removal and fitting of a PSU, just in case you need to know how.)

There are a few things to look out for in a good PSU, including power output, power consumption, and noise.

Power Output

The main consideration with a good power supply is the amount of power it can deliver. A PSU that can't deliver all the power your PC needs will cause you all manner of problems, from system lockups to crashes and random restarts.

FIGURE 3-10: A 350-watt power supply unit.

Power output is measured in watts, and different PSUs come with the ability to deliver different amounts of power. Forget PSUs rated at 230 watts. In fact, we recommend that you don't buy anything less than 300 watts. This level of power will ensure that the PSU has enough power for the motherboard, CPU, and all the hard drives and CD/DVD drives that you might want to add.

If you want something bigger, then 400-, 450-, 500-, and even 600-watt PSUs exist and are available — for a price.

Power Consumption

Table 3-3 shows a simple way to calculate the power needs for your PC. These figures are high-end averages; your devices may vary in power consumption.

Table 3-3   PC Power Consumption

Device	Power Consumption (Watts)
Motherboard	25
Floppy drive	5
Keyboard and mouse	3
CPU cooler fan	3
CPU	90–120
Video card	50–120
Memory (per module)	10
Hard drive (per drive)	25
Optical drive (per drive)	25
PCI expansion card (per card)	7
Each USB device (only if it draws power from the system)	5
Each FireWire device (only if it draws power from the system)	8
Case fans (per fan)	3

Total up what you have, and you have the maximum power consumption of your system. You need a power supply that can provide this much power.

Also, remember that you might want to add a few extras later on after the build (like a second hard drive or a CD drive, so make sure that you have some left-over power potential for your system because you don't want to have to upgrade the PSU too!

One Less Thing to Worry About

PSUs are capable of being adjusted to cater for different line voltages around the world. The power supply in your PC is designed to support both 110-volt and 220-volt line voltage. The United States uses 110 volts but other countries use 220 volts (or 230/240 volts, but in those cases 220 volts is close enough). To switch between line voltages there's a small red slider with the two voltages printed on it—take a look at the back of your PSU, near the power cord connector or the on/off override switch and you'll see the slider.

Noisy PSUs

The amount of noise a PSU is going to generate is something you can't really judge when you are buying a case in a store (unless you can persuade the sales staff to plug in the PSU and let you hear it in action), so you'll either have to take a chance on this or go out and buy a specifically designed quiet PSU (there are a number available). These are expensive but might be worth considering for a PC that lives and works in an area where other people are (den or living room, for example).

Summary

In this chapter, we've looked at two elements of a PC that are generally overlooked and underestimated. Choosing a good, sturdy case and a PSU that can deliver enough power to the system makes all the difference to your system in the long run.

Don't think of the case and PSU as unimportant components — they are as vital to the PC as anything else you add. Plan ahead and think about possible future upgrades, and make sure the case and power supply you choose will be ready to meet the challenges that your PC will face in the future.

Don't skimp on them, and get the best that you can afford.

In the next chapter, you will be looking at motherboards and CPUs.

Take Action

Before you move on to the next chapter, be sure you're prepared:

- Go looking in a PC store at cases and PSUs. Even if you buy mail order, the experience will give you an idea of what you are looking for.

- Consider the basic power needs of the PC you are planning. Nothing's fixed in stone yet, but get an idea of what you might need.

Choosing a CPU and Motherboard

I f there is one thing that keeps people from even considering building their own PCs, it's the confusion that exists over CPUs (central processing units, also known as processors) and motherboards. As you will see, there is a whole raft of considerations to take into account, so people often come away from looking in stores or catalogs with the feeling that it's easy to make a costly mistake by buying something wrong.

In this chapter, we will lift this veil of confusion and explain what all the different technologies and options really mean.

CPUs and Motherboards: The Brain and Nervous System of Your Computer

The *CPU* is the brain of the PC. This is the component where the data processing is carried out and where all the instructions are interpreted. This single component is at the heart of everything a PC does.

If the CPU is the brain, then the motherboard is the nervous system, responsible for carrying data to and from other devices in the PC and connected to it. The CPU fits into the motherboard via a socket called a ZIF socket. (ZIF stands for Zero Insertion Force, and the hundreds of pins on the base of the CPU are designed to slip effortlessly into the socket.)

The motherboard provides the circuitry that forms the pathways between the CPU and the RAM, hard drives, optical drives (CD/DVD drives), expansion cards, and other devices. As well as carrying data to and from other components, the motherboard is responsible for carrying power to these devices.

Both of these components are crucial to a PC and getting the right components will make the difference between an excellent PC, a good PC, and a poor PC.

CPU Terminology: The Roots of Confusion

Give people a set of choices and, rather than giving them options, you just end up confusing them! When it comes to choosing a CPU, a flurry of questions spring into mind, and these aren't readily answered:

- Why is there more than one option?
- What's the difference?
- What are the pros and cons of each?
- Which is best for me?

CPUs are one area that causes people a lot of confusion and frustration. Basically, there are two major corporations competing in the PC arena. These are:

- AMD
- Intel

Figure 4-1 shows a packaged CPU.

FIGURE 4-1: AMD Sempron 3000+ Socket A CPU (in protective plastic cover).

Both AMD and Intel make world class CPUs (see Figure 4-1). Both make CPUs that cover the whole consumer spectrum: budget CPUs, low-power consumption CPUs for mobile devices, midrange CPUs, and high-performance CPUs. Both manufacturers are very popular.

So what's the difference?

The Difference between CPU Manufacturers

The bottom line is that there's in fact very little difference between CPU manufacturers. Just as there are dozens of car companies all selling cars, the same is true of CPUs, but instead of there being dozens of companies manufacturing and selling CPUs, there are only two companies making and selling CPUs for the PC market: AMD and Intel. In fact, it's quite possible that if there were half a dozen or so CPU manufacturers, consumers would be more comfortable with the idea that AMD and Intel are competing manufacturers as opposed to making products that work differently.

 Note One of the reasons that consumers are confused by the difference between Intel and AMD products and have a belief that the CPUs are very different comes from the fact that the Apple Macintosh computers are so fundamentally different from the PC—so different that the Windows operating system won't run on a Macintosh. (However, Apple has now recently announced a shift from CPUs made by IBM to CPUs made by Intel, so things are bound to change.)

Choices, Choices, Choices . . .

From a point of view of performance and power, a case can be argued for both AMD and Intel CPUs. Take a look at computer magazines or surf the web for info, and you'll come across reams of reports and tests and comparisons — some independent, some not. Some will conclude that AMD CPUs (or more specifically, a particular AMD CPU) are better than Intel CPUs and that consumers looking for a good deal should choose AMD. Then within minutes, you'll come across another report or test that says that an Intel CPU is best and that's the CPU of choice and everyone should go for an Intel CPU.

Opinions are everywhere. The media, web, magazines, and newspapers fill their pages with them. And most are just that — opinions.

The truth is that both companies make powerful and reliable CPUs. Take two PCs of similar specification, and it's impossible to tell the difference without actually looking at the CPU or using software to tell you what it is.

For the purposes of this book, we are going to assume that there are no performance or power differences between AMD and Intel CPUs. For the project in the book, we will be using an AMD CPU, but you are free to choose either AMD or Intel for the PC you build. No matter which you choose, you'll get a high-quality CPU.

The Real Difference Is . . .

The real differences between AMD and Intel CPUs are in the underlying architecture of the CPU. This is the inner circuitry of the CPU, what makes it work.

A modern CPU is a mind-bogglingly complicated piece of engineering, and it crams a lot of sophisticated technology into a small space. Just as a Ford and Ferrari both have four wheels, have seats, and use an internal combustion engine to take people from A to B and back to A again, AMD and Intel do the same thing, but in different ways.

You can't take an engine out of a Ford and expect it to fit directly into a Ferrari, and the same is true of AMD and Intel CPUs. One of the main differences between the two manufacturers is that each CPU requires a specific motherboard.

What This Means to You

This means that no matter which CPU brand you choose, you need to make sure that the motherboard is designed to support the CPU. (That brand is, for example, whether you choose an Intel CPU or an AMD one. Each manufacturer will have a number of CPUs available covering the whole range, from budget to high performance.) And not only do you need to get a motherboard that's compatible with the CPU manufacturer you'll need a motherboard that's compatible with the type of CPU that you want.

If you want to use an Intel CPU then you need an Intel-compatible motherboard. If you go the AMD route, then you'll have to have an AMD-compatible board. There's no point buying a CPU and then buying a random motherboard — there's a good chance it won't be compatible.

After you know that your CPU brand is compatible with your motherboard, you need to make sure that your CPU model works with your motherboard. This is where things begin to get a little complicated, and you have to be careful so as not to make a mistake that could cost you money. Motherboards are designed to support a particular range of CPUs and no others. This is very specific, and it's important to get it right. Generally, it's not possible to fit an incompatible CPU onto a motherboard, but this doesn't stop people trying and then damaging the CPU, motherboard or both in the process. The main controlling factor is the CPU socket type (covered in the section "CPU Sockets" later in this chapter).

 Note   Motherboards and CPUs are closely linked, and this makes future upgrading of a CPU or motherboard difficult. CPUs change regularly, and every year or so new ones will replace the old and the manufacturers quickly stop making the old model, preferring to sell the newer technology. This means that as a general rule of thumb, if you try to upgrade a PC that is more than a year old, any upgrade involving the CPU or motherboard will be difficult because you will need to change both for them to be compatible (and there's a good chance that you'll need to swap out the RAM too at the same time).

RAM upgrades are much easier because manufacturers continue making old types of RAM long after the technology has been superceded.

Both Intel and AMD make motherboards, but don't be restricted by thinking that they are the only ones — there are half a dozen or so good motherboard manufacturers. Just a few of the names to look out for are:

- ASUS
- Abit
- Gigabyte
- Microstar
- MSI
- Tyan
- DFI

So, you either have to choose a CPU and get a motherboard to match or choose a motherboard and get a matching CPU. We recommend that you choose the CPU first because there are more considerations to take into account when buying a CPU than there are when buying a matching motherboard. Because of this we're now going to move on to examining how to choose the right CPU for you.

The Important Differences between CPUs

Let's take a look at some of the differences between CPUs that actually make a difference. These include:

- Speed
- Socket types
- Cache (built-in memory)
- Dual-core/hyper-threading/64-bit processors

CPU Speed

The most significant difference among CPUs is the *speed*. That is, how fast it can process instructions? The faster it can process instructions, the faster we perceive the PC to be.

Every PC is regulated by an internal clock. This clock regulates the rate at which instructions are processed by the CPU. This is known as *clock cycles*, and it determines the interval between successive instructions. The smaller the interval, the faster the CPU can process instructions and the faster the perceived speed.

A convenient way to measure the speed of a CPU is to say how many clock cycles the CPU can handle per second. A few years back CPUs were capable of millions of clock cycles per second, which was measured in *megahertz* (written as MHz). Mega is short for million (1,000,000) and Hertz or Hz is a shorthand way of saying "cycles per second." But progress has meant that CPUs now have a clock speed that's measured in thousands of millions of clock cycles per second (1,000,000,000), and this is called *gigahertz* (or GHz).

So, a CPU that's measured as 500 MHz (meaning the CPU can perform 500,000,000 clock cycles per second) is theoretically six times slower than a CPU that is rated as 3 GHz (3,000,000,000 clock cycles per second). Equally, a 3.6-GHz CPU is faster than a 3-GHz CPU or even a 3.4-GHz CPU.

In fact, the faster the CPU the smaller the perceived increases in speed. A 3.6-GHz CPU can carry out 200,000,000 more clock cycles per second than a CPU that's measured at 3.4 GHz. That's a difference of 200 MHz . . . it was only a few years ago that 200-MHz CPUs were top of the range!

Note The faster a CPU, the more expensive it is going to be.

CPU speed also isn't the end of the story. Because of different ways Intel and AMD CPUs work, AMD have decided to abandon CPU speed and instead go for model numbers to designate the CPU speed. This complicates matters when making your choice.

CPU Sockets

Remember how we said that the socket the CPU fits into determines the type of motherboard you can use? The reason for this is because CPUs fit onto the motherboard via a *socket*. The pins on the CPU have to fit into a specific socket on the motherboard. Different CPUs have different pin configurations and, therefore, need to be fitted into a different socket (see Figures 4-2 and 4-3).

Chapter 14 looks at CPU sockets and how they work in greater detail but for now it's important to understand that different CPUs fit into different types of sockets.

Table 4-1 lists the five popular types of CPU sockets. The socket numbers are significant. These indicate the number of contacts the socket has or, conversely, the number of pins on the bottom of the CPU. As CPUs become faster, the number of contacts required to connect the CPU to the motherboard also increases.

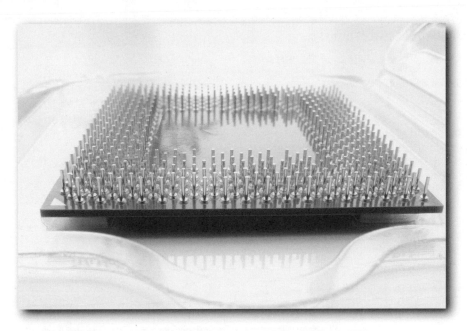

FIGURE 4-2: The pin side view of an AMD Sempron 3000+ Socket A CPU.

FIGURE 4-3: A Socket A motherboard socket.

Table 4-1   CPU Sockets

Socket	CPU Brand That Fits Socket	Example CPUs
Socket A/462	AMD	AMD Sempron 2800+ AMD Sempron 2500+ AMD Duron 1.8GHz
Socket 754	AMD	AMD Athlon 64 3400+ AMD Athlon 64 3200+ AMD Athlon 64 2800+
Socket 939	AMD	AMD Athlon 64 FX-55 AMD Athlon 64 FX-53 AMD Athlon 64 3800+
Socket 478	Intel	Intel Pentium 4 3.4GHz Intel Pentium 4 3.0GHz Intel Celeron D 340 2.93Ghz
Socket 775	Intel	Intel Pentium 4 660 / 3.60GHz Intel Pentium 4 640 / 3.20GHz Intel Pentium 4 550 3.4Ghz

So, for example, if you decide you want your PC to use an AMD Athlon 64 FX-55 CPU, this will make use of a Socket 939 socket, and you will need to get a compatible motherboard for this (for example, the MSI K8N Neo4 SLI Socket 939 ATX motherboard).

Cache

When looking through specifications on CPUs, you will undoubtedly come across mention of "cache," "on-board cache," "on-die cache," or "L1" and "L2" cache. These terms all refer to the amount of memory built into the CPU. The more memory that is built into the CPU, the faster the CPU and the better the performance.

The size of the cache varies for different CPUs, from 256 KB for the lower performance budget CPUs to 1 MB for high-performance CPUs such as the AMD Athlon 64.

Note   The more cache the CPU has, the faster the CPU. And, of course, the CPU will be more expensive.

Dual-Core/Hyper-Threading/64-Bit Processors

AMD and Intel both have a range of processors called "dual-core," which basically means two CPUs in one that offer greater power. Intel on the other hand has Hyper-Threading Technology; this allows the CPU to run some applications faster because it can run multiple computer instructions in parallel, which increases speed. (This can be a bit hard to understand. Think of it as a person who can carry on two telephone conversations at once and is able to get more done than the person who can only handle only one call at a time.)

AMD and Intel both also have a range of 64-bit processors that can run 64-bit applications, which also means greater speed. CPUs incorporating these latest technologies are all much more expensive than standard CPUs and are aimed at high-performance systems or business servers. Be aware that the performance gains you see may or may not justify the hefty price difference.

Choosing the Right CPU for You

So, how do you go about choosing the right CPU? There are a number of ways you can go about choosing a CPU. Some require a little skill and research; others are quite simple.

No matter what method you choose though, shop around before you buy a CPU. Both online and offline there can be a massive difference in price ranges for a particular CPU, within a range (and not a small difference — you might find a 100% difference in price, or possibly more). Don't just buy the first one you come across!

Budget

The single most common method of choosing a CPU is based on price. People building a PC usually have a final budget that they are aiming for, and they use this as a basis for choosing the CPU.

CPUs can be pricy and will probably be the single most expensive component of a PC. There's a huge difference in price between the cheapest budget CPU from Intel or AMD and their high-performance CPU offerings, which are going to be expensive, so it's no wonder that people use budget as a way to choose. It makes life so much easier — choose to spend $XXX on a CPU and go out and find a CPU that costs something near to that estimate and buy that CPU.

There is a certain logic to using price to determine what CPU to buy. It has always been the case that the top-of-the-range, fastest CPUs are always artificially overpriced. Wait a few months and the same CPU will have been superceded by a faster one and the price will drop dramatically.

Buying a CPU based on budget alone might seem like the easy option, but there are some very important considerations to bear in mind:

- **Shop around.** If you are buying your CPU based on price, then do make sure that you shop around for the absolute best deal you can get. Nothing is more depressing for people than to go out and buy a CPU only to find that they could have had the same CPU for far less (or could have had a far more powerful a CPU for their money).

- **Consider the motherboard.** Be sure to factor in the price of the motherboard. Expensive CPUs generally require more expensive motherboards, so it's vital to consider the total cost.

- **Factor in delivery costs.** Sometimes, what you gain on price you lose on delivery charges. Elevated delivery charges can be a trick used by stores to allow them to have a competitive price yet claw that money back on the delivery charges. If you are buying on a budget, then find out how much delivery is going to be before placing the order.

- **Look for bundles.** Many stores now sell CPUs and motherboard as a bundle (sometimes also including RAM). This can be a cheaper alternative to buying the components separately (and you also save money on delivery costs).

Performance

For some people there's nothing more important than having the biggest, fastest, latest technology. There are a number of reasons why people go for the latest technology. Some commonly quoted reasons are:

- Longer technology lifespan (longer before they have to upgrade).

- They want to play games or run software that demands high performance.

- They want the latest and best technology.

Going for the best in terms of performance is going to be expensive. Here are a few tips to help you get the best deals.

Determine How Much Speed You Need

How much CPU power you need depends a lot on what you are going to be doing with your new PC. Only you can truly decide how much power you need, but Table 4-2 will help you decide what range of CPU power you should be looking for, depending on the likely tasks you will be doing with your PC.

Table 4-2   CPU Power

CPU Speed Range (GHz)	Application	Cost
1.5–2.0	General office application Low-end gaming Internet	Budget
2.0–3.0	High-end gaming	Midrange
3.0+	Performance gaming High-performance photo/video editing 3-D wire frame and rendering applications	High

Make Sure That "Top of the Range" Is Really "Top of the Range"

Seems obvious, but in the fast moving world it's easy for technology to take a step forward without your noticing. Also, never trust salespeople to either be honest or have the full facts (sounds harsh but it's true — they are there to sell products to you).

Do your own research, on the web and in magazines. Get information from more than one source, and try to find out if there are any imminent CPU releases from either AMD or Intel that would mean you might be better off waiting a few weeks to get the very latest technology.

Know That Performance Is More Than Just the CPU

Take a top-of-the-range CPU and put that in a PC that is otherwise made up of inferior products, and you will get mediocre performance at best. A high-quality CPU needs a high-quality motherboard and other high-quality components to enable it to work at its best. If you want to build a top-performance PC, you are going to have to spend a lot of cash. Expect it to cost you at least 10 times what a basic PC might cost (you're looking at the CPU alone costing around $1,000!).

Keep Your CPU Cool

The faster a CPU runs, the more power it needs to keep it going. The more power it consumes, the more heat it generates. If you don't want your CPU to suffer premature death, you have to find a way of moving that heat away from the CPU.

High-performance CPUs generate a lot of heat. Make sure that you get a high-quality CPU heatsink and cooling fan to go with the CPU (see Figure 4-4). The purpose of a *heatsink* (which is normally a machined block of copper or aluminum) is to carry the heat away from the CPU, while the purpose of the *fan* is to drive cooler air over the heatsink to carry away the heat.

FIGURE 4-4: An AMD heatsink and fan cooler assembly.

Tip   Many CPUs are now sold complete with a suitable heatsink and fan.

Along with a cooler, you will need to use quality thermal grease to bridge the small air gap that will otherwise exist between the heatsink built on the fan and the CPU. This air gap, although tiny, can act as an insulator and cause the CPU to overheat, which could damage or destroy the CPU.

Buying a Midrange CPU

Most people will want to build a midrange PC that contains a midrange CPU. Price here is generally a good guide, and paying a midrange price for a CPU (a price somewhere between the high and the lows) will get you a good-quality CPU with enough power and performance for you to be able to do most things with it and have a reasonable lifespan before becoming obsolete.

Here are a few points to bear in mind when buying a midrange CPU.

Make Sure the CPU Will Do Everything You Want It To

When buying a midrange CPU, it's important to make sure the CPU is capable of doing everything you want it to. If you have a particular application in mind for running on your new PC, then make sure that the CPU is fast enough to give you good performance.

Games especially can have quite dramatically high system requirements, and having a system that meets the CPU requirements is crucial if you want to get good game play. If you are unsure of the system requirements, then take a look on the box, case, or cover for details. Often two values are listed — a minimum CPU speed and a recommended CPU speed. For example:

```
Processor/CPU
```

```
Minimum:
```

```
1 GHz Intel Pentium 3 or AMD Athlon or equivalent.
```

```
Recommended:
```

```
1.5 GHz Intel Pentium 3 or AMD Athlon or equivalent.
```

It's recommended that you never go for the CPU with a speed lower than the recommended speed. The minimum recommendation is frequently far too low, and performance will be poor. We'd recommend that you consider the recommended value the minimum value and base your purchasing assumptions on that. Remember, the faster the CPU the better the application or game will run.

Be on the Lookout for Good Deals

Sometimes, you will find that an extra $10 or so will buy you a better CPU and that for $20 you can get a better one still. Be on the lookout for deals like this and buy accordingly. Also, there are many times when older technology can cost more than newer technology, generally because the seller is basing their prices on the final recommended retail price for the item before the item was discontinued by the manufacturer; newer models are cheaper but the retailer is still selling it at the last recommended price. You will see this quite often among online retailers. Beware and shop around!

Motherboard Features

Now that you've looked at the different kinds of CPU available and looked at the terminology that cloaks them, it's time to take a look at the motherboard.

There are two types of motherboard features — standard features that are found on every motherboard (see Figure 4-5) and additional features only found on some motherboards.

FIGURE 4-5: The Foxconn K7S741GXMG is a typical motherboard.

Standard Motherboard Features

Standard motherboard features include:

- CPU socket
- RAM slots
- Chipset

- PCI expansion card slots
- AGP/PCI Express expansion slot (for video adaptor)
- Hard drive/optical drive connectors (IDE/SATA)
- Floppy drive connector
- Power connectors (to accept power from the PSU)
- Connectors for CPU and case fans
- Keyboard socket
- Mouse port
- Serial/parallel port
- USB ports

Most people wonder what the battery on the motherboard does (see Figure 4-6). This battery serves two purposes: it powers the PC system clock that keeps track of the date and time, and it also provides power to the CMOS (complimentary metal oxide semiconductor) to store the BIOS (basic input/output system) settings. You will see more of the BIOS and the importance of the CMOS during the building phase of the PC.

These batteries are very reliable and will last for many years.

FIGURE 4-6: Motherboard battery.

Optional Motherboard Features

Additional features that may or may not be present on a motherboard (depending on price and quality) include:

- **On-board video adaptor.** Buying a motherboard with an on-board video adaptor saves on your having to purchase a separate video adaptor. On-board video adaptors are usually poorer quality and provide less power than a separate video adaptor, but they are ideal for office PCs or PCs that play low-specification games.

  On-board video adaptors use a portion of system RAM for graphics processing (usually between 8 and 64 MB, the more RAM they use, the better they perform) so you might want to purchase additional RAM for the system. (See Chapter 5, "Choosing the Right RAM.")

- **On-board modem.** For those who still use a modem or connect to the web or send faxes, this can save on having to buy a separate modem.

- **On-board network adaptor.** More and more PCs connect to a network nowadays, and an on-board network card can be a useful feature.

- **Additional USB ports.** With so many USB devices you can't get enough USB ports!

- **FireWire ports.** Some devices (especially video cameras and external hard drives/optical drives) either require a FireWire port or can make use of either a USB or FireWire port. Having a couple of FireWire ports on a system is handy in case they are needed in the future.

Additional Motherboard Considerations

Here are a few other points to bear in mind when looking for the right motherboard for you.

Chipset

You will hear a lot about chipset when looking for motherboards. The *chipset*, put simply, is the main chip on the motherboard that controls the on board features (think of it as a helper to the CPU, but directing operations rather than processing instructions). Some people will advocate one chipset over another, claiming better performance or reliability. We recommend that you not get caught up in worrying about the motherboard chipset for your first PC. Let budget dictate your choice of motherboard and use this as a guide to performance of the board — the more expensive the board, the faster and better it will be.

RAM

Know what kind of RAM the motherboard takes. DDR and DDR2 are the most common types available nowadays. DDR2 is faster than DDR and because of that more expensive.

Also, know how much RAM your motherboard can hold. Most motherboards have a ceiling on the amount of RAM they can take, and if this value is low it might mean that you might hit the limit quickly and have to upgrade the motherboard if you want to add more. Consider a limit of 1–1.5 GB about normal.

Motherboard Speeds

The CPU speed isn't the only place where you're going to come across clock speeds. Just as CPUs have an operating speed (nowadays measured in GHz) motherboards have an operating speed, or, more accurately, the motherboard communicates with different devices at different speeds. There are two speed terms to bear in mind:

- **FSB or Front Side Bus.** The Front Side Bus connects the processor, chipset, RAM, and video adaptor AGP socket and the speed (measured in MHz) refers to the data transfer speed. The faster the speed, the faster the motherboard (and more expensive the motherboard).

- **RAM speed.** The RAM operates internally at a specific speed (measured in MHz, like FSB). The faster the speed, the faster the system.

Warranty

No one wants to think about things going wrong, but they do. Check out the warranty on any motherboard you buy. Also, check out any additional warranties that the store might offer. However, don't be tempted to purchase an additional store warranty—boards drop quickly in price, and the price you pay for an extra 12 month's warranty is likely to be more than the board is worth. Also, store warranties are filled with legalese and jargon that make it tricky to make a claim on the warranty.

Bundles

You might find that even if the store doesn't offer motherboard/CPU bundles they might have other bundles available (motherboard/RAM, motherboard/hard drive, etc). Be on the look out for bargains!

CPU and Motherboard Care

You've bought your CPU and motherboard in anticipation of building your PC. Here's how to keep your investment safe until they are ready to go into the PC.

- **Double-check that the CPU and motherboard are compatible.** Check the specification carefully before opening the items because you might not be able to return them if incorrect after opening.

- **Keep CPUs in their packaging until required.** A modern CPU can have almost a thousand pins on the base to allow it to connect up to a motherboard. These are very small, thin, and fragile, and very easily damaged. When it comes time to take the CPU out of the packaging, take great care not to damage the CPU (or to cut yourself—CPUs can be well packaged and difficult to remove from the plastic bubble packaging).

- **Store the motherboard in the original packaging.** Feel free to look at and examine your motherboard, but be careful not to flex or bend it the board (minute cracks and fractures can wreck a motherboard); take precautions against zapping it with static electricity and return it to the ESD bag and box for storage (see Figure 4-7).

FIGURE 4-7: Safely store your motherboard in an ESD bag until you're ready to use it.

- **Never store anything any other parts in the motherboard box.** The box is there to protect the motherboard and the motherboard alone.

The safest place for a motherboard is fitted correctly into a PC case, and the safest place for a CPU is fitted into the appropriate socket on a motherboard that's fitted into a PC case. If you want to skip ahead, this process is covered in Chapter 14, "Fitting the Basic Parts."

Summary

In this chapter, you've looked at two of the most critical components of a PC — the CPU and the motherboard. These are the brain and nervous system of the PC, respectively, and they form the structure onto which the rest of the PC is built.

Take your time choosing a suitable CPU and then in choosing a good motherboard to fit that to.

In the next chapter, you look at choosing the right RAM for your PC and the differences between the different types of RAM available.

Take Action

Before you move on to the next chapter, be sure that you're prepared:

- Consider the kind of PC you're building. Is it a budget PC or a high-end PC? Let that be your guide as to what CPU you want.

- Find a range of CPUs to suit your needs. Find out what "socket" they need.

- Find corresponding motherboards with the appropriate CPU socket.

- Get a short list of motherboards to fit your chosen CPU and make sure that they have all the features you want.

Choosing the Right RAM

W e've looked at the relationship between CPU speed and overall PC speed. Basically, the faster the CPU, the faster the PC will run applications. Think of your CPU like a car engine. The bigger the engine, the more power the car will have. When the PC isn't working very hard, you might not notice this extra CPU power (you don't notice that a car has a big engine when you are driving at 30 mph, but you do notice it when the going gets tough).

If CPU power is analogous to the size of an engine in a car, then RAM is comparable to the overall size of a vehicle. In much the same way that you can get more people into a big car, if you have more RAM you can run more programs simultaneously. Engine size is still important if the vehicle is going to drive smoothly under a heavy load.

In this chapter, we are going to be looking at RAM, different RAM types, and how much RAM you should install into your PC.

Understanding RAM

RAM (an acronym for random access memory) is a working memory space that PCs use to load data and programs that are regularly accessed. The data stored in RAM can be accessed in any order (hence the word "random") as opposed to, say, data stored on magnetic tapes, which has to be read sequentially (this format is uncommon nowadays other than for backups). The "random" in the name is a historical throwback much like the terms "hard" drive and "floppy" drive (early floppy disks were made of soft material and were floppy).

The main reason for loading data into RAM as opposed to accessing data directly off the hard drive is that it's much faster to access data from RAM than it is from a hard drive. To give you an idea of just how different the access speeds are, data access speeds from a hard drive are measured in milliseconds (thousands of a second); RAM access speeds are measured in nanoseconds (billionth of a second).

The First Rule of PC Building

Never assume that a term only means one specific thing. The term "bank" is used to describe the slot that memory modules fit into. However, you might also come across it being used in relation to the inner workings of memory modules.

For the purposes of this book, the term bank will be used exclusively to describe the slot into which a memory module is installed.

There's another crucial difference between RAM and hard drives. While there's no doubt that RAM is much faster than hard drives, hard drives have the upper hand when it comes to capacity. While hard drives can now be measured in hundreds of gigabytes, RAM modules are at mostly around 1 GB. Commonly used RAM modules sizes range from 128 MB to 512 MB.

RAM comes in the form of memory modules (or chips) mounted on circuit boards. These circuit boards are fitted onto the motherboard via the RAM module slots on the board, known as *banks*.

It used to be that RAM modules had to be installed in pairs of similar modules, so if you wanted a PC that had 64 MB of RAM you had to install two 32 MB modules. Three drawbacks of this system were that:

- You always needed two modules instead of one, which meant that manufacturers had to keep a larger inventory of modules.
- An upgrade sometimes meant throwing away two modules.
- There was twice the chance of being affected by a faulty memory module when adding new RAM modules.

Technology has progressed and now modules can be installed singly, which is both cheaper and less hassle overall. However, be aware that you might get better performance from having RAM in both banks because the motherboard makes use of a technology known as "dual-channel."

Types of RAM

A number of different types (or styles) of RAM are available. These different types come about from advances in technology as older types are replaced by newer, faster technologies. Here you'll take a tour of the RAM types supported by current motherboards. This means that if you are using this book to help you upgrade a current system, the RAM you have may not be mentioned here.

Tip A good site for anyone wanting to upgrade memory and wanting information on compatible RAM is www.crucial.com.

DDR

Currently, the most popular type of RAM in use is called DDR RAM. DDR stands for "Double Data Rate" and the "double" comes from the fact that it utilizes technology that makes it twice as fast as regular SDRAM (Synchronous Dynamic Random Access Memory) upon which it was based.

DDR does this amazing trick of being able to transfer data at twice the standard operating speed of the RAM by transferring data on every rising edge and falling edge of the clock pulse. This is a huge advantage compared to SDRAM. For example, if you assume a clock speed of 100 MHz, SDRAM will transfer data only on every rising edge of the clock pulse, thus having an effective transfer rate of 100 MHz. DDR, being able to transfer data at the rising *and* falling edge of the clock pulse, has an effective transfer rate of 200 MHz.

Keeping everything else equal, this doubling of the transfer rate alone represents a huge gain in performance. However, as with most things, more was demanded from RAM.

DDR2

The "2" in DDR2 refers to the fact that this new technology again represents a doubling of the data transfer rate when compared to DDR. This additional doubling of the speed of the RAM is due to improvements made on the chip rather than additional transfers made per clock cycle.

DDR2 also requires less power than DDR and SDRAM, reducing system power consumption and heat generated (making it handy in laptops).

How to Identify DDR and DDR2 RAM

DDR and DDR2 modules come in a variety of sizes (both memory capacity and physical size) and can have different numbers of connector pins, as shown in Table 5-1. You will need motherboard support for whatever RAM type you choose.

Table 5-1   DDR and DDR2 Pin Counts

DDR	DDR2
100-pin	200-pin
172-pin	240-pin
184-pin	244-pin
200-pin	

The most common DDR module is the module with a 184 pins, as shown in Figure 5-1. The most commonly used DDR2 module is the 240-pin module.

FIGURE **5-1: A 184-pin DDR memory module.**

You can easily tell the difference between DDR/DDR2 RAM and earlier SDRAM by counting the number of notches on the connector edge. DDR and DDR2 modules have one notch in the connector edge, while SDRAM has two notches. This notch keys how the module fits into the bank on the motherboard (it can only fit one way). See Figure 5-2.

Different DDR and DDR2 modules are identified by a specification code based on speed and data transfer rates. See Figure 5-3.

Tables 5-2 and 5-3 list the common codes for DDR and DDR2.

FIGURE 5-2: A single connector edge notch on a DDR module.

FIGURE 5.3: DDR RAM banks on a motherboard. Physically, you can fit any DDR module type, but the motherboard supports only PC-2100 and PC-2700.

Table 5-2   DDR Codes

Specification Code	Speed (MHz)	Bandwidth (GB/s)
PC-1600	100	1.6
PC-2100	133	2.1
PC-2700	166	2.7
PC-3200	200	3.2

Table 5-3   DDR2 Codes

Specification Code	Speed (MHz)	Bandwidth (GB/s)
PC2-3200 (DDR2-400)	100	3.2
PC2-4200 (DDR2-533)	133	4.2
PC2-5400 (DDR2-677)	133	5.2

Remember that the speeds of all of these DDR modules are doubled to 200, 266, 333, and 400 MHz, respectively. The speed of each of these DDR2 modules is quadrupled to 400 and 533 MHz, respectively.

There are faster DDR2 RAM modules available but they are rare, expensive, and limited to specialist motherboards. These include:

- DDR2-667
- DDR2-800
- DDR2-933
- DDR2-1066

The Bottom Line — Speed — Maybe Not!

So is the bottom line of all this speed? No, it's not. In fact, from a random data access speed point of view, the performance of DDR2 is worse than that of DDR. This is because of the way DDR works, and it's quite complicated. But, you can see clearly from the preceding tables that the overall data transfer rates for PC2-3200 is the same as for PC-3200.

So, what are the benefits of using DDR2 if it's not performance?

The benefits come from the fact that you can run a module at a slower clock cycle speeds and get better performance. To you and me this means lower power consumption and less heat generation, and it also means that it's easier to build motherboards that can handle the data transfers at lower clock speeds.

Expect to pay more for DDR2 memory modules than for the equivalent DDR modules, although this price difference isn't great.

Note An important thing to bear in mind about the overall speed of a PC is that it is similar to the analogy "a chain is only as strong as its weakest link." A fast PC requires all the parts to be of a high quality and performance, and it's not possible to speed up a PC made out of slow parts simply by adding more RAM.

Determining the Type of RAM That's Best for You

You've bought a motherboard and a compatible CPU, and now you want to buy RAM. How can you find out which type of RAM you should you buy to make sure that everything is compatible? Despite there being a number of different DDR and DDR2 specifications, it's not actually hard to buy the right RAM for your system.

Here are some ways to make sure that you get the right RAM.

Check Your Motherboard Documentation

Referring to the documentation that came with your motherboard is the simplest way to find out what RAM your motherboard is compatible with. Your motherboard's documentation should tell you the RAM specification along with the maximum RAM it can work with. Look for something like:

```
2 x 184-pin DDR PC-2100/PC-2700/PC-3200, Max 2 GB
3 x 184-pin DDR PC-2700/PC-3200, Max 3 GB
```

The first example shows that the motherboard is capable of taking two modules of 184-pin DDR PC-2100, PC-2700 or PC-3200, up to a maximum of 2 GB (basically two 1-GB modules), while the second motherboard can take three modules of 184-pin DDR PC-2700 or PC-3200 up to a maximum of 3 GB (in other words, three 1-GB modules).

Buffered/ECC/Parity

Look through a listing of RAM modules, and you'll come across terms such as buffered and unbuffered, ECC (which stands for Error Correction Code) and non-ECC, parity and nonparity. This can all be confusing. *Buffered memory* contains a special buffer that allows it to cope with the high electrical demands of a system that has a lot of memory. *Parity* and *ECC* both refer to a chip on board the RAM module that handles error corrections.

To cut through all the confusion, most standard motherboards require memory that is:

- Unbuffered
- Non-ECC
- Nonparity

As a rule, buffered memory, memory that uses ECC, and parity memory are reserved for server systems or critical PC systems. They are also slower in terms of data transfer speeds, and most normal PCs don't need this and won't benefit from this more expensive form of RAM.

Buy a Bundle

You can find plenty of good bundle deals. This is where you can buy a motherboard, CPU, and RAM for less than the selling price of the individual components. This way, not only are you guaranteed compatibility, but you also get a good price.

However, be careful of deals that include only a small amount of RAM. Buying a bundle that comes with only 256 MB of RAM could mean you later have to spend more on additional RAM for your system. (See the section "Deciding How Much RAM to Install" later in this chapter for a guide on how much RAM is needed for the machine you're building.)

Buy from a Memory Vendor

If you are buying memory and want to be guaranteed high quality memory, I recommend that you go to a memory vendor such as Crucial (www.crucial.com). Not only do these people stock the whole range of memory modules that you might need, but they also have an amazing online Memory Advisor™ tool that guarantees you get the right memory for your motherboard. Enter your motherboard details, and it quickly finds you the right type RAM for that board, along with details of the maximum RAM that the board can take.

Buying from a memory vendor is a simple, no-nonsense, and cheap way to buy memory. Not only do you get convenience, but you also get a product that's backed by high-quality tech support and a good warranty. Also, a high-quality memory vendor will test every module prior to shipping to ensure the highest standards possible, and the RAM will be shipped taking all the proper anti-static precautions to ensure that it reaches you in perfect working order (see Figure 5-4).

Tip

One of the great things about DDR and DDR2 modules is that later ones are backward compatible (as long as the number of pins matches). So, a board that can take PC-2100 modules is also compatible with PC-2700 and PC-3200, and a board that is compatible with PC-2700 will also be able to work with PC-3200 (but not PC-2100). The same is true for DDR2, although DDR and DDR2 modules aren't interchangeable (there's no danger of doing this by accident because the number of pins is completely different).

FIGURE 5-4: A well-packaged RAM module shipped from Crucial.

Deciding How Much RAM to Install

After you know what kind of RAM your system needs (or you decide to use a vendor to supply the right RAM), you come to the question of how much RAM to install.

Modern motherboards can all take in excess of 1 GB of RAM, while the smallest RAM module you can buy these days is 128 MB. Typical motherboard limits are somewhere around 1 to 3 GB. Don't try to exceed this figure because things will go wrong (at the very least your system won't recognize any amount over the limit, the worst case scenario being that it won't boot up at all).

So, your motherboard maximum is one ceiling to bear in mind. However, there's another memory limit, and that is the one imposed by the operating system you plan to install. Table 5-4 lists the memory limits for current popular PC operating systems.

Table 5-4   Operating System Memory Limits

Operating System	Max Memory (GB)
Microsoft Windows XP (Home and Pro)	4
Windows 2000	4
Windows ME/98	1.5
Linux	64

This operating system limit is another ceiling you are up against. As a rule, your motherboard will be able to take less RAM than the latest versions of the Microsoft Windows can so it's unlikely to be a problem unless you plan on using Windows ME or earlier (which is not recommended because you are likely to run into all sorts of compatibility issues).

RAM modules come in a variety of sizes. Common RAM module sizes are:

- 128 MB
- 256 MB
- 512 MB
- 1 GB

Note   You can buy memory modules larger than 1 GB, but the price is currently high for these modules.

Price of RAM modules can be confusing. The smaller RAM modules are cheaper than bigger ones, but the price isn't linear. One 256 MB module is cheaper than two 128 modules, and one 512 MB module is cheaper than two 256 MB modules. However, once you get to 1 GB you begin to pay an additional premium. For example, at the time of this writing, a 1-GB DDR module costs about three times as much as a 512-MB module.

It's not, however, all about price. Most modern boards that can take DDR and DDR2 memory have a feature called *dual-channel*. This means that you will get better system performance if you install two smaller modules than one big one. For example, if you want a system with 1 GB of RAM, installing two 512 MB modules will give you better performance.

So, how much RAM do you really need? Use Table 5-5 as a quick guide to help.

Table 5-5   How Much RAM Do You Need?

Amount of RAM	Notes
64 MB	Minimum support RAM for XP. Ludicrously low and totally unfeasible.
128 MB	Minimum recommended by Microsoft for Windows XP. Rather low and will seriously degrade performance. Not recommended.
256 MB	The minimum that we would recommend for a PC running Windows XP and applications such as word processors or spreadsheets. 256 MB of RAM is ideal for an office PC.
512 MB	This will give you a PC with more power. Not only will it run applications better and faster than a PC installed with 256 MB of RAM, but it will also be better placed to run games and future applications.
768 MB	This is a serious amount of RAM, and your PC will be able to handle task such as professional-level video editing and photo editing and also high-end games.
1 GB	Seems like a lot of RAM, but some people (especially those who use programs such as Adobe Photoshop) consider this a starting point! If you intend to use your PC extensively for video editing, sound editing, or manipulating large or complex graphics, then this extra RAM will come in useful. It will also come in useful for gaming.
Over 1 GB	Performance gains continue to be felt well over 1 GB. The more RAM you have installed, the more the more high-performance applications you will be able to run. Also, the more RAM you have, the more future-proof your system will be and the more likely that it will continue to be able to run the latest software for a number of years (assuming the CPU is powerful enough).

If you're not sure how much RAM to install, then we recommend you install 512 MB. Whether you install that as a single module or two paired modules depends on whether you think you will add more in the future. If you plan to add more, install a single module and take advantage of the added power of dual-channel later rather than installing RAM you may quickly need to throw out to make room for more. However, if you feel that 512 MB is all that you need for the foreseeable future, install two 256-MB modules because this will give you better long-term performance. However, the choice is ultimately up to you.

Note Never skimp on the amount of RAM you install. It's far better to have more RAM installed in your new PC than too little! Using a PC that doesn't have enough RAM is a miserable, unsatisfying experience—not the kind of PC you want to build for yourself!

You will find more information on fitting RAM in Chapter 14, "Fitting the Basic Parts."

Summary

In this chapter, we've looked at RAM and its function in a PC. We've also looked at the different types of RAM available (DDR and DDR2) and what these differences mean. We've seen how to ensure compatibility between motherboard and RAM modules and how you can get the right amount of RAM for your new system.

In the next chapter, we're going to move on to look at hard drives and floppy drives.

Take Action

Before you move on to the next chapter, be sure that you're prepared:

- Find out what RAM your short-listed motherboards support.

- Find out what RAM you need.

- Decide how much RAM you want to install into your PC.

- Find out the cost of the RAM from a reputable vendor.

Choosing Hard Drives and Floppy Drives

I f the PC's RAM is the short term memory of the system, then the hard drive and (to a lesser extent) the floppy drive represent the long-term memory of the system. Data stored in long-term memory remains well beyond when the file was created or last used. When you switch off the PC (or the power goes out for whatever reason) whatever information was stored in RAM is lost forever, while data stored on the hard drive is safe and can be accessed when the system is switched on again.

When you save a letter you've typed, an email you've received or a digital photo you've taken you want that data to be stored safe until it's needed again rather than deleted as soon as the PC is switched off. For this you need a storage mechanism that is permanent, which is what hard drives offer.

Moving things from one PC to another is a lot easier nowadays in this connected world. Homes that have more than one PC generally have both networked together and connected to the Internet so that sharing files is easy, but there are times when being able to transfer small files (an important document, say, or perhaps drivers for a piece of hardware) is quicker and easier if you have a floppy drive and a few disks.

Let's begin by taking a look at hard drives.

Hard Drives

The *hard drive* is a computer's main storage device and is used to store data such as the operating system, the applications, and the user's files and documents, as well as system settings particular to the user. A hard drive is non-removable in the sense that after it has been installed into a PC, it is left there until the user upgrades it or it becomes faulty.

What goes on inside a hard drive is not important information when it comes to building a PC, but it's useful to have a basic idea of how it works. Here's a quick rundown.

Never Open a Hard Drive

Take a look in any catalog or online at hard drives and the sales literature always shows the hard drive with the top cover removed and the platters and heads exposed. This is probably done to give the buyer an insight into the marvels of technology hidden in the metal box and also perhaps to reduce on curiosity. Problem is, this also tends to give some people the idea that it's okay to open a hard drive (it's not hard, you normally just need a TORX bit to open the screws) and have a look.

But resist the temptation! There's a very good chance that if you open a drive that you will let in dirt and thus kill the drive (and there's no need to mention that this will certainly invalidate any warranty you have). If you are curious as to what goes on inside a drive, then take apart an old one (you can buy second hand drives really cheap online).

Inside a Hard Drive

A hard drive consists of three major components:

- **A set of platters.** This set of platters is the main component, and the platters are made of either an aluminum alloy or glass/ceramic, and coated with a magnetic medium. Modern platters are double-sided, and all hard drives have more than one. In modern hard drives the platters are spun at 5,400 RPM (revolutions per minute) or faster. It is onto these platters that the data is written.

- **Drive heads.** The reading and writing of the data on the platters is carried out by the drive heads. Each platter surface has a head that does the reading and writing. These heads are fitted onto an actuator arm and driven by a motor.

- **Motor.** Finally, there's a motor that spins the platters around so that they can be written to and read from.

The entire hard drive is then encased in a metal box, and the connectors for it are all at one end.

A modern hard drive is a magnificent feat of engineering. With the platters spinning at full speed, the distance between the read/write heads and the platters is around 50 nanometers (50 millionths of a meter). Compare this to a human hair, which is about 2,000 times thicker than this. The inside of a hard drive has to be free of dust and debris (they are assembled in a clean-room environment) because given the speed of the rotating platters and the small tolerances involved, even the smallest particle of dust getting trapped between the head and the platters could cause tremendous damage to the drive, damaging both the head and the surface of the platters.

Hard Drive Care

Here are a few common sense hard drive care steps you can take to protect your drive from damage.

- **Store your hard drive in a well protected box and wrapped in an antistatic bag.** Likely, this will be the way the drive is stored when you purchase it (if not then consider the drive to be suspect). Keep it stored like this until it is required.

- **Protect your hard drive from falls and sharp knocks.** After all, a hard drive is a mechanical device.

- **Protect the connectors at the end of the drive from damage.** These connectors consist of small pins that are easily bent or broken off. A bent pin can be straightened with a pair of tweezers if you are careful (and very lucky!), but a broken pin means a dead drive.

- **Install your hard drive at room temperature.** If your hard drive has been stored in a cold, humid environment, then allow the drive to come up to room temperature naturally over a few hours before installing it. This will dramatically reduce the amount of wear and tear that the drive will experience when first switched on. It's also a good idea to do this too if it's just been delivered to you after transit in the mail.

- **Never peel any labels off the drive.** This can invalidate your warranty.

Types of Hard Drives

There are three kinds of hard drives that you will come across when considering your purchase:

- SCSI (Small Computer System Interface)
- SATA (Serial ATA, where ATA stands for Advanced Technology Attachment)
- PATA (Parallel ATA)

Of the three, the PATA hard drive interface is by far the most common (see Figure 6-1). SCSI hard drives (pronounced "scuzzie," this is a communication standard for peripherals) have been around for years but are rarely made use of in home PCs. While SATA hard drives are much newer, motherboard support for these isn't as widespread as for PATA.

Most motherboards will come for support for PATA drives, and some hard drives come with additional connectors for SATA drives (this will be stated clearly). To make use of SATA, you need a SATA-compatible motherboard, a SATA drive, and SATA cables to connect the drive to the motherboard. While SATA drives are a little faster than PATA drives, the gains are negligible unless you have a really fast SATA drive. The PATA hard drive is the most commonly available hard drive, and for simplicity, it is the type that we will be concentrating on in this book. If you wish to fit a SATA drive, then the process will be almost identical to that of fitting a PATA drive (we'll mention any differences as we go).

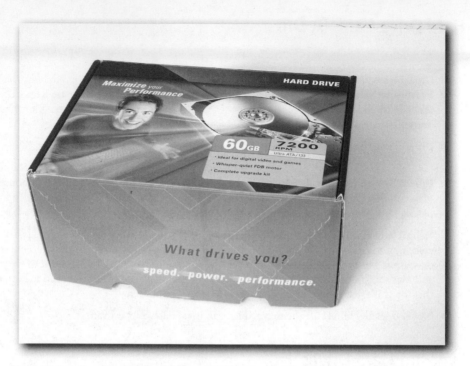

FIGURE 6-1: A Parallel ATA hard drive retail kit: Maxtor DiamondMax Plus 60 GB drive.

PATA drives come in two different sizes (physical dimensions, as opposed to data capacity):

- 2-1/2 inch
- 3-1/2 inch

The difference is the width of the drive bay they are designed to fit. Desktop computers make use of 3-1/2–inch drives, and the smaller 2-1/2–inch drives are reserved for use within laptop computers.

Note   When you are looking for a PATA drive you might see them referred to by a number of different names. Most vendors are good and now use the terms "PATA" or "Parallel ATA," but some still refuse to change and refer to them generically as "IDE drives," "EIDE drives," "internal IDE," or "internal EIDE" (IDE stands for Integrated Device Electronics and EIDE for Enhanced Integrated Device Electronics). If you are in any doubt, then either call the vendor and ask or choose another vendor who uses the right terms.

Anatomy of a PATA Drive

One PATA drive looks much the same as any other PATA drive. Figure 6-2 shows a PATA that, apart from branding, looks like any other. The outer casing is approximately 4.0 x 5.8 x 1.0 inch (100 x 147 x 25 mm). It comes as a surprise to many that the drives aren't 3-1/2-inch wide because they fit into what is called a 3-1/2–inch drive bay. The bay doesn't get its name from the dimensions of the bay, but rather from the size of the floppy disk that the floppy drive bay was meant to fit (3-1/2–inch drives, which are still in use, and the older, now obsolete 5-1/4 inch drive). A typical drive weighs about 1.5 lb (680 g), but this varies between models and manufacturers.

FIGURE 6-2: The Maxtor DiamondMax Plus 60-GB drive.

The base of the casing is a cast alloy, while the top is made of pressed sheet metal. Into both sides of the drive are cut six threaded screw holes (three on each side). These are used to mount the drive into the drive bay.

On the rear of a drive are two blocks of connectors and a set of jumpers. The larger connector is the data connector and has 39 pins, as shown in Figure 6-3. It looks like 40 pins, but years ago one was removed because it wasn't used, and this also helped people not to attempt to attach a cable the wrong way. The smaller 4-pin connector, shown in Figure 6-4, is a power connector. If you take a close look at both of these connectors, you will find that they are keyed to prevent the improper fitting. The key for the data connector is in the middle at the bottom, while the power cable isn't actually square but cut off at the corners at the top.

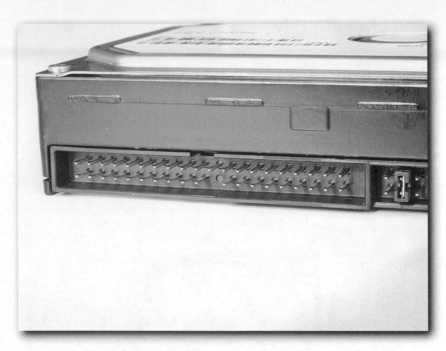

FIGURE 6-3: Data connectors have 39 pins.

FIGURE 6-4: Power connectors have 4 pins.

The *jumper* is a primitive switch (see Figure 6-5). A jumper consists of pin connectors, and two of them are joined together with a small metal bridge. Jumpers are there for you to select whether the drive is a master (also called primary) or slave (also known as secondary) drive on the data cable. There is also a setting for "cable select," where the drive can determine the correct setting from its position on the cable.

FIGURE 6-5: Drive jumpers allow you to set the primary or secondary drive for the data cable.

 Note You can find much more on the drive settings in Chapter 15, "Adding Storage."

Hard Drive Cables

A PATA hard drive needs two cables, one to carry data to and from the drive (called the data cable) and a power cable. If one of these cables is missing or incorrectly plugged in, then the drive won't work.

Data Cables

The data cable generally comes in the form of a ribbon with three connectors on it, one at each end and one not quite in the middle.

Ribbon or Round?

In addition to the standard ribbon data cable, there are a number of round cables also available for hard drives (where the wires are routed into a round trunk rather than a ribbon). The idea behind this is that these cables, being round, have less of an effect on the air flow through the PC case and help prevent devices from overheating. That might be true, but being round they are also a lot stiffer than ribbons, and they can be rather more difficult to bend and can easily pop out of the back of drives. This is why we recommend ribbons.

Despite what many people believe, round cables are not faster than ribbon cables and offer nothing in the way of performance gains.

The data cable cannot exceed 18 inches (460 mm) in total length, 12 inches (300 mm) from first to second connector, and six inches (160 mm) from second to third. If the cable is any longer than this, signal integrity along the cable is impaired.

These connectors are color coded on most cables. Table 6-1 lists the most common colors for data cables.

Table 6-1   Data Cable Color Coding

Color	Position on Cable	Connected To
Blue	End	Motherboard IDE connector
Black	End	Master or primary drive
Gray	Mid-ribbon (approximately)	Slave or secondary drive

These colors aren't fixed in stone. You might see cables with all the connectors a different color. (The standard isn't much of a standard at all when it comes to this, and this can lead to a lot of confusion.)

Cable confusion doesn't end there. There are two types of cable: the modern 80-wire cable (see Figure 6-6) and the older 40-wire cable. It's quite easy to tell them apart because the wires are finer and feel softer in the 80-wire cable. The difference is that the newer 80-wire cables have additional wires to separate the signals to achieve the faster communication speeds.

Don't bother with 40-wire cables. If these are supplied with any device discard them and replace with 80-wire cables (sometimes referred to as ATA 100 IDE cable). Figure 6-7 shows a ribbon data cable connected to a hard drive.

Note

Remember: 80-wire, not 80-pin! Many people get confused and call 80-wire hard drive cables 80-pin or 80-connector. They are all still 40-pin cables!

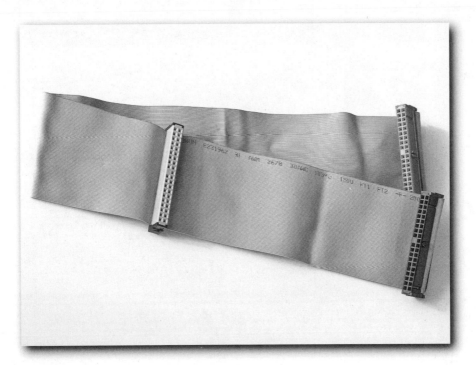

FIGURE 6-6: An 80-wire, 40-pin ribbon data cable.

We'll go into more detail on connecting devices to ribbon cables in Chapter 14, "Fitting the Basic Parts."

Power Cables

The second connector to look at is the power cable. This cable originates from the power supply unit and consists of four separate wires, as described in Table 6-2.

Table 6-2   Power Cable Color

Color	Signal
Red Pin 4	+5V
Yellow Pin 1	+12V
Black Pin 2	Ground
Black Pin 3	Ground

FIGURE 6-7: Ribbon data cable connected to hard drive.

Why two different voltage inputs? Because the electronics on the circuit board needs 5V, while the motors powering the actuator arm and spinning the platters both need 12V.

This connector is also keyed, and there is no risk of plugging it into the hard drive incorrectly (or CD/DVD drive, since the cable is the same).

 Note Carefully check the plastic housing around each of the power cable connectors. When the cover is intact, there is little or no danger of the cable shorting against the case or another device, but where the plastic is damaged there's a risk of short circuit. Don't use any connectors that are damaged (cover them in insulating tape for added safety).

Keyed Cables

Now take a look at the cable connectors that fit these connectors on the hard drive. In Figure 6-8, you can clearly see the keying and how this prevents improper insertion into the drive.

FIGURE 6-8: You cannot incorrectly attach a power cable to a hard drive.

The Right Hard Drive for You

Choosing the right hard drive for your system isn't easy. Ideally, you need to weigh up three different variables:

- Drive capacity
- Drive speed
- Number of drives

Drive Capacity

Hard drives are now measured in gigabytes. The larger the hard drive, the more data it can hold and the more expensive the drive. Typically, onto a gigabyte of space you can save, on average, about 650 digital photos (assuming that they are each about 1.5 MB) or about 400 MP3 songs (assuming that each is 2.5 MB).

Shop around because the difference in price between two or three drives can be very low. For example, the difference in price between a 60 GB, 80 GB, and 120 GB drive can be as little as $20 or so. If in any doubt and your finances allow, always go for the larger drive — you'll be amazed how quickly even a drive that seems massive at first will fill up!

How do you know how big a drive to buy? Use Table 6-3 to help you decide what drive capacity you might need.

Table 6-3   Drive Capacity

Application	Suggested Capacity
Office PC	40–60 GB
Home PC	40–60 GB
Gaming PC	120 GB
Serious gaming	200 GB
Digital photography	200–350 GB
Video editing	500 GB+

The suggested capacities in Table 6-3 are all average figures based on estimates of different types of PCs. If in doubt, err to a higher capacity. Better to have it and not need it than want it and not have it!

Drive Speed

Drive speed is determined by two factors:

- The RPM of the drive (that is, how fast the platters turn)
- How much on-board cache (memory) the drive has

Platter RPM speed plays a key part in overall drive speed because it determines how fast the platter can move the portion of the surface that holds the data to the heads for reading.

Imagine that you are sitting at a huge circular table that rotates and the food that you want is placed on that table exactly opposite to you. You have to rotate the table to bring the food to you — the faster you rotate the table, the quicker you'll get your food. That's how it works with hard drives. The faster they rotate, the less lag there is in reading or writing the data. RPM values range from about 5,400 RPM to 12,000 RPM and above. The faster the RPM the faster the drive (and the more expensive it will be).

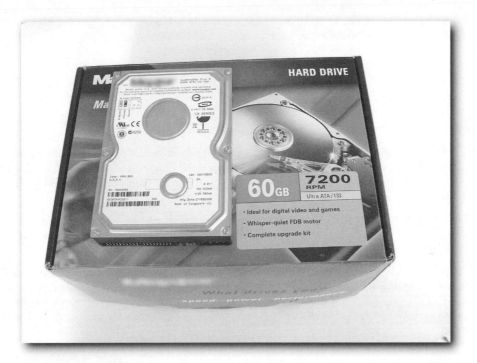

FIGURE 6-9: 7200 RPM drive.

The average time that a drive takes to find a spot on the platter is called *seek time* and is measured in milliseconds. Seek times vary from drive to drive but usually fall between around 5 ms (very fast!) and 10 ms (pretty slow).

The *cache* is the on-board memory a hard drive uses to speed up drive operations, especially writing data to the platters. In general, the bigger the cache, the faster the drive will be. Typical cache values range from 512 KB to 16 MB.

Number of Drives

A standard PC can have up to four hard drives installed, two IDE cables connected to the motherboard, and two drives per cable (then there would be no room for CD or DVD drives). With capacities going up to 500 GB and beyond, having more than one hard drive might be seen as an indulgence. However, there are a number of good reasons to have multiple drives. Here are some good reasons:

- Additional storage capacity
- Backup (store your data on one and your backup on the other, so if one drive fails you've still go your data)
- Multiple hard drives as an organizational tool
- Upgrade the computer with more storage capacity without having the hassle of moving data

Note Not sure if you want one hard drive or two? Install one and see how you get on. It's easy to install a second (or third) hard drive later if you find that the need arises.

Floppy Drives

For years the humble 3-1/2–inch floppy drive has been gracing the front of all PCs. While the hard drive was the mainstay of high-capacity storage, the floppy drive represented a quick and easy way to carry data to and from the PC system before computers became linked by networks and the Internet.

Back in the days when hard drives were measured in megabytes, the 1.44 MB of read and write storage capacity of a single floppy disk held was a fair amount of storage. Many files, and even whole applications, could fit on a single floppy.

Times have changed. Both hard drive capacities and file sizes have increased manyfold, and now the 1.44 MB offered by a single floppy disk seems almost too small to bother with. Some big PC makers are now not installing floppy drives on their systems, and instead are relying solely on the CD/DVD drive.

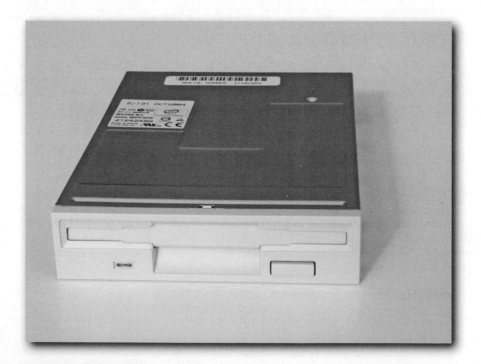

FIGURE 6-10: Floppy drive.

The Need for Floppy Drives

So, do you still need a floppy drive? We believe that it is best that you do. The truth is that you are unlikely to need it very often, but for the $10 or so that it's likely to cost, you can look at it as insurance.

In day-to-day PC use, the floppy drive is not likely to see much use at all, but if you ever need to troubleshoot the system, then a floppy drive where you can make use of boot disks and diagnostic software could save the day.

Floppy Drive Basics

Floppy drives can be fitted into any 3-1/2–inch drive bay in the PC that has a removable faceplate that allows the front of the drive to be accessed.

A floppy drive is approximately 4 x 5-3/4 x 1 inch (100 x 145 x 25 mm) and is set up so that the floppy disk fits into the front and the connectors are at the rear. Along the side of the drive are six threaded screw holes (three each side), and these are used to attach the drive to the PC case.

You might also be interested in a floppy drive that has a built-in reader for various removable memory used in digital cameras and PDAs. These are now quite cheap and add more validity to having a floppy drive installed!

Floppy Drive Connections

At the rear of the floppy drive are two connectors, one for a data ribbon and one for the power connector.

Data Cables

The floppy drive cable is a strange cable indeed. It looks at first like a standard PATA hard drive cable, but on closer inspection you'll notice that near one of the connectors a number of the wires are twisted.

The cable is a 34-pin, 34-wire cable (as opposed to the 80-wire PATA hard drive cable), and seven of the wires are twisted near to one of the connectors. The connectors on the cable are keyed in a similar way to those on a hard drive cable to prevent the cable from being incorrectly fitted. The connectors are shown in Figure 6-11.

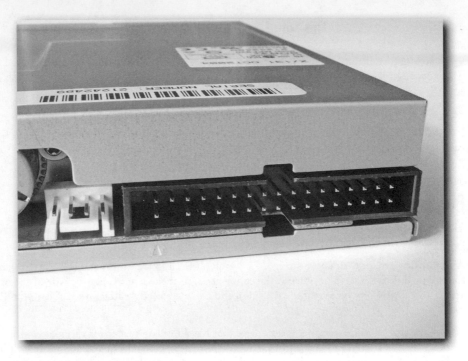

FIGURE 6-11: Floppy drive connectors.

The connector opposite the twist is fitted to the floppy drive connector on the motherboard, and if your system has one floppy drive installed (and there's no reason to have more than one fitted) that is fitted to the connector closest to the twist (the middle cable is not used).

Tip   In case you're wondering, that twist in the cable is used to determine which drive is drive A: and which is drive B:. Drive A: is always connected to the connector closest to the twist.

Power Cables

The power cable that feeds power to the floppy drive from the power supply unit is smaller than the connector that feeds the hard drives and CD/DVD drives. The connector is keyed and it is fed by four wires. Table 6-4 helps you distinguish the power cable colors.

Table 6-4   Power Cable Color

Color	Signal
Red Pin 1	+5V
Yellow Pin 4	+12V
Black Pin 2	Ground
Black Pin 3	Ground

Cable Care

Cables represent the arteries of the PC, so it's important to take care of them so that they can do their job.

Here are some top cable care tips:

- Never harshly twist or bend cables. They might seem flexible, but the inner wire strands on most of the cables are very delicate and easily damaged.

- Never tug on cable connectors.

- Store cables flat until needed.

- Never crush a cable underneath a heavy weight and try to avoid trapping them between devices or in the case lid.

- Never tie back a cable with wire ties. These ties can easily cut through the outer sheathing and cause a short circuit that will damage components or could even start a fire.

Removing a Stuck Connector

The power cables and data ribbons are prime candidates for becoming stuck after being fitted (they have a knack for becoming almost instantly stuck). Never tug on the wires to remove them because this can easily damage the cables.

To safely remove the connector, firmly grasp the connector and pull on it gently, gradually increasing the force until it gives way.

It that doesn't work, grasp the sides of the connector and gently rock it side to side to loosen it while pulling. Be careful how much force you use to remove it—it will give way quickly and leave your hand flying with great force toward something that's both important and fragile (or sharp!).

Summary

In this chapter, we've looked at the two commonest types of data storage devices — the hard drive and the floppy drive. We've looked in particular at PATA (Parallel ATA) drives as these are by far the most common drives. We've looked that the typical hard drive (inside and out) and at the cabling required to connect them to a PC. We've also looked at typical hard drive capacities and looked at ways to help you decide what kind of hard drive you need.

We also looked at floppy drives, the reason behind why they're still important, and looked at what cables are used to connect them up to the PC and how they connect to the PC.

In the next chapter, we move away from hard and floppy drives and look at how to choose the right optical (CD or DVD) drive for your system.

Take Action

Before you move on to the next chapter, be sure you're prepared:

- Decide on how much storage you want for your new PC in terms of hard drive capacity.

- Do you need one hard drive or two or possibly three?

- Are you going to use PATA or SATA drives? What does your motherboard handle?

- Find hard drives that are suited to your needs. Remember, if you are interested in SATA drives your motherboard will need to support SATA (or you will need to buy a separate expansion card to support SATA).

- Do you need a floppy drive?

Choosing CD/DVD Drives

A s you've already read, the floppy drive is considered by many to be pretty much dead. It's rare that you find anything shipped on floppy disks (in fact, it's hard to find a program small enough to fit onto a floppy now!). They were also fragile and quite susceptible to damage from heat, cold, magnetic fields, and bending.

Today, the main physical data storage and dissemination system is the CD or DVD. These discs (notice the spelling difference — a "c" at the end as opposed to a "k," which indicates that the media are optical rather than magnetic) can hold much more data than the paltry 1.44 MB offered by a floppy disk and are far more robust, with a much longer lifespan. Because they hold so much more data, they also take up far less room than floppy disks did!

In this chapter, we'll look at CD and DVD drives and at ways for you to decide which is for you. There are a lot of drives to choose from, and because they all look roughly the same, this can present the buyer with confusing choices. In this chapter, we aim to clear up the confusion!

Note In this chapter, we are only going to consider internal drives, that is, drives that fit into a drive bay in your PC.

The Difference between CDs and DVDs

Once, an optical drive was looked upon as a luxury, but nowadays having a CD or DVD drive is a PC essential (see Figure 7-1).

in this chapter

☑ CD and DVD differences

☑ The basics of optical drives

☑ Choosing optical drives

☑ Drive speeds

☑ Writable CD drives

☑ Different CD formats

☑ Writable DVD drives

☑ Different DVD formats

☑ What kind and how many?

FIGURE **7-1: A typical optical drive.**

Physically, a CD and a DVD look the same, although if you're eagle-eyed you will have spotted that a DVD is slightly thicker than a CD.

Another obvious difference is the name!

- CD – Compact disc
- DVD – Digital versatile disc (sometimes known as a digital video disc)

The main differences between a CD and a DVD are overall capacity and data bandwidth (or how much data you can get off the disk in a given time).

A CD can hold between 650 and 700 MB of data, while a DVD can hold a minimum of 4.7 GB, enough for a full-length movie. Capacities of DVD discs vary because they can store data in two different layers on the disc and also because they can be double-sided (have data on both the top and the bottom of the disc). Table 7-1 lists the capacities of DVDs.

Table 7-1   DVD Capacities

Type	Capacity (GB)
Single-layer, single-sided	4.7
Double-layer, single-sided	8.54
Single-layer, double-sided	9.4
Double-layer, double-sided	17.08

Note Capacities don't double as you add a layer. This is because data has to be written to the disc to cover the transition from one layer to another, which consumes space, making it unavailable for data.

DVDs also have the bandwidth to transfer data fast enough to play a movie full-screen in high quality, and the DVD drive you can buy to fit into your PC is compatible with discs that you play in your home cinema DVD player.

DVDs aren't just for movies—you can find all sorts of content on them, from files and applications to music.

The choice you have to make is to whether you have a PC that can read (and write) CDs, DVDs, or both.

Optical Drive Basics

CD and DVD drives are collectively known as *optical drives*. They are optical because they use a small laser to read the discs. Data is stored on the disc in the form of pits in a thin aluminum sheet (or dark dye spots in the plastic for recordable discs) written in a spiral pattern from the center outwards. The discs are rotated in the drive, and a laser beam reads the patterns of pits and transforms this digital information into information the computer can understand.

Drives are fitted to the IDE (Integrated Device Electronics) cable inside the PC (the same ribbon cable to which parallel ATA hard drives are connected). Likewise, optical drives are powered by standard 4-pin hard drive power cables.

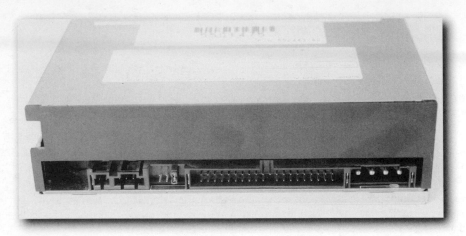

FIGURE 7-2: Optical drive connectors.

Optical drives are fitted to the 5-1/4 inch drive bays and require front access on the case (which will generally be covered initially by a blank plastic fascia).

How to Choose an Optical Drive

The choices that you have to make when choosing an optical drive revolve around what capability you want your PC to have in terms of CD or DVD support.

To make things simple, we recommend that you provide your new PC support for both CD and DVD. This can be done by simply buying and fitting a DVD-ROM drive into your system. (ROM stands for read-only memory, since standard discs are read only and cannot be written to.) DVD drives are backward compatible with CDs and can read both types of disc. You don't have to do anything special when you change disc types — the drive detects the disc, recognizes the format, and reads the data. All this is handled automatically and doesn't need any user input.

When choosing an optical drive, apart from the format it supports, the other important consideration is speed.

Take a look at the front of most CD or DVD drives, and you'll see numbers such as:

- x16
- 12x2x24
- 52x32x52

These numbers indicate the speed of the drive in question. When the number is on its own, as in the case of x16, this indicates the read speed of the drive in question as a multiple of the basic read speed of a disc, which would be x1. The basic read speed is different for both CD and DVD drives.

- CD – 150 KB/s or 0.15 MB/s
- DVD – 1.3 MB/s

As you can see from those numbers, the basic read speed of a DVD drive is much higher than that of a CD. A x16 DVD drive would read data at 16 x 1.3 MB/s, giving a read speed of 20.8 MB/s, while a CD drive with that speed rating (a very low speed for modern driver) would read data at only 2.4 MB/s.

On CD-ROM or DVD-ROM drives, you see only the single speed rating. Speed ratings such as 52x32x52 are seen on drives that can write (or burn) CDs or DVDs. These are collectively known as "recordable," "writer," or "rewritable" drives. Before we look at the speeds for drives capable of creating discs, let's take a look at the drives themselves.

Optical Writer Drives

A *writable drive* allows you to take data from your PC and write or burn it to a CD or a DVD disc. Given the capacity of these discs, this can be a very cheap and convenient way to make copies of your data.

Note CD and DVD writers require special "writable" discs to write the data to.

Writer drives look like standard optical drives (apart from the fact that the labeling will indicate that it is a drive capable of burning discs) and fit into the PC in the same way. Internally, however, the drive has a laser that is used to change the color of a dye impregnated into a recordable disc.

Note Writer drives need special software in order to burn data to the disc. The drive you buy might be supplied with the software or you might have to buy your own. CD burning is supported by Windows XP, so you can also burn CDs through the operating system.

Optical drives break down into three broad categories, as shown in Table 7-2.

Table 7-2 Types of Optical Drive

Type	Use
CD writer	Burn CDs
DVD writer	Burn DVDs
CD/DVD writer combo	Burn both CDs and DVDs

However, things are never as clear as they first appear. These drive types can be further broken down into different categories.

Types of CD Writers

There are two different CD writers:

- CD-R
- CD-RW

The key to understanding these drives is in the R and RW. Different drives support different formats. When buying a drive, consider whether you want R or RW capability. The price difference between R and RW drives is small, and it's a good idea to get a DVD drive that supports rewriting of discs. See Table 7-3.

Table 7-3   Writable CD Drives

Type	Description
R (recordable drive)	Used for recording a CD (known as CD-R discs). Once recorded, the data is permanently stored on the disc.
RW (rewritable CD drive)	These can record a CD and also be used to erase and rerecord certain CD discs (known as CD-RW discs) numerous times. These discs are generally more expensive when compared to regular CD-R discs.

DVD formats are even more complex as there are a number of formats. See Table 7-4.

Table 7-4   Writable DVD Drives

Type	Description
DVD+R	This is a recordable format similar to CD-R. Used for recording a DVD (known as DVD+R discs). Once recorded the data is permanently stored on the disc. It is supported by Philips, Sony, Hewlett-Packard, Dell, Ricoh, Yamaha, and others.
DVD+RW	This is a rewritable format similar to CD-RW or DVD-RW. These can record a DVD and also be used to erase and rerecord certain DVD discs (known as DVD+RW discs) numerous times. It is supported by Philips, Sony, Hewlett-Packard, Dell, Ricoh, Yamaha, and others. These discs are generally more expensive when compared to regular DVD discs.

Type	Description
DVD-R	This is a recordable format similar to CD-R. Used for recording a DVD (known as DVD-R discs). Once recorded the data is permanently stored on the disc. It is supported by Panasonic, Toshiba, Apple Computer, Hitachi, NEC, Pioneer, Samsung, and Sharp.
DVD-RW	This is a rewritable format similar to CD-RW. These can record a DVD and also be used to erase and rerecord certain DVD discs (known as DVD-RW discs) numerous times. It is supported by Panasonic, Toshiba, Apple Computer, Hitachi, NEC, Pioneer, Samsung, and Sharp. These discs are generally more expensive when compared to regular DVD discs.
DVD-RAM	DVD-RAM discs can be recorded and erased repeatedly but are only compatible with devices manufactured by the companies that support the DVD-RAM format. DVD-RAM discs are typically housed in cartridges.

It's wise to choose a drive that supports a number of formats as this gives you better scope and you encounter far fewer hassles when you come to buying blank discs. Drives that support a variety of formats are quite common nowadays and prevent the user from being locked to a specific format.

Note When you buy a drive, check for format support carefully. If in doubt, ask for more information.

Writable Drive Speeds

So, now that you've covered the discs, let's go back to drive speeds. Let's decipher the following speeds:

52x32x52

You can break this up into three speeds: 52, 32, and 52. These speeds refer to write speed, rewrite speed, and read speeds, respectively.

This means that a drive marked at 52x32x52 writes data at 52 speed (7.8 MB/s), rewrites data (on rewritable discs) at 32 speed (4.8 MB/s), and reads data at 52 speed (7.8 MB/s).

Write speed of 52	0.15 MB/s multiplied by 52 = 7.8 MB/s
Rewrite speed of 32	0.15 MB/s multiplied by 32 = 4.8 MB/s
Read speed of 52	0.15 MB/s multiplied by 52 = 7.8 MB/s

DVD writer drive speeds seem slower on the face of it than CD writer speeds, but this is not the case. A 16x speed DVD writer would write data at 20.8 MB/s.

Disc Writing Process

The process of writing a disc requires both software and hardware. The process is simple.

1. Have a writable drive!

2. Insert a blank writable disc into the drive (you can erase a CD-RW/DVD-RW/ DVD+RW; all others have to be blank).

3. Launch your CD-burning software (you might have had software supplied with the drive, have bought your own, or use the feature built into Windows).

4. Select the files for burning to the disc.

5. Start the burning process.

6. When the burning process is finished the disc will be ejected from the drive.

7. Label the disc (using a special CD labeling pen or a labeling system).

8. Store the disc safely.

The Right Drive for You

So, what do you choose? Price-wise there's very little difference between ROM drives and writable and rewritable drives, and because of this we strongly recommend that you buy a rewritable drive, preferably a DVD drive since this gives you the greatest flexibility and choice—you can burn CDs when you want sub-700-MB storage capacity and DVDs when you want more. It's now possible to buy a good quality multiformat DVD rewritable drive for under $50.

Another important question is how many drives to fit in the system you are building. Many people find that two drives (either two writable drives or one writable drive and one read-only drive) offer greater flexibility and convenience—especially if you might be copying a lot of discs.

If you don't think that you need two optical drives then just get one—it's easy enough to install a second at a later date.

Note The usual rule applies. The more expensive the drive, the better the quality generally (in terms of reliability and compatibility with discs). However, in our experience cheap drives can be just as good as expensive ones. If you're buying online, be sure to read all the other customer reviews so that you can get a general feel for the quality of what you are buying.

Summary

In this chapter, we've looked at optical drives, in particular writable CD and DVD drives because these offer the best in terms of flexibility for you as the user. We've taken a look at the technology behind optical drives and looked at and deciphered the bewildering variety of formats present.

In the next chapter, you will look at video adaptors and the choices that are open to you there.

Take Action

Before you move on to the next chapter, be sure you're prepared:

- Consider your optical drive needs. Do you need only drives that can read discs or do you need writers?

- If you need a writer, how much storage do you need? Will a CD be enough or do you need DVD?

Choosing Video Adaptors and Monitors

Without a video adaptor and monitor, you won't have a window into what's happening with your PC. Your PC will need both a video adaptor and a monitor. In this chapter, we examine the options available to you when building a new PC.

Note Clearing Up Terminology: We're going to be calling the card that lets you hook up a monitor to your system the *video adaptor*. However, you might find this particular item referred to by many different names in different places:

➤ Video card

➤ Graphics card

➤ Graphics adaptor

➤ VGA (Video Graphics Array) card

And any number of other word combinations too! These all refer to the same thing—a device that allows you to connect a monitor to the system.

Types of Video Adaptors

There are a number of different video adaptor options that are open to you. Here are the main options, listed in increasing price:

➤ Using an "on-board" video adaptor

➤ AGP (Accelerated Graphics Port) video adaptor

➤ PCI Express video adaptor (PCI stands for Peripheral Component Interconnect)

Let's take a look at each of these options in a bit more detail.

"On-Board" Video Adaptors

Motherboards now come loaded with all sorts of extras that a few years ago had to be bought separately, and along with network adaptors and modems, one commonly bundled feature is an "on-board" video adaptor.

An *on-board video adaptor* provides support for a monitor that's been built directly onto the motherboard. There are two ways that you can tell whether your motherboard has an on-board video adaptor:

- Look at the ports available. Along with a serial port and parallel port, you might find the DB-15 port (see Figure 8-1). This is easily recognizable from the other ports because the connector has 15 holes in it. It looks a little like a serial port connector, but if you look closely, you'll notice that unlike a serial port it has holes instead of pins.

- Check the documentation for your motherboard. Look for mention of "on-board" video.

FIGURE 8-1: A DB-15 port on a motherboard.

Pros and Cons of On-Board Video Adaptors

Is an "on-board" video adaptor good enough? This is a question most people ask themselves when they are building a PC. The answer depends on what you intend on doing with your PC.

There are several things to bear in mind about on-board video adaptors. They revolve around quality, performance, and price.

The odd thing about on-board video support on motherboards is how the pros and cons switch places depending on how you plan on using the PC you are going to build. For example, the first thing to bear in mind about on-board video support is that you're not paying much for that extra. For a lot of people this is a "pro" point. In fact, it's now pretty much a standard on most boards that you might actually find it costs more to find a board without an on-board video adaptor.

Problem is, in the PC world cheap rarely means high performance or high quality, and nowhere is this more true than for video adaptors. This means if want high performance, the "pro" point of low cost becomes a "con" point in that you are going to have to buy a separate video adaptor.

On-board video adaptors generally use low-quality components. Although they work and will allow you to connect a monitor to the system, don't expect much in the way of speed or performance. An on-board video adaptor will be fine if your PC is destined for word processing and Internet use (making it a "pro" point), but if you want to play games on the PC or use your system for movies or video, then forget the on-board video adaptor because it's not going to have enough in the way of power or performance and the results you are going to get will be disappointing. "Con."

One of the main reasons on-board video adaptors cost so little is that they don't have their own RAM (as you will see later in this chapter, video adaptor cards have RAM on the card to handle the needs of the card) and instead share a portion of the system RAM. Obviously, a "pro" point. However, this results in much lower performance from the video adaptor, and it also means that your system will need additional RAM — bought and installed — to cater to the RAM consumed by the on-board video adaptor. I think you'll agree that this is a big "con" point!

The Bottom Line

So, what do you do?

If you are building a machine that's going to be used for playing games or playing videos or DVDs or if you are going to be doing graphics or image manipulation, then dismiss the idea of using the on-board graphics adaptor. In this case, you will get at best disappointing results, and at worst things won't work at all.

If all you think your PC will be doing is running word processors and spreadsheets, processing email, and surfing the web, then on-board video support might be everything you need. However, bear in mind that $20 well spent will likely get you a separate video adaptor that will offer far superior performance and reliability than anything you get on a motherboard.

For everyone else, we recommend steering away from using the on-board video adaptor and getting a separate video adaptor.

Upcoming Windows Vista

To get the best out of Microsoft's upcoming Windows Vista operating system, you will need a video adaptor with at least 64 MB of on-board memory and reasonable 3-D performance. Windows Vista will more than likely run on systems with a lower performance, but users will not be able to take advantage of features such as the new Aero Glass interface.

AGP Video Adaptors

AGP stands for Accelerated Graphics Port. This is a video adaptor expansion port that is present on the motherboard and allows you to connect an AGP video adaptor card to the system. AGP was designed by Intel, and its purpose was to replace slow PCI-based video adaptors with something capable of delivering the performance required for gaming and video.

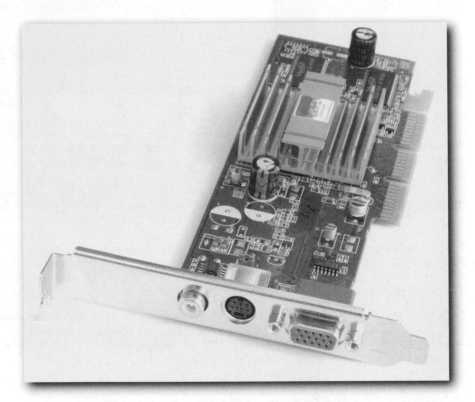

FIGURE 8-2: An AGP video adaptor (Crucial Technology Radeon 9200).

Note PCI-based video adaptors (video adaptor cards designed to fit into a PCI expansion card slot on the motherboard) are all but extinct (they are still for sale in many places but either as replacements for systems prior to AGP support or to allow users to hook up two cards to one PC—more on that later!) and have been replaced by AGP.

AGP is faster because it allows for greater bandwidth between the motherboard and the video adaptor card, meaning that the system can display and update complex graphics faster and with less load on the CPU.

FIGURE 8-3: An AGP slot on motherboard.

An AGP expansion card slot is easily distinguished from a PCI slot. The AGP slot has a small catch on the front to hold the card in place (see Figures 8-4 and 8-5).

FIGURE 8-4: Clip at the front of the slot to hold the AGP card in place.

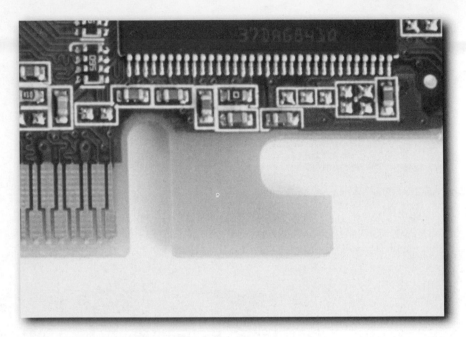

FIGURE 8-5: Slot for clip on AGP card.

AGP is currently very popular, and you will find support for it on many motherboards, and you will have a wide choice of AGP-compliant video adaptor cards from a large number of manufacturers and at a wide range or prices. However, there is an alternative to AGP that is gaining ground fast. This technology is called PCI Express.

PCI Express Video Adaptors

PCI Express takes the lessons learned from PCI and improves on them. PCI Express is faster than AGP (about 2.5 times faster) because it utilizes greater bandwidth, and it is quickly gaining ground on AGP. It is also more versatile because the technology isn't just limited to video adaptors. All new video adaptor cards from ATI Technologies and NVIDIA make use of PCI Express, and for cards that connect to AGP, a bridge chip is used.

Physically, a PCI Express slot looks similar to an AGP slot, but check for motherboard support. Your motherboard will either support PCI Express or AGP, not both. Motherboard support for PCI Express is limited to mid- and high-range motherboards.

An easy way to tell the difference between the two slots is to measure the distance between the back of the slot and the back edge of the motherboard (see Figure 8-6). For an AGP slot this will be 2-1/2 inches (6.35 cm), while for a PCI Express slot the gap is less, 1-5/8 inches (4.13 cm). Another way is to look at the adjacent slots — all the other PCI Express slots are small.

FIGURE 8-6: To tell the difference between AGP and PCI Express slots, measure the distance indicated by the double-headed arrow shown here.

How to Choose between AGP and PCI Express

How do you decide what you need?

If you want to build a PC that uses the latest technology and has a long lifespan before becoming obsolete, then choose a PCI Express-based motherboard and video adaptor. However, you are going to pay extra for this, in particular the motherboard costs. You will also need to make sure that all your other expansion cards are PCI Express cards, which can increase your build costs (especially if you were thinking of moving some of the cards from an old PC into the new one). However, if you are into gaming in a big way and your new PC is destined to be a gaming rig, then you should consider PCI Express-based technology.

The AGP port is still a good, solid option to choose, and this will give you a good compromise between performance and cost. If you are building a budget or midrange PC, then choose a motherboard that has AGP support over PCI Express. As always, cost will be your guide. If you want performance, power, and the longest upgrade life, go for PCI Express. However, for budget systems you might be stuck with AGP (although you might be lucky and grab a bargain!).

Video Card Features

When you are looking for a good video adaptor to buy, there are a few features that you can check for.

First of all, as we've said already, decide whether you want an AGP video adaptor or a PCI Express video adaptor. This is either a choice you can make prior to buying a motherboard or you will have to buy whatever your motherboard supports.

Once you have this information you can then set about buying a suitable video adaptor expansion card.

Manufacturer

You will find a number of video adaptor manufacturers to choose from. Any good vendor will provide you with all the relevant information you need to make an informed choice (or at least they should be able to — if not, find another vendor).

Generally, you will find that at the core of the cards is a processor (known as a GPU or graphical processor unit) from one of only a handful of manufacturers. Two of the most common GPU makers are ATI and NVIDIA.

These GPU makers make chips for a number of companies, so you might find that even though you have a card with a GPU from, say, ATI, that the card was otherwise made and assembled by another company.

Don't worry too much about brands — most brands carry similar lines and if you are buying from a good, reputable store, you can use price as a guide to performance and quality. The more expensive the card, the higher performance it will be and the better quality the card will be overall.

2-D or 3-D

You also need to decide whether you want a card that's capable of 3-D (or, more accurately, 2.5-D, which is as close to 3-D as you can get on a flat screen). 2-D cards are much cheaper than 3-D cards, but they have limited scope. 2-D cards are fine on machines that are going to be confined to office work (word processing, spreadsheet work, or databases). For anything like gaming or video work, you will need a card with greater capabilities, and 3-D becomes essential.

We recommend that unless you are building a system designed for office use (where perhaps you might even want to discourage gaming!) that you steer away from 2-D-only video adaptors.

Speed

Just like CPUs, the on-board GPUs (shown in Figure 8-7 under a heatsink) come in a variety of speeds. The faster the speed of the GPU, the better the performance of the card. Again, without burdening you with too many confusing terms, you can let price guide you. The more the card costs, the faster the overall card will be.

The price range can be incredible — from a few tens of dollars to hundreds of dollars. You can buy a budget card for about $30, while a good midrange card will cost less than $100. For high-end gaming, you might want to spend upwards of $300 just on the video adaptor.

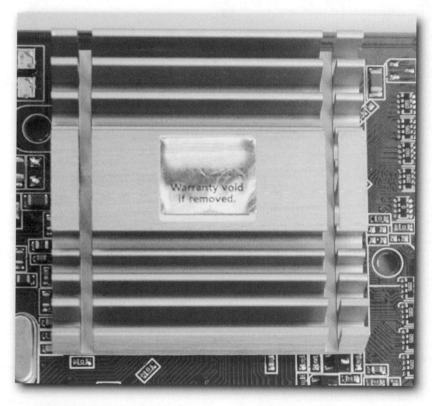

FIGURE 8-7: GPU hidden beneath heatsink unit. This is the processor at the heart of the video adaptor!

Memory

Video adaptor expansion cards come equipped with RAM memory modules built onto the card itself (see Figure 8-8). This gives the card a place to hold data for fast access by the GPU. The more memory that's installed, the higher the performance of the card in question.

You'll need to equip your general home/gaming PC with a card that comes with at least 128 MB on installed RAM.

As with GPU speed, the more memory installed on a video adaptor, the more the card will cost.

FIGURE 8-8: Memory modules on a video adaptor.

Multi-Monitor Support

You will find that some video adaptors offer you the ability to connect up to two monitors to a single PC. This will allow you to have greater on-screen work area, which can be very useful if you find yourself needing to work with a number of documents at once without the hassles of swapping between documents.

With a video adaptor that has multi-monitor support, all you have to do is connect two monitors to the ports and use the software to activate the second one.

There is another more complicated way of getting multi-monitor support of your PC and that's to fit it with two video adaptors. To do this, you will need two expansion cards:

- An AGP card (this arrangement doesn't work with PCI Express)
- A PCI card

The main monitor will be fitted onto the AGP expansion card, while the second monitor is hooked up to the PCI-based video adaptor card.

There are some points to bear in mind when attempting this:

- **Complexity!** It can be tricky to get multi-monitor support to work on some systems. If you are not prepared to experiment then buying a specific card with multi-monitor support is a lot easier.

- **Compatibility.** Not all card combinations work. You'll have to carry out some research on the web to find suitable cards.

- **Operating system support.** For this to work you will need to be running the Microsoft Windows XP (or higher) operating system.

DVI

DVI is a connections standard for hooking up flat panel screens and digital projectors to a PC. DVI stands for Digital Visual Interface, and it was developed by the DDWG (Digital Display Work Group).

DVI connectors come in two formats:

- 24 pins that carry digital video signals only, called DVI-D
- 29 pins that carry both digital and analog video, called DVI-I

Different systems need different connectors, and it's important that if you buy a flat panel that you get one with a compatible connector. This is getting easier nowadays because many come with both DVI and standard DB-15 connectors. You get a better image when using DVI connector over DB-15, but some monitors are incompatible with certain DVI connectors.

TV/S-Video Out and Other Features

Some video adaptor cards have support for TV and S-Video out to allow you to connect your PC to the TV or to other video devices (such as a DVD player, video recorder or camcorder), as shown in Figure 8-9. Other video adaptors come with a built-in TV tuner card, allowing you to view TV channels on your PC. All these features cost extra and generally only appear on higher-end video adaptor cards.

FIGURE **8-9: Video out connectors.**

That's the video adaptors covered, let's now move on to monitors.

Monitor Choices

After you've chosen your video adaptor, it's time to choose what you are going to connect to the video adaptor — the monitor.

There are two types of monitor you can choose from:

- Traditional tube-based CRT (cathode-ray tube) monitors
- Flat-screen panels

Opinions vary as to which is best. As with most things, the best guide to quality is cost and the higher the price, the better the quality of the display and overall quality of the monitor will be. However, there are some basic considerations to keep in mind when choosing a monitor:

- Flat-screen panels take up far less desk space than CRT monitors. This means that you can have more desk space for other things.

- CRT monitors are incredibly heavy and need a much stronger desk to support them than a flat-screen panel.

- Flat-screen panels consume far less power than CRT monitors, meaning that if you use your PC a lot (or have a number of PCs running) you can reduce your electricity bills by choosing flat-panels.

One other important decision to make when buying a monitor is to choose a screen size suitable to your needs and your budget. Screens are traditionally measured diagonally across the screen and displayed in inches. Table 8-1 lists the most popular monitor sizes.

Table 8-1   Monitor Sizes

Size (inches)	General Usage
15	Low-end PC. Suitable only for word processing, web, etc.
17	Midrange. Suitable for a variety of applications.
19	Extra viewing area makes work and leisure applications easier and more enjoyable.
21+	High-end, high-priced screen.

Note For a midrange PC, we recommend a screen of no less than 17 inches. Overall, the more you use your PC, the more vital the screen becomes. If you use a PC a lot you don't want to be squinting at a 15-inch screen.

The bigger the screen viewing area, the more expensive it is going to be. CRT monitors 17 inches and bigger are very big (in terms of depth, because the bigger the tube, the longer it has to be too) and also they get progressively heavy and unwieldy.

Caution CRT monitors are very heavy, but you also have to be careful when lifting them because the weight is unevenly distributed (the majority of the weight is at the front of the screen). Always lift CRT monitors with the screen facing toward you.

Summary

In this chapter, we've looked at video adaptors and monitors for your new PC. We've looked at different video adaptor port technology (including on-board video adaptors built onto the motherboard) and looked at some of the more important aspects of video cards, such as GPU speed, memory, and additional features.

We also looked at monitors and toured some of the important pros and cons of flat-screen panels and CRT monitors as well as looked at different screen sizes and suitable applications.

In the next chapter, you will find out how to get good sound from your PC.

Take Action

Before you move on to the next chapter, be sure that you're prepared:

- Consider your video needs. Are you building a basic office PC or will your PC be used for gaming? Do you use your PC for long periods?

- Check whether your motherboard supports AGP or PCI Express.

- Is upgradeability to Windows Vista important?

- Draw up a short list of possible cards that suit your needs.

Choosing Sound Capability

L ike a CD or DVD drive, having a sound-capable system (which used to be referred to as a "multimedia" system) was optional and generally reserved for gaming systems. Nowadays however, games aren't the only source of sound on a PC — you have the web, music, messaging programs, and a whole lot more. Without having sound output, a big part of the PC experience is lost. Having the capability to output audio has moved from being optional to being essential.

In this chapter, we're going to look at what you need to add stereo sound output to your PC and how the choices you make at the build stage can affect the overall quality of your audio experience.

What You Need for Sound

To get audio output from a PC you need two things:

➤ Audio output facility (provided by an expansion card or facility built onto the motherboard)

➤ Speakers and cables to connect them to the PC

What You Get by Adding Sound Capability

When you add sound capability to a PC, you get a number of different capabilities all from one system.

➤ **Speaker output.** This is the most obvious capability. Generally, you get stereo output from a sound card via a 3.5 mm stereo jack plug connector, as shown in Figures 9-1 and 9-2.

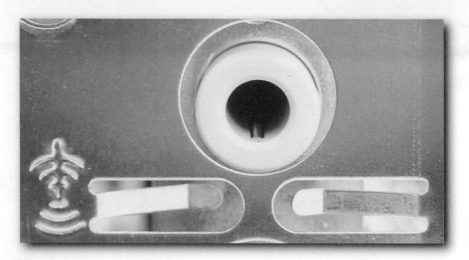

FIGURE 9-1: Speaker output.

FIGURE 9-2: A 3.5-mm jack connector.

- **Sound input.** This is for audio input into the PC from other devices, such as TV cards, again making use of a 3.5 mm stereo jack plug connector.

- **Microphone input.** A sound card will give you a separate input for a microphone. This again makes use of a 3.5 mm stereo jack plug connector.

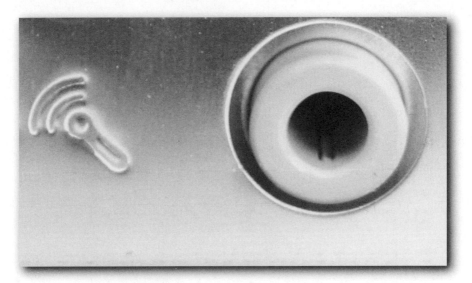

FIGURE 9-3: Microphone input.

- **Joystick port.** This might seem like an odd thing to find provided by a system designed to output sound, but this betrays the origins of the sound card being based in gaming. The joystick port is a 15-pin connector but nowadays this isn't used as often because many joysticks are USB devices.

Audio Output Facility

To be able to output sound, you need a way to be able to hook up speakers to the PC. This is done by using an audio output device on the PC. The device outputs sound when instructed to do so by software on the PC.

A PC has three ways to output audio:

- Through an on-board sound system built onto the motherboard

- Through a sound card that is fitted to an expansion slot

- By using a USB speaker system

Let's take a closer look at these three options.

"On-board" Sound

Many motherboards now come with sound capability "on-board" the motherboard (see Figure 9-4). This means that a system with *on-board sound* capability doesn't need any additional cards or attachments in order to output sound (apart from speakers).

FIGURE 9-4: On-board audio connectors.

On-board sound has a couple of advantages:

- **Price.** Because the sound system is built onto the board, it is cheaper than a separate sound card because fewer fittings are required. (Generally it involves little more than adding a chip to the board and output connectors at the back.) There is also a hidden advantage to PC builders — they need to have fewer items in stock and assemble fewer parts together to make a working PC!

- **Convenience.** No need to bother to buy and fit a separate component to the PC.

You may recall that when we looked at on-board video adaptors in the previous chapter we said that overall we weren't that thrilled by them and that on the whole you could get much better performance from a separate video adaptor card costing not much more than $30 or so. However, it seems that on-board sound capability is generally of better quality than its video counterpart. This is due in part to the fact that sound card technology is simpler than video technology. (Put simply it's easier to create a sound processor and output system than it is a video adaptor.) However, another important reason is that, overall, there is less stress and demand placed on the sound system, and thus lower-performance and lower-quality devices are still capable of performing acceptably.

Because of this, many people, including those who use their PC for gaming and playing videos or DVDs, might find the sound system provided by the motherboard to be adequate for their needs.

However, sound generated by on-board systems will never be as good as what you will get with a separate, dedicated, sound card.

Sound Cards

The most popular choice in PC sound systems is the PCI-based sound card that will slip into an expansion slot. By far the most popular range of sound cards you will see for sale are manufactured by Creative Labs and distributed under the SoundBlaster™ label. In the SoundBlaster product range you will find a variety of cards.

FIGURE 9-5: A generic sound card.

The PCI-based sound card is very much like any other expansion card. The sound card has connectors along one edge that fit into the expansion slot, and the metal back plate of the card has the connectors and jack ports for speakers, microphones, and other devices.

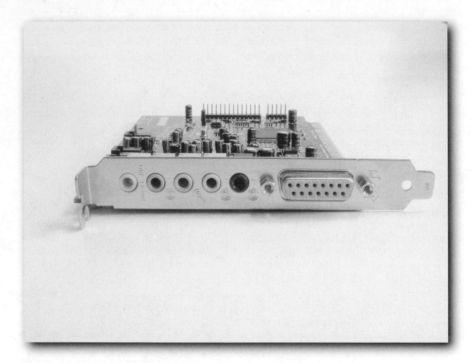

FIGURE 9-6: Close-up of card connectors.

A broad range of sound cards are available, ranging from budget cards that have an acceptable sound quality output to expansive cards that are capable or high-quality audio output for the discerning gamer or music listener (although to get good output you will need good speakers).

The best guide as to quality is price. As with video adaptors, sound card technology moves quickly and what is innovative today will be midrange in a few months and budget in a year or so. The basic rule is that the more you want out of a card, the more you are going to have to pay. At the budget end, you will find cards that cater for those requiring basic stereo audio output, while at the higher end you'll find sound cards packing technology such as surround sound and front panel controls that fit into a free 5-1/4-inch drive bay and give you controls such as volume, balance, and even graphic equalizers.

The main advantage of opting for a PCI-based sound card over an on-board system is that you can choose exactly what you want. If your needs are basic you can stick with the on-board sound system or buy a budget PCI card. If you want more, you'll have to spend more to get extra features. However, there's no doubt that a separate sound card will give you greater overall performance.

USB Speakers

One new innovation is the USB speaker. These are USB speakers that don't require a separate sound card. They plug into a free USB port and work directly from that.

Although innovative, we don't recommend these for a new system. Although they are handy for upgrading the sound system on a laptop or for giving a new lease on life to an old system where you might not have the space for a separate sound card (when you are upgrading from on-board sound), the cost can be quite high and the results from them unpredictable. Sound card technology is also far more robust and less prone to compatibility problems that can affect some systems using USB speakers.

"Out-the-Front" Sound

Some sound cards give you the ability to have jacks at the front of the PC for things like microphones and speakers, while others even allow you to control the card through a panel that consists of knobs and dials such as volume, balance, and so on. Cards that incorporate these features are more expensive than regular cards, but they are worth considering if you are someone who feels you will be using your PC a lot for music or home entertainment. Having an easy-to-reach and non-software way of controlling basic audio functions can be very useful indeed (and climbing round the back of the PC to reach the connectors can be a major headache at the best of times!).

 Note Some cases come with front panel connectors for microphones and speakers too, but these either plug into the connectors at the rear of the sound card or require specific motherboard or sound card support.

Speakers

No matter what the quality of your sound card, it's the speakers that actually do the job of turning the electrical signals from the card into air movements that we then detect as sound. A good pair of speakers isn't going to improve on a bad sound card, but poor speakers can give you a poor audio experience from even the best sound system.

FIGURE 9-7: A set of generic speakers.

A number of different types of speaker are available. The most popular and most common is the standard stereo speaker; however, because the PC is slowly becoming part of the home entertainment system, there is now also a good range of surround sound speakers available for the PC. These require specific sound card support, but they can be used to create that all-round audio effect otherwise only found in real life and in the best cinema theatre. Such system are normally called "5.1 surround sound" systems and come with six speakers:

- One front speaker, called a "center" channel
- Two speakers at the front, one on either side
- Two speakers at the rear, one on either side
- One low-frequency speaker called a *subwoofer* to add low bass to the overall sound (handy for deep rumbles from games or DVDs)

These systems not only come with speakers (and note that the subwoofer is usually quite large), but they also come with a control box that connects to the PC. Out of the control box comes all the speaker wiring. Surround sound systems involve trailing a lot of wiring about, and care needs to be taken to route the wires in such a way that they don't get damaged or trip up people.

How to Choose Speakers

There are three aspects of a set of speakers that are important to consider when buying speakers:

- Build quality
- Power
- Cabling and connectors

Build Quality

You can spot cheap speakers just by looking at them. They will be small and made of plastic, and when you tap them they will sound tinny or hollow. (The best sound that a speaker can give out when tapped is a dull, dead thud but this is rare from PC speakers.)

By now you probably know what we are going to say before we even say it — as with most things, you get what you pay for. You can't expect to get rich tones and natural highs and lows from a $10 pair of speakers. However, don't despair because even poor speakers can actually output quite decent audio, but the problem with small, light speakers is that they have a tough time keeping up with the low frequencies. It all depends on what you expect your PC speakers to do.

For general office use and a PC that is going to see a lot of Internet use, then a budget pair of speakers will suffice. However, if you want good sound output (say, for a gaming PC or a home entertainment PC that is going to play a lot of DVDs and video), then you are going to need better-quality speakers and expect to pay $50–$100 for a reasonable set and more than $250 for a good-quality set. A high-quality 5.1 surround sound system can cost much more. It all depends on what you want from the system.

Tip   A Cheaper Option: Don't want to bother getting high-quality speakers but want good sound output from your system sometimes? A simple answer is to get a good-quality pair of head-phones and use them. Good-quality headphones will set you back a lot less than good-quality speakers and won't bother your spouse, parents, or neighbors as much!

One thing that is absolutely vital on a set of speakers is that they have decent feet on them. Without these the speakers will rattle or vibrate when working, and this will add unwanted sound effects into the audio. Speakers must sit firmly on the surface on which they are going to be resting on. Rubber feet on speakers are generally a good idea. They improve the sound quality and stop the speakers from sliding about the place.

Power

How are your speakers powered? There are several options:

- Unpowered speakers
- Battery-powered speakers
- Mains-powered speakers

Unpowered speakers are handy, but the output from them is more than likely to be poor and they won't be up to gaming and video. Generally these are no good for anything other than office PCs.

You can completely dismiss the idea of battery-powered speakers. These will cost you a fortune to run, and the batteries will die at exactly the wrong time.

That leaves mains-powered speakers as the best choice for most PC owners. These give the best audio output and won't be silenced by dead batteries. Also, to reduce on cabling some come with an adaptor that slots between the power supply unit and main code and draws its power needs from there, eliminating the need for a separate power outlet.

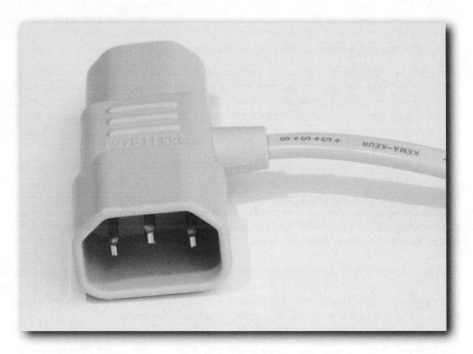

FIGURE 9-8: Power adaptor.

Cabling and Connectors

Good-quality speakers will have good cabling and high-quality connectors. Budget speakers will have cabling and connectors of variable quality. In order to get decent audio output, you will need speakers that have good cable fitted with decent molded connectors on the end.

A good test of cable quality is to hold the cable near the connector and see how far away from the connector you can hold it without the wire flopping over. Good-quality cable should be able to hold the weight of the connector and at least 6 inches (15 cm) of cable without flopping over.

Check the cable and connector for cuts in the sheathing, bad kinks in the cable, and damage. All these will have an adverse effect on audio output.

Summary

In this chapter, we've looked at the PC sound output system and looked at different ways that you can get your PC to output sound.

As well as looking at on-board sound, sound cards, and USB speakers, we've also looked at different kinds of speakers that are available and looked at simple ways to tell the difference between good speakers and poor-quality speakers.

In the next chapter, you will be looking at the variety of cabling and fittings that are present inside a PC.

Take Action

Before you move on to the next chapter, be sure that you're prepared:

- Spend some time now considering your audio needs. Is the PC going to be a general office PC that will need little in the way of audio? Or will you use it for gaming, playing music, and so on?

- Factor the pros and cons of a separate sound card as opposed to on-board sound. Remember, if in doubt, you can always add a separate sound card at a later stage.

A Tour of Cables and Fittings

To someone unfamiliar with the inside of a working PC looks like, it has countless cables and fittings that snake from one component to another in a random, haphazard maze (people expected a lot of "tech" crammed into a small space, but they don't expect all the cabling that goes with it!). Thankfully, it isn't as haphazard as it may seem at first and there is logic to it all! Once you know what you are looking at and understand what connects to what and why you'll begin to notice that everything is laid out quite logically!

In this chapter, we'll look at the cables and fittings that connect everything inside a PC and look at how you can identify each cable and know what they are for and where each one goes.

Power Cables

A PC has three different types of power cable supplying power to three different devices:

> **Motherboard power block.** This is the largest power connector block—a long, broad connector with 20 or more pins (see Figure 10-1). Some motherboards have a 20-pin connector, while others have a 24-pin connector. Some have 20-pin connectors and a separate 4-pin block—ultimately, it depends on the motherboard. This fits onto the motherboard and supplies all the power needs of the motherboard and the attached expansion cards.

Most new motherboards that support high-power processors actually have 24-pin power connectors, and it's critical to know the difference and get a power supply that matches your motherboard. You can convert down from 24-pin to 20-pin, but you can't convert up.

> **Hard drive/CD/DVD drive power cables.** These cables provide power for the drives. Also, these cables can be used for case fans and to provide additional power for other devices (see Figure 10-2).

> **Floppy drive power cable.** This provides power for the floppy drive (see Figure 10-3).

FIGURE 10-1: Motherboard power block.

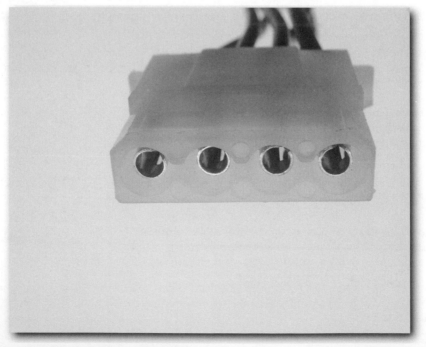

FIGURE 10-2: Drive power connectors.

FIGURE 10-3: Floppy drive cable.

 Note Some of the photos you will see in this chapter are of a single type of motherboard, so there may be some significant differences between what you see here and what you have at home. Check the manuals for your devices for specifics relating to connector location on the board and specific pin layouts.

Each of these three cable types stem from the power supply unit. Generally, you will find that you have one motherboard power connector, four cables for drives and two for floppy drives (although only one of these is ever used nowadays). See Figure 10-4.

FIGURE 10-4: Full wiring loom from a 350-watt PSU.

On some motherboards, you may also find auxiliary power cables. Each of these cables has a distinct connector at the end, so there is no chance that you will get confused. In addition to the connector, each cable is keyed to prevent it from fitting incorrectly into the device (see Figure 10-5).

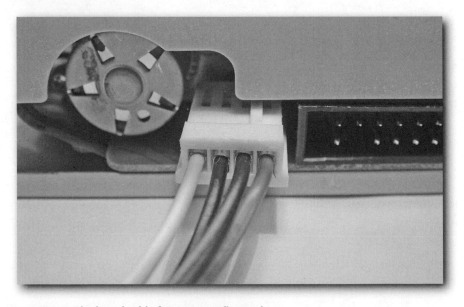

FIGURE 10-5: The keyed cable fitting into a floppy drive.

These are all little touches that make life much easier for people who build and upgrade computers, and they eliminate problems and damage caused by incorrect wiring.

 Note When you are building your PC, you should have a basic set of cabling all ready. The PSU will supply all the cabling when it comes to power needs.

That's all the power cabling inside a PC. You can easily spot them all because they all come from the PSU.

Let's now look at the front panel connectors.

Front Panel Connectors

When you look at the front of a PC, you'll notice that there are a number of LEDs and buttons there to control or get feedback from the PC. Typically, you will find a:

- Power on switch
- Reset button
- Hard drive LED
- Power on LED

Although these aren't essential items (well, okay, the power on button is if you want to get your PC going, you can live without all the others), it's a good idea to hook them up to the motherboard in order to make sure that everything works.

 Note LED is short of "light-emitting diode." An LED is a little component that glows brightly when power is put through it.

Each of these will have cables reading from the front panel that need to be connected to the appropriate head on the motherboard:

- Hard drive LED (see Figure 10-6)
- Power switch (see Figure 10-7)
- Power LED (see Figure 10-8)
- Reset button (see Figure 10-9)

FIGURE 10-6: Hard drive LED lead.

FIGURE 10-7: Power switch lead.

FIGURE 10-8: Power LED lead.

FIGURE 10-9: Reset button lead.

These four connectors are all attached onto the PC case and fit onto the motherboard. Each of the connectors on the ends of the wires should be clearly labeled, as should the connections on the motherboard (see Figure 10-10). Generally, these are on cables that are long enough to reach the back of the case because the case makers don't know where the motherboard makers will put the connector heads. Typically, if you have a good case, these will all be marked up nice and clear to make fitting easy, but there are a few case makers that just stick labels on the cables that can fall off and become illegible.

Tip If your case cables are marked with paper labels, then do yourself a favor and cover these labels with tape so that they last longer. This will prevent them becoming dirty and unreadable.

FIGURE 10-10: Front panel connector head on the motherboard.

Both of the cables for the LEDs require fitting the right way. You must match the polarity on the connector with the polarity on the motherboard; otherwise they won't illuminate. The orientation of the power and reset switch connectors is unimportant, however. These cables just connect to a simple switch.

The case will have all the front panel wiring already hooked up. All you will need to do is connect it to the motherboard.

Hard Drive Data Cables

After the PSU, the hard drive and optical drive data cables add the greatest cable bulk to the inside of a PC. A lot of this bulk is due to the fact that these cables usually come as a ribbon that can be inflexible and hard to take control of. It is possible to get round data cables, but the main problems with these is that what you gain in terms of a smaller cross-section you lose in terms of ease of use and flexibility. Round data cables can be very hard to bend into shape because they are so stiff.

Note   Serial ATA (or SATA) cabling is much smaller and easier to route than the wide IDE cables for PATA drives.

The typical PC makes use of up to two hard drive data cables. Each cable that is used to carry data to and from PATA (Parallel ATA) drives has three connectors (see Figure 10-11):

- **One that fits onto the motherboard.** These connectors are generally colored-coded blue for easy recognition.

- **Two for devices.** The master or primary device, which is generally a hard drive, goes on the end.

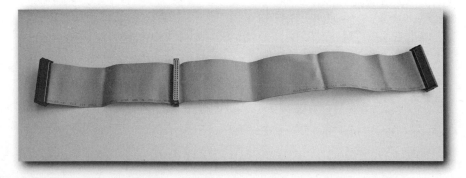

FIGURE 10-11: PATA hard drive/CD/DVD drive 40-pin, 80-wire cable.

Hard drive data cables are 40-pin, 80-wire cables (avoid older 40-wire cables) and are usually in the form of a ribbon. However, many places now sell them as a round cable instead of a ribbon (see Figure 10-12).

FIGURE 10-12: An 80-wire cable (left) and 40-wire cable (right).

All the hard drive data connectors are keyed to prevent them from being improperly attached (see Figure 10-13), but there's also another feature to help prevent mistakes — the cable running from pin 1 is generally marked with a red line on the cable and pin 1 on the drive is usually highlighted by a small mark or stamp (see Figure 10-14).

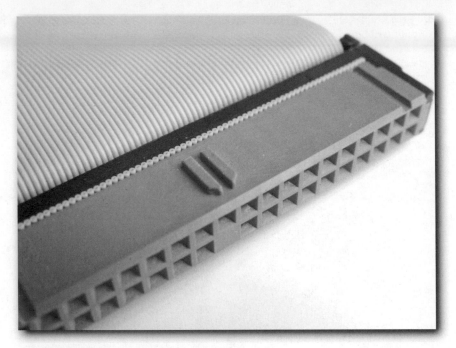

FIGURE 10-13: Keyed motherboard connector.

FIGURE 10-14: Red stripe indicating pin 1.

Generally, you can expect to be supplied with cabling when you purchase the motherboard (you should be supplied with at least one 80-wire, 40-pin hard drive ribbon, and a separate floppy drive connector). If you buy a hard drive retail kit, as opposed to a bare drive, then more than likely you'll get another ribbon there.

Check in case you need additional hard drive data ribbons before you begin the build. It's irritating holding up the build just for a cable!

Tip Sometimes the marks on the drives can be hard to spot, so here's a quick and easy tip to ensure that you're fitting the cable correctly. Hold the drive upright and facing away from you (you are now looking at the back of the drive). Pin 1 will be on the left, so keep the red line on the cable on the left, and you'll be sure of matching it up correctly!

Floppy Drive Data Cables

Okay, you might not be planning on installing a floppy drive, but you still need to know where it goes!

The one thing that catches people out about the floppy drive data cables is that they are similar in appearance to hard drive cables, but instead of being 40-pin they are 34-pin, 34-wire cables (see Figure 10-15). Floppy drive data cables are however instantly recognizable from hard drive data cables because seven of the wires in the ribbon have a twist in them (the twist is before the connector that connects to the drive that will become drive A:). You will never see this on hard drive cables.

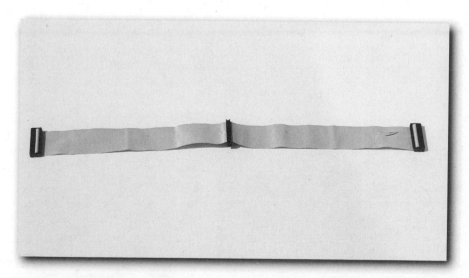

FIGURE 10-15: Floppy drive cable.

Floppy drive data cables are keyed in a similar way to hard drive cables and also have the red line indicating pin 1, which comes in handy when fitting them.

The connector nearest the twist is the one fitted to the floppy drive, and the one farthest away from the twist is hooked up to the motherboard.

Fans and Coolers

Cooling is vital to a PC and without effective active (that is, assisted) cooling, modern PC components would overheat and die very quickly.

Generally motherboards provide support for two types of fans:

- CPU cooling fan
- Case fan

Both of these fans connect to the motherboard by a separate connector head that both provides the power for the fan and also monitors the speed of the fan (see Figures 10-16 and 10-17).

Both of the connectors are keyed to prevent incorrect fitting. Generally, however, given the distance between the connection points on the motherboard, it's not usually possible to fit the CPU fan to anything other than the CPU fan connector (see Figures 10-18 and 10-19).

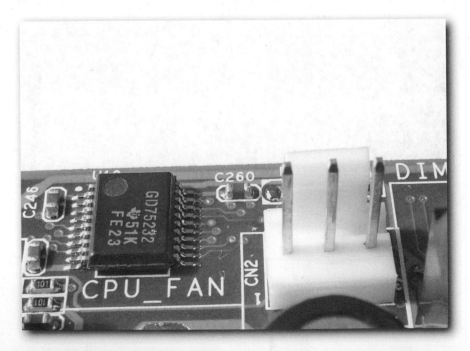

FIGURE 10-16: CPU fan connector head.

FIGURE 10-17: Case fan connector head.

FIGURE 10-18: Case fan keyed connector.

FIGURE 10-19: CoolerMaster case fan.

Note   Sometimes, you might want to fit additional case fans. For example, you might want to ensure that the inside of the case is as cool as possible (perhaps because you have additional hard disks). Or maybe just because you like the idea of a fan in the case with a cool LED on it! When this becomes necessary, the fans draw power from the hard drive power cables via a bridging connector that both taps power from the connector and allows it to be fitted to a device if required.

Case Speakers

Even in a modern, high-tech PC that has stereo or surround sound, the basic system beeps (used to diagnose problems) are supplied by a primitive case speaker that is connected to the motherboard. You won't hear any sound from this speaker other than a beep when it is switched on and for troubleshooting purposes. (Refer to your motherboard manual for an explanation of these diagnostic beeps.)

This case speaker is usually fitted to the front of the PC and is connected to the motherboard via a 2-pin connector (the connector, however, is a broad 4-pin connector where only two pins are actually made use of; see Figure 10-20).

FIGURE 10-20: Speaker connector lead.

This connector is not keyed, so make sure that you match pin 1 on the connector (sometimes marked "S", "SPK", or an arrow) on the cable with pin 1 on the motherboard (both of which should be clearly marked). See Figure 10-21.

Rest assured that an incorrect fitting won't damage the PC, but the on-board speaker might not work until it is connected properly. This is something that you can only check out properly when you test the PC.

FIGURE **10-21: Speaker lead properly oriented with connector head. Notice how the arrows painted on the connector and motherboard match up.**

USB Connector Head

Most modern motherboards have USB support already built in, but some cases also provide additional USB ports, usually on the front of the case. To take advantage of these ports, you will need an additional USB connector head on the motherboard (see Figure 10-22 and 10-23). This is a 9-pin header (1 pin is not required) that provides support for two ports. The connectors from the USB port on the case can seem rather daunting because you will be faced by four 2-pin connectors that must be mated up to this header.

These connectors are normally marked:

- **VCC1 and VCC2.** These are the voltage lines taking over to the USB device.
- **USB1+ and USB2+.** Wires carrying data to the USB device.
- **USB1- and USB2-.** Wires carrying data from the USB device.
- **GND and GND.** These are the grounds for the power.

FIGURE 10-22: USB connector head.

FIGURE 10-23: USB leads — thankfully all marked up well!

It is important that you make sure you connect up the connectors marked 1 (VCC1, USB1+, and USB1-) and 2 (VCC2, USB2+, and USB2-) to the appropriate header on the motherboard. (Don't worry how you hook up the GND connectors. They can be attached to either pin.)

Drive Fittings

Drives are fitted into the PC case in drive bays. As a rule, hard drives are fitted into 3-1/2–inch bays and CD/DVD drives are fitted into 5-1/4–inch bays (hard drives can be fitted into a 5-1/4–inch bay by making use of a separate converter). See Figures 10-24 and 10-25.

FIGURE 10-24: 3-1/2–inch drive bay.

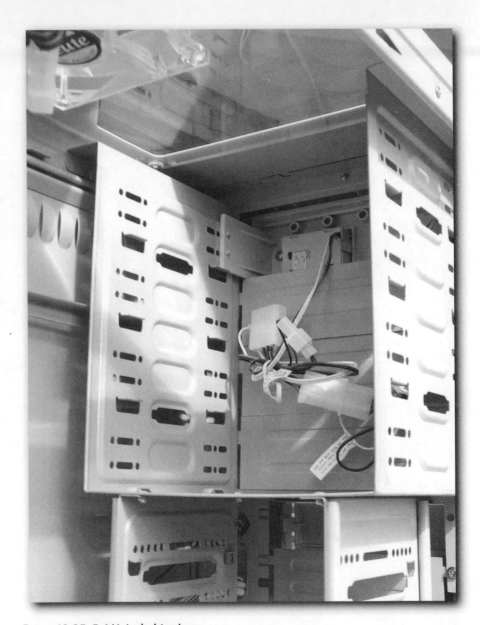

Figure 10-25: 5-1/4–inch drive bay.

Each drive bay is fitted with enough screw holes to make use of all of the threaded screw holes on the drive.

As a rule, hard drives are fitted into the drive bays from inside the case, whereas CD and DVD drives are fitted through the front of the PC case (because they are usually too big to be taken through the inside).

The main difference between a hard drive bay and a CD/DVD bay is that a CD or DVD drive needs to be accessed through the front of the PC, so the case needs to have a removable plastic fascia. After you've removed the plastic fascia (see Figure 10-26), you will see a metal plate attached to the chassis in such a way that it can be popped off (see Figure 10-27). Usually, this is accomplished by breaking off the small metal tabs holding the plate in place (use pliers or wobble the plate by hand until the tabs break).

FIGURE 10-26: Plastic fascia.

FIGURE 10-27: Metal plate behind fascia.

Take care after removing the plate as there can be some nasty edges present that are sharp enough to cut skin. Either try your best to avoid these (easier said than done), remove them by clipping at them with the nose of a pair of pliers, or cover them with tape.

You can dispose of the metal plate, but it's a good idea to keep any fascia plates you remove — you may need to put them back on again if you remove the drive. A case with a big hole in the front is really ugly, and it means that the airflow in the case is disrupted, which can cause hotspots to form.

Motherboard Fittings

The motherboard is fitted to the case using a number of screws and risers that create a flat, stable surface for the board to lie on, raised from the case chassis so that there's no chance of a short circuit. Different cases come with different fittings. Some come with metal fittings that use red fiber washers to insulate the board from the metal fittings, and others make use of plastic fittings.

Tip Metal fittings are best because they provide greater strength and stability. If your board comes supplied with plastic ones you can always buy metal ones.

The connectors at the back of the motherboard come out the back of the PC case through a surround, called a bezel plate. The PC case will usually come with a basic generic bezel, but you will also find that the motherboard comes supplied with its own bezel that is specific to the connector layout at the back (see Figure 10-28).

FIGURE **10-28: Motherboard specific connector bezel.**

Removing the bezel is easy. Simply unscrew the screw holding the generic plate in place and pop the motherboard-specific bezel in place (see Figure 10-29). This might be held in place by screws or just by friction-fit, depending on the board.

FIGURE 10-29: Generic connector plate.

Summary

In this chapter, we've taken a picture tour of the variety of cables and fittings that are inside a PC. The build will be a lot easier for you if you take the time now to familiarize yourself with everything and where it is supposed to go and what's used to connect it. Do this now before you move on and actually start assembling the parts to get your system going, which is what you will begin doing in the next chapter!

Take Action

Before you move on to the next chapter, be sure you're prepared:

- Take time to familiarize yourself with all the fittings and connectors that you are going to be using over the course of the build.

- Examine the cables and fittings and see for yourself the differences between the different kinds of cables and connectors and screws.

- Read through the motherboard manual and find out where all the connector headers you will need are located.

Checking and Testing Components

I f you are following this book with the intention of building a PC, by now you should have read the 10 chapters that came before this one and used the information there, along with information you've picked up from magazines, the web, and PC parts stores. You probably also come up with the blueprints for your PC and gone out and bought the parts that you need. If you are in that position you should be sitting (or standing) with this book in your hand, surrounded by boxes containing PC components.

At the very least, you should have these items:

➤ PC case

➤ Motherboard with on-board video and audio

➤ CPU

➤ RAM

➤ Hard drive

➤ CD/DVD drive

➤ Keyboard

➤ Mouse

➤ Monitor

Here we're assuming that you have on-board motherboard support for video and audio; otherwise, you'll have a sound card and video adaptor card, too. We're also assuming that you have access to a keyboard, mouse (although you're not going to need that for a while), and a monitor.

You're also probably starting to feel buried in manuals and CDs containing drivers. Keep these safe for now as you will need them soon.

How to Proceed with the Testing

Now, at this point in time you have two choices:

- Start with the build
- Take some time to examine the parts that you have looking for problems or defects

We suggest that you take some time to scrutinize the parts looking for trouble down the line. You're not going to spot some internal flaw in a CPU, RAM module, or hard drive doing this, but you are going to be able to spot a number of possible problems before they hold you up mid-build.

There are a number of things that you can look for that signal trouble, and in this chapter we'll show you how to spot trouble signs before they give you trouble. To give you the best chance of spotting problems before they happen we suggest that you get hold of a few items that will be of great use to you. We recommend:

- A magnifier
- A good flashlight

These will let you have a good view of the components and give you the best chance of spotting problems.

You might also find a digital multimeter handy for testing and checking the power supply unit for potential problems.

The Principles of Checking and Testing

There are a number of good reasons why you should take some time out of your PC building and examine components before you fit them. Some of the reasons just save you time, but others can save you money and the hassle from damaged components. The following list describes a few reasons why it's worth the time to examine your components:

- A damaged component will put your build on hold until you get a replacement.
- Some vendors might not accept responsibility for damage to components unless the damage is reported promptly.
- Damage to connectors or sockets can also damage whatever they are connected to, so it's wise to look for damage before hooking things up.
- Damage to circuit boards or circuit board connector edges can result in damage to the motherboard. Your warranty won't cover these types of damage and can leave you substantially out of pocket. Careful checking will save you money!

Checking and testing can be broken down into two stages:

- Visual checking
- Testing by using a second PC

Although we look at visual checking as a *must*, testing the components in a second PC isn't. Not everyone can or wants to test on a second PC. For example, you might not be happy taking apart your existing system or you might not be happy doing it in case you invalidate the warranty or lose data.

Another reason why it's not possible for everyone to carry out actual testing is that their PC might not support the new hardware. CPUs in particular are motherboard-specific, whereas RAM such as DDR and DDR 2 won't work unless you already have a relatively new PC. Motherboards are notoriously hard to test because you either need a PC that is otherwise working or you need to assemble all the parts around it to check.

Hassles also arise from driver issues when adding a new video adaptor to a system. If you allow the computer to boot as far as the operating system, then you'll enter into situations where you have to install drivers and such, making it a big hassle. However, if you do have access to a system that's perhaps not being used, then if your parts are compatible (after reading the book up to now you should be able to decide this for yourself now) you could save yourself a lot of trouble by testing to see whether the following components are at least working:

- PSU
- RAM
- Video adaptor
- Hard drives
- Optical drives

Given this, testing with a second PC is optional. We won't cover in-PC testing and will leave that for when the PC is being built. In this chapter, we will look only at visual checking and basic testing.

Visual Checking

Visual checking is the process of looking over your parts with an eye to uncover any problems before you get stuck into the building. To carry out this process, we're assuming that you have nothing better than normal eyesight, a magnifier, and a good flashlight. We're not going to assume that you have x-ray vision or a bionic eye installed (although both would be quite useful!).

When carrying out a visual check of components, the key is to look for the unusual, the unexpected, or oddities. At first sight, this might seem impossible given the complexity of PC components, but with a little guidance and some hands-on time you soon learn what to look out for.

Caution When handling PC parts and examining them for damage, take care not to damage them with ESD! Take precautions outlined in Chapter 1, "Staying Safe," and work in a way that eliminates the risk.

Checking Circuit Boards

Most people when it is suggested to them that they can visually examine circuit boards for problems just don't believe it. The sea of green board, wire pathways, connectors, and multitude of components can appear daunting if not completely overwhelming.

Don't worry if the parts you are looking at look like they might be more at home in the starship *Enterprise* rather than your PC. You don't need to know what all the parts are called or what they do, and there won't be a test at the end of this chapter either!

Despite their complexity, circuit boards are actually quite easy to look over for problems. Of course, with anything *that* complicated there are going to be problems that you will never spot by eye (even if you did have an x-ray eye and a bionic eye combined), but it's surprising how easy it is to spot many of the problems.

Here's a rundown of the problems to look out for.

Bends and Warps

Most circuit boards are supposed to be flat. Although the material that makes up the circuit board (the stuff usually colored green, called the *substrate*) isn't made of kryptonite and does bend and flex quite a lot, boards should be as close to flat as possible.

Check for bends and warps by placing the circuit board on a flat surface (on something nonconductive, like cardboard) with the components facing upwards. The board should lie flat. Twists and bends can signify problems and can cause you to have difficulty fitting the board later or even cause the board to crack or components to come loose when it is flexed back to flat. You can also check boards for bends and warps visually without having to lay them on a flat surface. Look along the edges and then from corner to corner — any significant bend or warp will show up clearly. See Figure 11-1.

Caution Store all circuit boards flat in their box until they are needed. This is the best way to protect them from damage.

Cracks

Remember how we said just now that circuit boards can bend and flex? Well, this isn't an invitation to go around bending and flexing them. Why? Because if you bend a circuit board too much, first they'll crack (see Figure 11-2), then a few components are guaranteed to pop off the surface (see Figure 11-3), and then the board will splinter before finally breaking completely.

FIGURE 11-1: Carrying out a visual check for warped circuit board.

FIGURE 11-2: A crack in a circuit board.

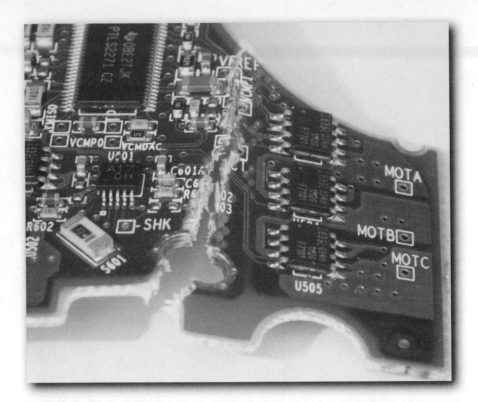

FIGURE 11-3: Components damaged by a crack.

None of these are good for a board, and prevention is a lot better than cure (which means a new board). Here are ways you can protect your circuit board:

- Store your board safely in its original packaging until needed.
- Support the board well when carrying it out of the box.
- Do not use circuit boards as trays to carry other things!
- Never place anything on top of a board.
- Never bend or flex the board.
- Be careful not to jam it when fitting.

There are a number of ways to check for cracks in a circuit board.

A good way to check for actual physical damage is to hold the board up to strong light (sunlight is ideal, but artificial light will work) and look through it. The light will stream through cracks and make them easy to spot.

If you see a crack, examine the area of the crack carefully with a magnifier and a flashlight. You might be lucky and find that the crack is somewhere away from components and the circuit pathways in the board. Damage to the circuit board substrate isn't in and of itself fatal to the device but if any of the pathways are damaged (see Figure 11-4) or if it has damaged the components on the board, that spells bad news for the device.

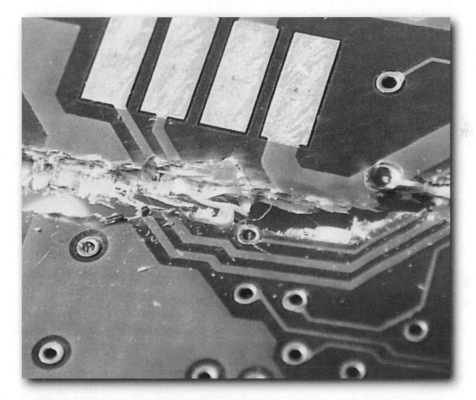

FIGURE 11-4: Crack through the circuit board wiring.

Component Damage

Generally, circuit boards have components mounted on at least one side of the circuit board. RAM modules, for example, quite often have components on both sides. These components are usually made up of a good mixture of capacitors, resistors, LEDs, chips, and other devices that are actually quite robust despite their small size and fragile appearance. But this doesn't mean you should go testing how robust these tiny components actually are — at least not with devices you want to later use. Destructive testing on dead devices, however, can be quite fun and educational.

There are two ways that a component can be damaged:

- It can be physically damaged or broken.
- It can be knocked off the surface of the circuit board.

Checking for component damage or missing components involves carefully examining the circuit board with a magnifier and a flashlight looking for anything out of the ordinary. This isn't as long a job as it might at first seem, but it is a bit tedious.

You can examine a circuit board in two ways:

- Start at one corner and go around the board in a spiral pattern until you reach the middle.
- Start at one end and work across the board in strips.

Both methods work equally well, but the method where you work in a spiral pattern around the board generally means handling the board a lot less, which is preferable.

A broken component is quite easy to spot. You will notice that components are generally smooth but that a broken component is rough and jagged. Missing components often leave solder remnants on the circuit board (see Figure 11-5).

FIGURE **11-5:** Missing component on circuit board.

It's worth noting that sometimes it appears that components have been knocked off a circuit board when in fact they were never placed there in the first place (see Figure 11-6). Circuit boards are quite often designed to cater for a number of models in a range, and the difference in models is due to the components fitted. You can normally tell the difference because no solder remnants will be present at the site of the component.

FIGURE 11-6: These are unused mountings that make the board look like capacitors have been knocked off.

Pins and Connectors

Both pins and connectors are susceptible to damage both during manufacture and transit and also from sloppy or careless handling. A bent pin on pretty much any device that you connect to a PC will mean that that device will probably not work. And because pins are small and it's hard inside a PC to test for continuity, it can be difficult to troubleshoot problems caused by bent pins.

The same is true for connectors. A damaged connector can, while it is being inserted into a connector, damage the pins on the connectors, too. Because of this real risk of bending or breaking off pins, it is important to check pins for straightness and connectors for any damage.

There are a lot of pin-style connectors in a PC. The main circuit board component that has the most pins is the motherboard.

To check your pins and connectors, you'll need your magnifier and flashlight. With both of these items handy, carefully check all the pins, paying special attention to any that seem bent. If you happen to come across a bent pin, the best fix is to try to straighten it with tweezers. Work slowly and don't overbend the pin as this is a sure route to breaking it. A bent pin is bad enough, but a broken pin spells real trouble and can be virtually impossible to fix.

Tip

A broken pin can spell death for a component, but if you are handy with a soldering iron (or know someone who is), then one possible fix is to try to solder the broken pin back on. It's not easy and the joint has to be very good, but it is a possible "last resort" fix for any broken pins you might come across.

Connector Edges

Check all the connector edges on circuit boards, especially the connector edges on expansion cards (see Figures 11-7 and 11-8). Look for twists or kinks in the board, which could harm the motherboard slot (this damage usually occurs when cards are dropped). The edges of the connectors are usually smooth and straight, so you are really looking for anything that might prevent the card from slipping into the expansion slot.

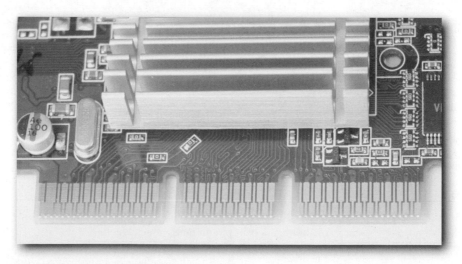

FIGURE 11-7: Good connector edges.

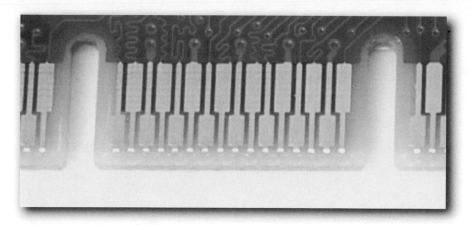

FIGURE 11-8: A notch on an AGP connector. This is normal.

Note Notches on the connector edge of the expansion card are common and nothing to worry about.

Checking Hard Drives

Because all of your data is going onto your hard drive, it's important to give your hard drive a thorough check over before fitting it into the PC.

We're assuming here that the drive that you have bought has been well packaged while in the store and during any transit in the mail or by carrier. The drive should be packaged in such a way that there is at least one good inch of insulation all around the drive. If you suspect that a drive has been mistreated in transit or while in the store, avoid it and get another from somewhere that takes better care of them.

Note The advice here can also be equally applied to internally fitted CD or DVD drives. The main difference is that label damage on a CD or DVD drive doesn't matter and that there normally isn't a visible circuit board on optical drives.

The following sections provide advice for the things you want to look for on a hard drive.

The Drive Exterior

Check the outer casing of the drive for any obvious signs of physical damage (see Figure 11-9). Knocks and dents to the outer casing are not usually good news, and even the smallest dent to the metal cover of the drive can mean that the drive has a much shorter life than it should have. You need a significant amount for force to make a dent in the metal case, and this translates into a lot of energy being carried into the drive to cause damage (especially causing the heads to scrape across the platters). Also, a dent may warp the casing, allowing air to leak into the drive, carrying with it harmful dirt and dust.

FIGURE 11-9: Even a small dent in the casing is bad for a hard drive.

Of equal importance is looking for damage to labels. Although these might seem cosmetic, it can void your warranty or even damage the drive. Some of the labels on a drive hide actual holes into the drive, which, if you uncover them, can allow in dirt that will damage the drive.

Pins and Connectors

Check the pins on the rear of the drive for damage (bearing in mind that pin 19 is not usually present on hard drives). Carefully straighten any bent pins that you find (see Figure 11-10), both on the data connector and the power connector (bent power connector pins are rare given their thickness). Again, the best fix is to try to straighten the bent pin with tweezers (see Figure 11-11). Work slowly, and don't overbend the pin. Broken pins usually mean a replacement drive.

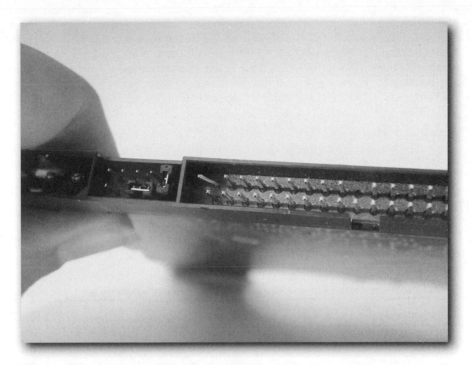

FIGURE 11-10: Bent pin on hard drive connector.

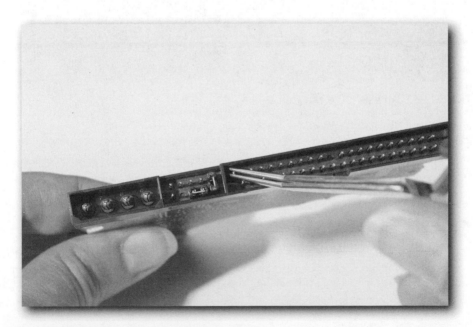

FIGURE 11-11: Using tweezers to straighten the pin.

Circuit Board

Check the circuit board on the base of the hard drive. On some drives this will be covered by a rubber or metal plate. If this is the case, don't remove the rubber or the plate to have a look because this might void your warranty. If the circuit board is uncovered, refer to the information covered in the preceding "Circuit Boards" section. Visually inspect your circuit board before progressing, looking in particular for component damage.

Checking the CPU

There's not a lot to check on a CPU, but nonetheless it's an important part of the checking process.

Pins

The area most prone to damage on a CPU is the sea of pins on its underside (see Figure 11-12). This isn't as hard to spot as you might think, because one pin out of alignment actually stands out against the hundreds of straight pins!

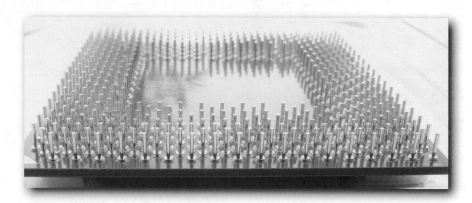

FIGURE 11-12: All pins 100% straight!

Exterior Physical Damage

Quickly inspect the CPU for any exterior damage. This is extremely rare and only happens where either the CPU has been dropped when out of the protective packaging or where the packaging has been extensively damaged in transit.

Checking RAM Modules

RAM modules are basically small circuit boards, like mini-expansion-cards. They have circuitry on the board and a connector edge. Inspect RAM modules as you would inspect any other circuit board. Check in particular for bending and cracks.

The most common type of damage to affect memory modules is invisible damage sustained from electrostatic discharge (ESD). Take extra precautions when handling memory modules against ESD. For more information, see Chapter 1, "Safety First."

Checking the PSU

The power supply unit is the component that takes the mains power and changes the voltage to suit the components in a PC. PSUs are normally tested before shipping from the factory, but because damage can occur in transit and because your PSU is a critical component, it's important to carefully check it to make sure that it is undamaged.

There are two types of check that you can carry out on a PSU:

- Visual inspections
- Powered tests using a multimeter

We're well aware that not everyone is comfortable testing components when plugged into the electrical supply. We would recommend that if anyone is unsure or doesn't feel they are ready to attempt this kind of testing to bypass these tests and assume that the PSU is okay, and only undertake these tests if the system isn't working (or return the PSU to where you bought it).

Visual Checks

Check the exterior of the PSU for any damage such as dents. Reject any PSUs that show signs of external damage as they might be malfunctioning and destroy other components attached to them.

Also, check all of the power cabling on the power rails (the cables that feed power to the motherboard and drives) coming from the PSU for signs of wear, sharp kinks, or cuts to the outer sheathing of the wires. Check all the connectors carefully and look for any that might have suffered crush damage in transit.

Finally, give the PSU a little shake and listen for anything that sounds loose inside or any rattling. There's a lot of space inside a PSU, and screws and other small items can work their way inside and cause a short when switched on. Reject the PSU if it sounds like it has something loose inside.

Power Checks

Carrying out power tests on a PSU will give you a definitive answer as to whether the PSU has suffered any damage while in transit and whether the output voltages provided by the power rails conform to the specification required.

These tests involve the PSU being connected to the mains and switched on. This means that mains power is flowing into the PSU and that low-voltage outputs are present in the drive rails.

Technically, the PSU in this state is no more dangerous than when plugged into a PC and running, but there is a slightly increased risk of electric shock if you touch anything inside the PSU with a screwdriver or tweezers (or if something like a screw or wire finds its way into the PSU). Also, because the power rails are free and unconnected to anything, you also need to keep them away from liquids or metal surfaces in case of a short circuit.

If you follow the instructions here carefully, then you can carry out these tests safely but never take short cuts or guesses. If you are unsure about anything, backtrack, reread the instructions, and check again.

If you are in any way uncertain about carrying out these tests or don't feel that your skills with a multimeter are good enough, then do not perform these tests and assume that the PSU is okay.

To carry out these tests you will need a:

- Multimeter (see Figure 11-13)
- Surface to place the PSU on while running (a wooden surface, heat resistant kitchen work area, or a ceramic tile is best as the PSU might get a little warm)
- Power cord for the PSU
- Nearby power outlet
- Small length of insulated wire
- Hard drive or two 20-ohm (or higher) resistors (all will be revealed shortly!)

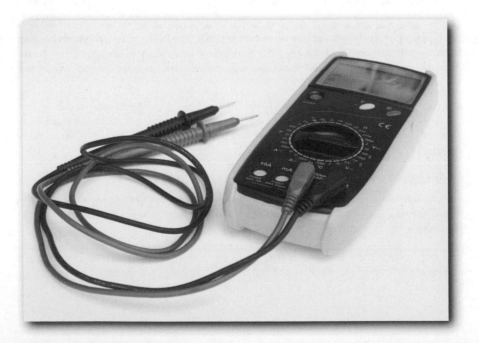

FIGURE 11-13: Digital multimeter.

The purpose of these tests is to ascertain that the power output from the power rails on the PSU falls within a range acceptable for a PSU.

Table 11-1 lists the three specific voltages you are testing.

Table 11-1	ATX (Advanced Technology Extended) Power Output Specification		
Power Rail Voltage (Volts)	Allowable Variance (%)	Minimum Voltage	Maximum Voltage
3.3	5	3.14	3.47
5	5	4.75	5.25
12	5	11.4	12.6

If your PSU has any of the output that falls outside of these values, you will need to get it replaced before using it. As a rule, power supply units are quite well behaved, but some (especially cheaper ones) might not be constructed to a high enough standard.

 Caution Never, ever, connect a PSU that is delivering too much voltage to a PC. The additional voltage can harm or destroy the CPU, motherboard, RAM, and hard drives.

Testing the PSU

Testing the PSU is probably one of the most complicated things that we have covered so far. It's not a case of just plugging the PSU into the mains and probing it with the multimeter probes. There are a few precautionary steps that you have to take to properly load the PSU before testing along with a small temporary modification that you have to do to get the PSU to start when out of the PC.

Loading the PSU

First, it's not a good idea to run a PC without any load on it (that is, without connecting the PSU to anything to draw power from it). While the ATX specification relating to power supplies indicates that a PSU should be able to run indefinitely without any load, some people encounter problems resulting from this, possibly because the PSU they have purchased is not totally ATX-compliant. These problems range from a high-pitched noise being emitted by the PSU to overheating and cutting off.

Because of this, it's a good idea to put a load on your PSU. The easiest way to do this is to attach a hard drive to the PSU power rails and let that take the power (see Figure 11-14).

If you are loading a PSU with a hard drive, then make sure that the drive is on a nonconductive surface. Better still, fit the drive into the PC, even if only temporarily.

Caution   Because you are testing the PSU for power output, if your PSU is damaged the output might spike and damage the hard drive. If you have an old hard drive, it's a good idea to keep it for testing. If you don't want to risk damage to your drive try the method below instead.

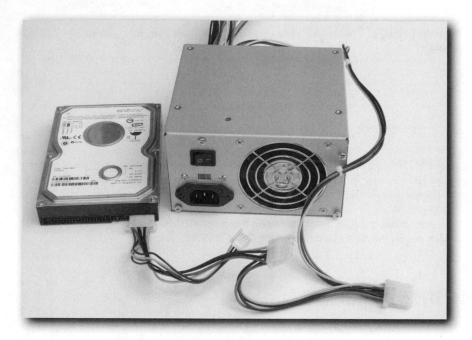

FIGURE **11-14: Loading the PSU using a hard drive.**

Another way to test the PSU is using two resistors of 20 ohm (or greater). You can use these to load the 5-volt and 12-volt hard drive power rails to simulate a hard drive.

Connecting the resistors is easy (see Figure 11-15). Take the hard drive connector and use one resistor to bridge one of the outside connectors fed by either the yellow wire (12 volts) or red wire (5 volts) to one of the two ground connectors in the middle (black wires). Then simply repeat for the other connector. This will provide load for the PSU and simulate a hard drive.

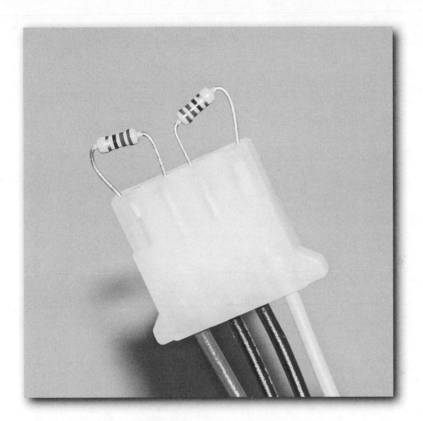

FIGURE 11-15: Loading the PSU with resistors.

Don't touch! These resistors will get hot when the PSU is switched on. Also take appropriate precautions so that they do not touch other PC components or damage surfaces.

Jumpering the On Switch

A PSU is designed to be switched on and off by the switch on the front of a PC. Because of this, if you plug in the PSU without connecting it to a motherboard, nothing will happen. In order to activate it, you have to bridge one of the motherboard connectors to a ground wire. Fortunately, this is easier than it sounds.

Take a look at the big 20-pin motherboard connector block on the PSU. Hold it so that the keyed connector faces you and the wires are at the bottom and the connectors facing upward. Now look at the seventh pin along from the left. This one is fed by a green wire and either side of this is a pin fed by a black wire (ground) as shown in Figure 11-16. What you need to do is take that piece of wire that we mentioned earlier and strip off a bit of the insulation at each end and bridge the pin fed by the green wire to either of the pins alongside. This will simulate the PSU being connected inside a PC and the PC being switched on.

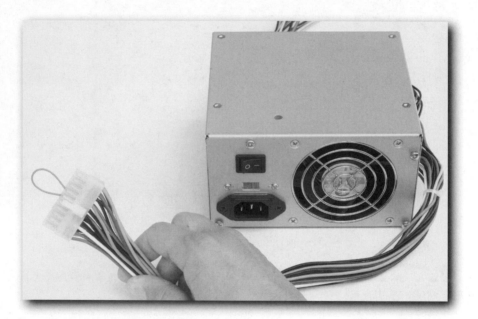

FIGURE 11-16: Jumpering pin 14 to ground.

Performing the Tests

There are three voltages to test inside a PC. These are:

- 12-volt supply
- 5-volt supply
- 3.3-volt supply

The best place to test the 12-volt and 5-volt outputs is from the hard drive power connector. You do this by bridging the pins with your multimeter. To test the 12-volt supply, you will bridge the pins supplied by the yellow and black wires. To test the 5-volt supply, bridge the pins for the red and black wires (either black wire will do).

To easiest way to test the 3.3-volt output is to use the auxiliary connector. With the multimeter, bridge one of the pins fed by the orange wire (pins 4 or 5 on the connector if you look at it with the key facing you and the wires at the bottom) to either of the pins fed by the black wires (pin 1, 2, or 3).

But before you can carry out any testing, you need to set up your multimeter, which you will see how to do next.

Multimeter Setup

The first thing you need to do is set up the multimeter to measure DC voltage in the 20-volt range. All multimeters are different, so consult your documentation if unsure how to do this.

What follows are generic instructions for setting up a multimeter:

1. Plug the black probe into the socket labeled COM.

2. Plug the red probe into the socket labeled V (see Figure 11-17).

FIGURE **11-17: Probes connected to multimeter.**

3. Set the multimeter to measure a range around 20V DC. Your number may vary but make sure that it is set to measure DC volts. See Figure 11-18.

FIGURE 11-18: Multimeter set to correct range.

You're now ready to switch on the multimeter and test the three different output voltages!

12-Volt Supply Tests

Here are the steps necessary for testing the 12-volt output from the PSU:

1. Place the PSU on its side on the heat-resistant surface, taking care not to obstruct any fans or air input or exhaust vents.

2. Prepare the PSU as described in the preceding section — connect a load to one of the hard drive rails and jumper the on switch on the motherboard.

3. Connect the red probe to pin 1 of the hard drive power connector (fed by the yellow wire).

4. Connect the black probe to either pin 2 or 3 (fed by black wires). See Figure 11-19.

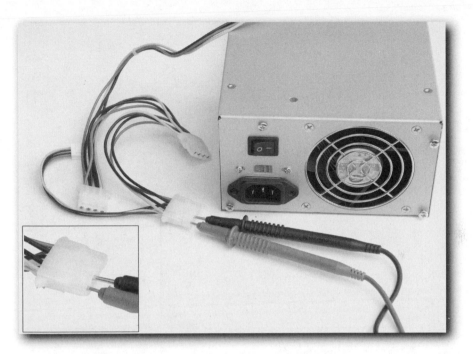

FIGURE **11-19: Probes inserted correctly.**

5. Switch on the PSU and take a reading. You are looking for an output that falls into the range of 11.5–12.6 volts.

6. Switch the PSU off again soon afterward.

5-Volt Supply Tests

Here are the steps necessary for testing the 5-volt output from the PSU:

1. Place the PSU on its side on the heat resistant surface, taking care not to obstruct any fans or air input or exhaust vents.

2. Prepare the PSU as described, connecting a load to one of the hard drive rails and jumpering the on switch on the motherboard.

3. Connect the red probe to pin 4 of the hard drive power connector (fed by the red wire).

4. Connect the black probe to either pin 2 or 3 (fed by black wires). See Figure 11-20.

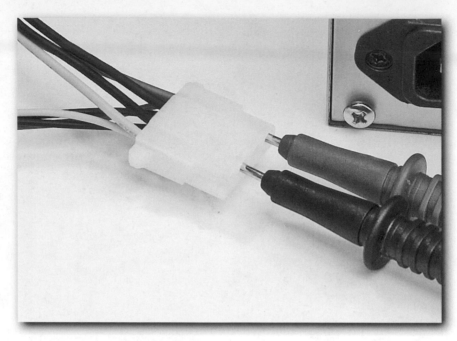

FIGURE 11-20: Probes inserted correctly.

5. Switch on the PSU and take a reading. You are looking for an output that falls into the range of 4.75–5.25 volts.

6. Switch the PSU off again soon afterward.

3.3-Volt Supply Tests

Here are the steps necessary for testing the 3.3-volt output from the PSU:

1. Place the PSU on its side on the heat-resistant surface, taking care not to obstruct any fans or air input or exhaust vents.

2. Prepare the PSU as described, connecting a load to one of the hard drive rails and jumpering the on switch on the motherboard.

3. Connect the red probe to pin 4 or 5 of the auxiliary power connector (fed by the orange wires).

4. Connect the black probe to either pin 1, 2, or 3 (fed by black wires).

5. Switch on the PSU and take a reading. You are looking for an output that falls into the range of 3.14–3.47 volts.

6. Switch the PSU off again as soon as possible. Don't leave it on unnecessarily.

If you find that any of the voltages fall outside the ranges specified, we recommend that you exchange the power supply unit. An unreliable power supply is not going to get any better with use and will likely deteriorate, causing you problems like lockups, crashes, or even fried components!

Summary

In this chapter, we've looked at how to check and test certain key PC components for problems before they are installed in the PC. You'll no doubt save time, money, and frustration by checking your components before you begin the installation process.

Much of the testing involved only simple visual checking of the components for cracks, defects, and broken pins. But for the PSU, given its importance, we covered physical testing using a multimeter to measure various output voltages along the power rails.

Now that the testing is over, let the building begin!

Building Your PC

part

Top 10 Things You Don't Want to Forget before You Begin the Build!

There's no worse time to realize you've forgotten something than when you need it in order to be able to proceed with the job. Things seem to be coming together well and you feel you're on a roll, and then you find you need something small but important, and the job is delayed until you can get it. Not having everything ready can cause big delays. At minimum, it's a delay until you can take a trip to the local computer store; at most, it's a wait of a few days while you have to wait for it to be delivered. A wait of a few hours is disruptive enough, but a wait of a few days can really put your PC project off course.

So, be prepared and get everything ready before you start. In this chapter, we're going to look at the top 10 things people forget when building a PC.

This chapter is in this book to prepare you so that your build doesn't get delayed by making simple mistakes!

No. 1: Compatible Parts

By now, you should be sitting in the middle of a whole heap of PC parts all waiting to be connected up together to make one working PC. You can think of the pieces as the pieces of a jigsaw puzzle, each piece having a specific place to go and playing a key role in the end product (the final picture in the case of a jigsaw puzzle, or a working PC in the case of your PC parts).

Just as with the jigsaw, you've seen in previous chapters that PC parts aren't all interchangeable. You can't mix up random pieces from two jigsaw puzzles and expect to get them to fit together, let alone make a sensible final image. The same is true for PC parts.

The three main components you need to make sure will fit together are:

- CPU
- Motherboard
- RAM

These are the three critical components and are the same ones you are most likely to encounter compatibility problems with.

Check the documentation. The information supplied with the motherboard is likely to cover the type of CPU and RAM that it is compatible with. Check the details carefully and confirm that the RAM and CPU are compatible. When building a PC, there's no equivalent to the jigsaw puzzle world where you can bash a piece into place or chew a lug off! Things have to fit, and they have to fit smoothly. Otherwise, the project is going to go wrong, components will be broken or damaged, and you will end up out of pocket.

However, don't become too paranoid about things fitting — if the documentation says that things are all going to come together then there's a really good chance that they will. Sockets and connectors can be quite deceptive, and a socket and connector that are perfectly compatible can look incompatible to the eye (especially when they're still in their packaging). If later you find that your components aren't coming together right when the instructions says they should, then you have a good case for an exchange. (RAM is the most likely candidate to give you troubles. There are times when even the best vendor gets its lines mixed up and supplies the wrong parts.)

Newcomers to building a PC have a tendency to want to handle the parts that they've bought — a lot. It's easy to understand why — the parts are not only cool but they look exciting. No matter how excited you are, please do try to limit your handling of the parts to a minimum. By handling them, not only do you increase the risk of damage to them from electrostatic discharge but also damage from dropping them or careless handling.

Also, never bring parts up to one another when one or more of the components are still in their antistatic bags to check for fit. It's very easy to damage connectors in this way, and also remember that the static charge is designed to skip across the surface of these bags. If one component is protected and the other isn't, there's a greater chance that the unprotected item could be destroyed by ESD.

No. 2: Instructions and Drivers

One thing you're definitely going to find when building a PC is that you quickly become buried in instructions and in the CDs that contain software drivers for your devices (see Figure 12-1). Drivers aren't too bad because they are usually labeled clearly — if not, label them yourself to avoid confusion and hassles later.

FIGURE **12-1: Piles of instructions!**

Instructions come in all shapes and sizes. Single sheets, booklets, CD, even things that look and feel like whole books. It's actually rare to come across a component or device that doesn't come with some sort of documentation these days.

Tip

Don't decide to be tidy and keep all your documentation and instructions tidy in a folder or box. Keep them with the components. That way you won't have to go searching through a box or folder each time you want something, and identical-looking pieces of paper won't become mixed.

It's also not unusual for extra notes containing important additional instructions or warnings that have been left out of the main documentation to be added to the box in the final stage of the packaging process. Because these are printed as an afterthought, they may not carry the name or number of the product they are referring to (or even the manufacturer's name), so separating this paper from the component will mean that you are missing vital instructions that could affect your warranty should things go wrong.

However, don't let the weight or thickness of the paper you get supplied with impress or overwhelm you. There are a few things that you need to check before you start building the PC.

Are the Instructions in Your Language?

It's quite possible to get a component or device that has a lot of instructions shipped with it, but when you look closely, you discover there's nothing written in any language that you can read and understand! Some things ship with paperwork in numerous languages, but sometimes critical languages are omitted. Check through all the paperwork you've received carefully (it's at times like this that you'll be glad that you didn't throw anything away!) and don't assume that your language will be the first one listed in whatever book or leaflet provided. In fact, you may have to hunt for it.

Still can't find instructions you can read? Take a look through any CDs or DVDs that came too as they might be on that. There're a number of different file formats to look out for.

The main file types likely to contain instructions are:

- Text files (.txt)
- Rich text files (.rtf)
- Portable document format (.pdf)
  Requires Adobe Reader to be installed

Still no success? Try the website if there's one listed (there usually is). There may be documentation available for download there.

If you have no joy finding instructions on the web, you can check for a support email or telephone number in your country and give them a call or send an email. Before you call, make sure that you know what components or products you have (make a note of the model numbers). Avoid overseas calls — these are going to be expensive and are unlikely to be unsuccessful. In an email, be clear in detailing what items you have and the problem that you are having.

Note If you can't find any instructions that you can understand you can always turn to the web for help. The search engines Google (www.google.com) and AltaVista (www.altavista.com) both have excellent translation tools on their sites that might be of use to you.

Do the Instructions Make Sense?

Read through the instructions in advance of actually needing them. Finding instructions in a language that you can understand is no guarantee that the instructions are actually going to make sense, as they may have been poorly translated.

Note Better quality products usually have better written, clearer, easier to read instructions included.

What's much worse and far more annoying than instructions that make no sense are instructions that seem to make sense until you get to a point and then become vague (usually at a crucial step or during a complicated procedure). This is why it's vitally important to read them through well ahead of time.

Read all instructions in advance and clarify any vague aspects! Read with a highlighter pen in hand and highlight any areas of ambiguity so that you can come back to them later and see if you can work it out.

Tip Reach Out for Support: Remember that tech support is not only there for when things go wrong. You can get in touch with tech support to clear up ambiguities and problems with the documentation. You've paid for support so use it!

Are the Instructions Current?

Stop press! Over time, things change. Well, everything except the instruction manuals!

Manufacturer's don't like changing their instruction or installation manuals until they have to because it's not a cheap process (it's a long process that usually involves testing, translation, and chucking away the old manuals). They can do this not only for small changes but also big important ones. But, rather than incorporating information relating to the changes in the manual, what they do instead is include a "Stop press!" or late breaking information sheet.

Because there will be no indication of this in the manual, be sure to check through all the paperwork. Also, just to confuse, they may have not included it on paper but may have just added this important information to a readme file on disk or CD that you'll have to find yourself (or just post it to their website — always worth checking out to see in case there's anything new there!).

No. 3: Keyboard

We can't count the times we've seen someone start building a PC and then realize that he or she hasn't got a keyboard! As odd as it sounds people have quite a blind spot to realizing that a PC has a keyboard attached!

It's not the end of the world if you forget one — if you have another PC you can always borrow it in the interim, but as you get deeper into the build you begin to need the keyboard more and more.

When you're building and subsequently testing a PC, a basic keyboard without any fancy buttons or features is a lot better because it doesn't require any special drivers to be installed. The same is true of mice — build and test with a basic one if possible.

Tip   If you are planning to make building PCs into a hobby or small business, then it's a good idea to have a spare keyboard or two handy (same goes for mice and monitors). Basic keyboards are cheap (you can get one for under $5) and are perfectly adequate for testing purposes.

Another option is to keep your old keyboard the next time you upgrade to a better one.

No. 4: Power Cord

Again, a power cord is something that every PC has yet few people think about when they're building one. Your PC is going to start needing power pretty quickly, so you'll need a power cable to connect the PSU to the mains line, and without a suitable power cord you're not going to get very far (see Figure 12-2).

FIGURE 12-2: Power cord.

You might have already been supplied with one. Sometimes a case comes with a power cord; sometimes it doesn't. If you don't have one, then you can borrow the one off an existing PC until you get a spare.

Note There's also a pretty good chance that if you have been supplied with a power cord that it's the wrong one for your country (especially if you live outside the United States or the United Kingdom). Don't bother trying to find an adaptor for an incorrect power cord; it's far cheaper and safer to buy a new cable.

No. 5: Internal Cabling

As you're about to find out, the inside of a PC houses a lot of cables, each of which is important and serves a vital purpose. Be short one cable, and you're going to have to delay the build.

A lot of the cables you need are going to be attached to the PC case or the power supply unit and aren't detachable, which does make life simpler. However, there are some cables that you might still have to source separately.

Here is a list of the standard cables you will need:

- **Cable to connect hard drive to motherboard.** Generally, these are ribbon IDE cables, but if you've chosen a SATA drive you'll need cables specific for this. (See Figure 12-3.) One IDE ribbon cable can connect up to two IDE devices (either hard drives or CD/DVD drives) to the motherboard. A SATA cable can connect only one device to the motherboard.

  If you buy a hard drive in what's known as a "retail kit" this will contain a cable, but "bare" drives come with nothing, and you have to provide your own cable.

Note We recommend that you get two cables even if you only intend on fitting two IDE devices (one per cable) because this will give you the best in terms of performance and scope for upgrade in the future.

- **Floppy drive cable (if you plan on fitting a floppy drive).** You will only need one of these.
- **CD/DVD to sound card audio cable.** Not all drives require this cable (most modern CD and DVD drives are capable of digital audio extraction). Generally, if you need this cable, it will be provided.

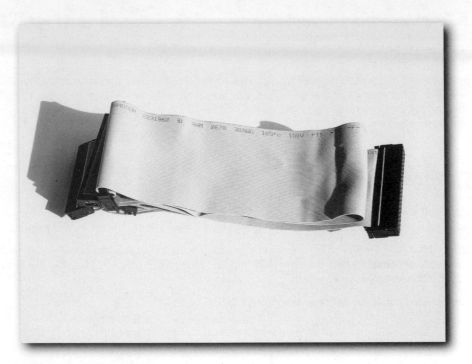

FIGURE 12-3: Internal cabling.

No. 6: Drive Rails

There are two types of drive bay in your PC:

- 5-$\frac{1}{4}$ inch drive bay
- 3-$\frac{1}{2}$ inch drive bay

The idea is that hard drives fit into the 3-$\frac{1}{2}$ inch bay and CD/DVD drives fit into the 5-$\frac{1}{4}$ inch drive bays. However, many people prefer to fit hard drives into 5-$\frac{1}{4}$ inch bays because they're generally better placed and it's easier to both route the cables that way, and also since the bays are bigger there's more space to work in.

Problem is, a 3-$^1/_2$ inch hard drive won't fit directly into a 5-$^1/_4$ inch drive bay because it's too large. The answer to this problem is to get drive rails that fit over the hard drive, making it fit into the 5-$^1/_4$ inch bay. The drive rail simply screws into the screw holes on the drive and makes the drive wider (see Figure 12-4).

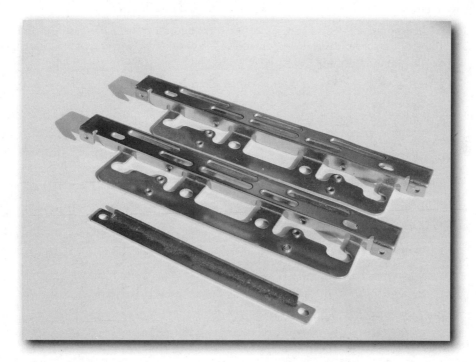

FIGURE 12-4: Drive rail set.

Some people prefer to fit hard drives into the bigger 5-$^1/_4$ inch bay because it allows more air to flow around the drive, helping to keep it cool. This does help when you have a midsized or full-sized tower and generally you have enough 5-$^1/_4$ inch drives to space a few for hard drives.

No. 7: Screws and Fittings

There are a lot of screws and other fittings that go into holding a PC together, and you don't want to be skimping on screws when it comes to the build just because you didn't plan ahead.

Note Some cases come with screws supplied, but these screws are generally low-quality "one-size fits all." It is preferable to use screws supplied with a particular device over generic screws.

Here are just a few of the screws and fittings that you will need to have:

■ **Motherboard to chassis fittings.** Because these can vary from case to case, generally they are supplied with the case. Sometimes "stand-off" type screws are used to keep the board from touching the metal case, and other times the stand-offs are built into the case. See Figure 12-5.

FIGURE 12-5: Metal motherboard to chassis fittings.

■ **Case screws.** These screws are six-gauge wire with 32 threads per inch American National Coarse Thread (UNC) machine screws that are cut to accept a both a Phillips No. 2 screwdriver and a ¼ inch hex driver and are ⁵/₁₆ inch long. See Figure 12-6.

FIGURE 12-6: Case screws.

- **Hard drive screws.** Hard drives are connected to the case using pan head screws that accept a Phillips No. 2 screwdriver. Specifically, these are six-gauge wire with 32 threads per inch American National Coarse Thread (UNC) machine screws, just like case screws, only the heads and length (3/16 inch) are different. See Figure 12-7.

Never mount a hard drive using case screw. It's too long and can damage the drive!

You can use a maximum of four screws per drive (two either side). At minimum, you can use is two (one either side), but this isn't recommended. Remember, if you are using drive rails you will need more screws (supplied with the rails).

FIGURE **12-7: Hard drive screws.**

- **CD/DVD drive screws.** These are similar to the screws that hold hard drives or drive rails in place. However, "similar" doesn't mean "same." These drive screws are 5 mm long M3x0.5 (3 millimeter wire with a 0.5 mm thread pitch) machine screws with integral washer and are cut to accept a No. 1 Phillips head screwdriver. Some also have a both a $^7/_{32}$ inch hex head (odd indeed for a metric screw!). Modern optical drives spin the discs at high speed and can generate a lot of vibration. It is vital then that drives are firmly attached by using all four screws. See Figure 12-8.

FIGURE 12-8: CD/DVD drive screws.

- **Drive rails.** Never skip on the screws used to attach the rail to the drive or the drive to the case. Use four screws to fit the drive to the rail and use four to fit the rail to the PC case. These come supplied with their own screws for fitting (they use hard drive screws).

- **Floppy drive screws.** Each drive is secured to the case with four screws that initially look like the same as the ones used to fit optical drives. The thread is the same as optical drives, but the head is different (these have a domed head that only accepts a No. 1 Phillips head screwdriver). Also, they are shorter, at 4 mm in length. See Figure 12-9.

FIGURE 12-9: Floppy drive screws.

 Note Don't forget the screwdrivers you need, either!

No. 8: CPU Cooler

Every CPU needs a cooler. Gone are the days where a CPU could safely be run without any sort of heatsink or fan. See Figure 12-10.

 Caution Never run a modern CPU without a cooler—even for a few minutes. The heat build-up occurs quickly and can easily wreck the CPU!

FIGURE 12-10: CPU cooler assembly.

These coolers consist of a heatsink (a fancy name for a machined block of copper or aluminum designed to carry the excess heat away from the CPU) and an electric fan designed to blow cooling air over the heatsink. Sometimes these coolers are bundled with the CPU and sometimes they're not. If you don't have one, then you'll need to get a cooler that's compatible with your CPU. There's a wide selection of types, ranging from small and cheap to massive and pricey! As long as you get a cooler designed for your type and speed of CPU, then it should be adequate for the job of keeping it cool. However, if you run your PC in a hot environment, it might require some more effort to cool, and you'll need to buy a bigger and more expensive cooler.

If you have to buy a heatsink/fan combo, then don't forget the thermal compound that goes between the heatsink and CPU (see Figure 12-11). This is vital for proper transfer of the heat from the CPU to the heatsink.

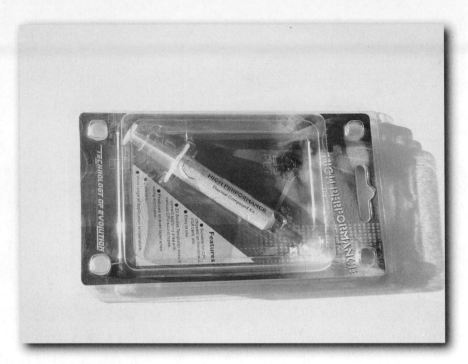

Figure 12-11: Thermal compound.

 Caution Never fit a fan without applying a thin coating of thermal compound to the joint because the heat build-up, at worst, can destroy the CPU and at best dramatically shorten its life!

No. 9: Boot Disk/CD

You're going to need some form of boot disk to bring the PC to life and load on the operating system. The old floppy disk has now given way to bootable CD-ROMs, which have a greater data capacity and are a lot less prone to damage.

No matter what you want to load onto the PC — Windows XP or a Linux distro — you will find the system will boot from the CD and will allow you to carry out the installation of the operating system.

However, the boot floppy disk shouldn't be considered to be totally obsolete — you will see us making use of one later on for testing the system for faults. They are quick to make, simple, and you don't need to have an optical drive connected.

For testing purposes, a boot floppy made from any PC and any version of Windows post-95 will do fine. Just make sure that the PC you use to create the disk is free from viruses that might damage your PC.

No. 10: Operating System

Make sure that you have an operating system lined up for installation on your PC, and make sure that you are legally licensed to install it. With a new, purchased copy, there isn't likely to be a problem, but if you are transferring it from one PC to another then make sure that you consult the license agreement on how to do this legally.

As mentioned previously, most operating system CDs are also boot discs, so if you have an operating system ready for installation you also have a boot disc.

Knowing in advance what operating system you are going to be loading onto your PC means you can tailor the PC components to suit (especially RAM and CPU).

You will be loading Windows XP onto your system as part of this build.

Have Fun!

Finally, don't forget to have fun while building your system! It's easy to get caught up in problems and worries about compatibility and forget to enjoy the process — after all, it's a big part of building your own PC!

You might find it fun to document the building process — maybe build a small website around the build or make blog entries. You might also like to take photos of the build so that you can see the progress you are making!

Summary

In this chapter, we've given you a heads up on some of the things people tend to forget when they are gathering the parts necessary to build a PC. There's every chance that if you've been reading the book so far you've got everything you need, but just in case you decided to jump ahead, this chapter's here to make sure you are prepared.

On with the building!

Assembling the Case and Fitting the PSU

With all the theory on PC components and inspecting and testing out of the way, it's now time to get your tools out and begin building your custom PC!

We're going to begin by looking at how to check the PC case you have bought and start planning where things are going to go. Then we'll fit the PSU and carry out some basic testing to make sure that we're ready to proceed.

Beginning with a Bare Case

You're going to start like everyone else starts when they build a PC — with a totally bare case.

Well, we say "totally bare," but that's not entirely accurate. Some elements of the case might already have been assembled for you (see Figure 13-1). These include:

➤ Wiring for the front on/off switch

➤ Wiring for the reset button

➤ Hard drive activity lights

➤ Case fan wiring

All of this should be in place for you, and what you're going to notice is a lot of loose wiring inside the case. If not, fitting these is generally only a matter of screwing a panel onto the front of the PC — they never expect you to do any wiring or soldering! Don't worry about this right now; we'll get on to that when we come to fitting the motherboard. For now, just tuck the wiring out of the way while we look at the power supply unit.

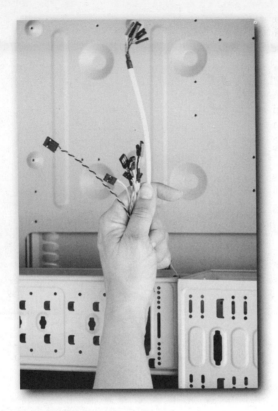

FIGURE 13-1: Case wiring.

One item that may or may not be fitted to your PC's case already is the power supply unit (PSU). Some cases come with these fitted ready for you, whereas others come with a PSU but it's not fitted. Still other times your case won't come with a PSU, and you'll have to buy and fit it yourself.

We're going to start with a PC case that doesn't have a PSU fitted. However, all of the wiring for the switches, buttons, and LEDs are already fitted and in place. If your case has the PSU prefitted, you can either just ignore the section that deals with fitting it or take the opportunity to check that it's been fitted properly! At the very least, an improperly fitted PSU can be very noisy indeed.

Checking the Case

You might have already checked the case in the store from where you bought it, but it's always a good idea to give it a check again at home.

It's time to lift your case out of the box, and get it out from all the packing it has been stored in and take a look at it. Leave on any plastic sheeting covering any transparent plastic windows or shiny parts on the case — these will help protect against scratches.

Inspect the Case

Take the PC case out of all its protective wrappings and place it on a firm, level surface and visually inspect for any damage that might be present. Look for dents, scratches, and signs of knocks. Remember that you are going to be looking at that PC case for a long time, so make sure that it's in good condition to start with.

Check that the case feels firm on the surface and doesn't wobble or vibrate (if it does check the feet as they might have either come off or have adjusters on them).

Another thing worth checking is the buttons — give them a quick press to be certain that they work properly. They should operate smoothly.

With the case out of the box and on a solid surface, now take the side panels off the case. You might have practiced this is in the store already, so it could be simple. However, if this is the first time, it might be a bit of a puzzle.

 Refer back to Chapter 3, "Choosing a Suitable Case and Power Supply," if you need guidance on cases.

At this stage, make sure that you find and keep safe any screws provided with the case — losing these can cause you headaches later!

Check For and Fix Sharp Edges

With the side panels off, check the case. Begin by looking for any sharp edges. If you did this earlier when you bought the case, you should not find many. Still, you'll soon learn that even the best made case will have at least one sharp or jagged edge waiting to catch you when you least expect it.

Along with jagged metal, look for pointy bits of plastic. Although plastic is not as sharp and nasty as metal, a plastic point or edge can give you an unpleasant surprise — not something you want to happen when you're handling the delicate CPU or motherboard!

Spend a few minutes checking for sharp edges. If you find any, you can:

- Temporarily put tape over the sharp edges. Although you can use insulating tape, this can leave a mess. A better recommendation is to use decorator's masking tape — get a bright or outrageous color so that it stands out! Above all, don't use anything with too much sticking power (like duct tape) or you'll never get it off. This way you can remove the tape when the building is done without making a mess.

- On the case, use a permanent marker to make a note of where the sharp edges are. Just be sure that these marks aren't visible from the outside of the case. You can use arrows or circles to show the snaggy spots.

Even after taking these precautions, keep a small first aid kit handy—just in case!

Fitting the PSU

Now it's time to move on to the PSU. If you have a tower style case, then the PSU fits at the top of the case at the rear (this is what we are using). With a desktop case, the PSU will go at the back of the case. No matter what kind of case you use, it will be apparent from the hole in the chassis where the PSU goes.

On first impression, the PSU might seem massive, too massive in fact to fit into the case. Rest assured, however, that it will fit! To put your mind at ease we'll try that now.

You have to fit the PSU before fitting the motherboard and other components. Trying to fit the PSU after fitting the motherboard is a very bad idea, because you will be trying to squeeze the bulky, heavy PSU past the delicate motherboard. Fit it now and save yourself a lot of trouble.

Check for Damage

Before fitting, check the PSU for any damage. (We looked at how to do this and also how to check the output voltages in the previous chapter.) A damaged PSU is a potentially dangerous PSU. If you haven't already done so, read through the previous chapter to make sure that your PSU is in proper working order.

Fit the PSU

After you have determined that your PSU is ready to go, you're ready to fit the PSU. The following steps guide you through this process:

1. At the back of the PSU (the back is the face the power connector is on and where you'll find the main power on/off switch and the little red voltage selector slider), you will find four threaded screw holes, as shown in Figure 13-2. In the pack of screws provided with the case, you should find screws that fit into these holes. Retrieve four screws that fit the threads on the PSU, and keep the remainder safe.

2. The PSU is fitted onto the case from the inside (there's no way to slot it into the carriage from the outside). Begin by first getting the PSU in the right orientation. You want the PSU with the fan and switches pointing toward the rear and with the two screws in the corner of the PSU at the bottom. Don't worry, you can't fit the PSU incorrectly—the holes in the case won't allow it.

FIGURE 13-2: PSU-fitting points.

Screw Tip!

Many people are worried about damaging the screws or threads when trying to find the right screw to fit the right thread.

Keep this in mind—you cannot strip a thread or damage anything if you try the screw by hand. All the screws that hold a PC together should screw into their appropriate threads by hand, and if they feel tight they are either not in the hole correctly or you are using the wrong screw.

Getting a screw to bite into the thread can be difficult to start off with too—a simple way to get it going is to turn the screw in the counterclockwise direction for a turn or two to clear the tips of the threads—this will help it bite easier.

Don't trust the labeling on the PSU to tell you how to fit it—the labels might be upside down!

3. Place the case on its side with the opening at the top. Move all of the case wiring—including the PSU wiring—out of the way so that you don't trap it. See Figure 13-3.

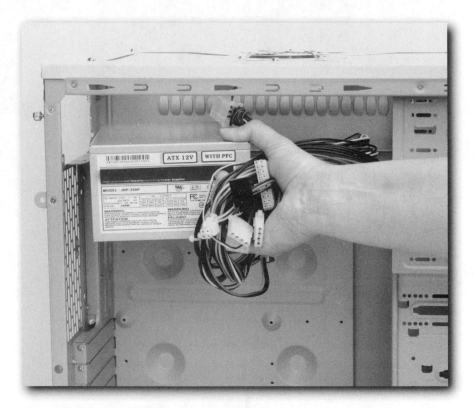

FIGURE 13-3: Keeping the wiring under control.

4. Take the PSU into the case and work it toward the top rear of the case (see Figure 13-4). Different cases make this easier or harder, depending on layout. Although it might be a tight fit, there should be no need to use excessive force or to bash or use pry bars or levers to get the PSU into place. If it's not fitting right, something is wrong, so you'll need to backtrack and start again.

5. After you have the PSU in the right spot, you'll now see not only that there is a handy metal rail to hold it in place but also that the holes in the case and the threaded screw holes in the PSU line up (see Figure 13-5).

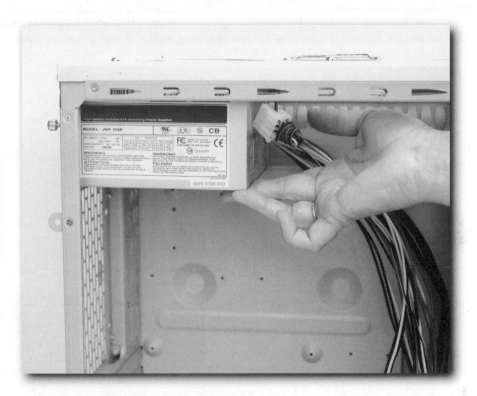

FIGURE 13-4: Fitting the PSU.

FIGURE 13-5: PSU screw points line up.

6. Take one of the screws and fit it. Do this screw up *hand tight* (don't overtighten the screw; it's not needed) and then add the other four, making sure that they are hand tight too.

7. Once you have all four in place, get your Phillips head screwdriver (size No. 1 for this job), and give each a half turn to tighten. Don't overtighten! See Figure 13-6.

FIGURE 13-6: Adding the screws.

That's the PSU fitted to the case!

Watch the Wiring

One thing that you are going to notice now that your PSU is fitted is a LOT more wiring in the case. Don't be tempted to knot this up or to tie it up with insulating tape or even cable ties. Why?

- You'll be undoing it all again real soon!
- Knotting the cables can cause damage.
- Insulating tape makes a real mess!
- Removing cable ties, especially with scissors, could mean that you cut a cable accidentally.

Note The easiest and safest way to cut the cable ties that hold your wiring in place is to use scissors. Slide one blade in under the cable tie along in the direction of the wires, and then slowly snip.

Instead of tying up the wiring, just loop the cables loosely and place them at the bottom of the case, out of the way for now.

What to Do If You Drop a Screw Inside the PSU

One nightmare scenario is dropping one of the screws that you planned to use to hold the PSU in place inside the PSU. This isn't easy to do, but it's doable (see Figure 13-7), and it's a major problem because there's no way you can start a PSU with a screw rattling around inside. Not only can it cause dramatic short circuits, but it could jam the cooling fan and possibly cause a fire.

If you drop a screw into a PSU, you'll have to get it out!

FIGURE 13-7: Screws CAN drop into the PSU!

Note Keep track of all the screws you have. Count them before you begin, and at every stage, after you've used a few, subtract these from the total. Check that you've not lost any—they might just end up somewhere you don't want them to be!

The trick is to get the screw out without opening the PSU, because this can void your warranty, but more seriously is that it can hold a charge after being disconnected from the electrical supply—a charge that's got enough power to kill you.

Lucky thing is that if the screw went in, you should be able to get it out the same way. It's not going to be easy, but with some precision shaking you will either get it out or get it to a point where you can use pliers to grab it.

Caution Make sure that the PSU is disconnected from the electrical supply and don't go digging inside the PSU with tweezers. Shake the screw to a point where you can grab hold of it easily.

Check the PSU for Proper Fit

With the PSU fitted, the first thing to look for is for trapped wires. These will need to be freed quickly and carefully, and the trapped cable will need to be checked for any damage.

Next, check that the PSU is fitted properly. Check in particular for rattling—try wobbling the PSU by hand. A rattle at this stage will only get worse and drive you nuts once the PC is running. If you find the PSU rattles, check first that it's fitted properly. The most likely cause of a rattle is that one of the screws is loose—do them up hand tight plus a $1/4$ to $1/2$ a turn extra to tighten.

Summary

In this chapter, you've begun the build of your PC by checking the case over and fitting the PSU. In many ways, this chapter is about confidence building and getting you started handling and assembling the parts that will come together to form your PC.

Everything covered in this chapter is both quick and overall quite easy, but it will get you started on the building process. And once you're done, it allows you to get on and add more components to your embryonic system.

In the next chapter, we'll look at how you fit the motherboard, CPU, RAM, and video adaptor! Because there's a lot to do in the next chapter, this might be a good place for you to take a break so that you can hit Chapter 14 refreshed and ready for more!

Build the Ultimate Custom PC

If you are going to be building a PC, then it's important to be able to know what all the parts are and how they fit together. Throughout the book we've used black-and-white photographs, but here we've added a little splash of color. The photographs here and throughout this book will help you get a true and accurate picture of what the components you will use are, what they're for and how they come together to make a working PC. What is the ultimate custom PC? It is a PC that is tailored exactly to suit your own needs, that can grow and change with you, and it is ultimately the sense of achievement of knowing that you designed it, bought the components and built it right from scratch. It is truly yours!

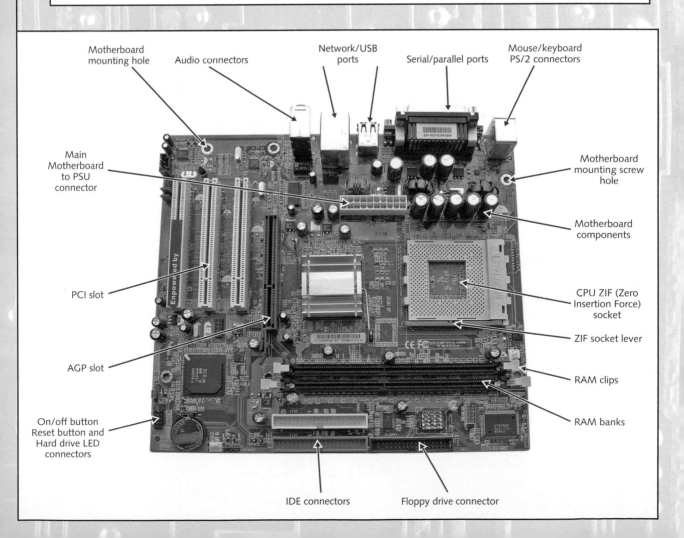

- Motherboard mounting hole
- Audio connectors
- Network/USB ports
- Serial/parallel ports
- Mouse/keyboard PS/2 connectors
- Main Motherboard to PSU connector
- Motherboard mounting screw hole
- Motherboard components
- PCI slot
- CPU ZIF (Zero Insertion Force) socket
- ZIF socket lever
- AGP slot
- RAM clips
- On/off button Reset button and Hard drive LED connectors
- RAM banks
- IDE connectors
- Floppy drive connector

Hard disk in an ESD bag. It's important to store all components in anti-static bags to protect them from the damaging effects of electrostatic discharge.

The hundreds of pins on the base of the CPU are designed to fit into the ZIF (Zero Insertion Force) socket on the motherboard with ease.

The CPU is held into the ZIF socket on the motherboard with a lever.

The notch on a 184-pin DDR module is used to line up the module with the corresponding notch on the RAM bank of the motherboard.

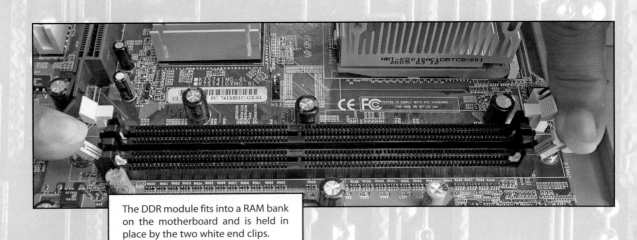

The DDR module fits into a RAM bank on the motherboard and is held in place by the two white end clips.

The clip at the front of the AGP slot holds the graphics adapter card in place on the motherboard.

The Crucial Technology Radeon 9200 is an AGP video adaptor. The aluminum heatsink cools the GPU (Graphical Processor Unit). At the back of the card are three ports for connecting monitors and other video devices: video out (colored yellow), S-video (black), 15 pin VGA port connector (blue).

Many motherboards come complete with on-board sound, which saves you the need for a separate sound card. External cabling for line-in (blue), speakers (green) and microphone (pink) will connect to these sockets on the rear of the PC when it is completed.

The PC case has a built-in speaker, which is very important in diagnosing errors. The speaker lead must be correctly oriented with the connector head on the motherboard. The letter "S," "SPK," or an arrow indicates pin 1 on the cable.

Test the power supply by using two 20 Ohm resistors to load the 5 volt and 12 volt hard drive power rails. This will simulate a hard drive attached to the PSU.

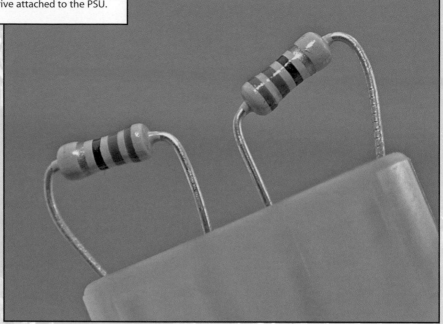

Jumpering pin 14 to ground (pin 13 or 15) will simulate the PSU being connected inside a PC that is switched on.

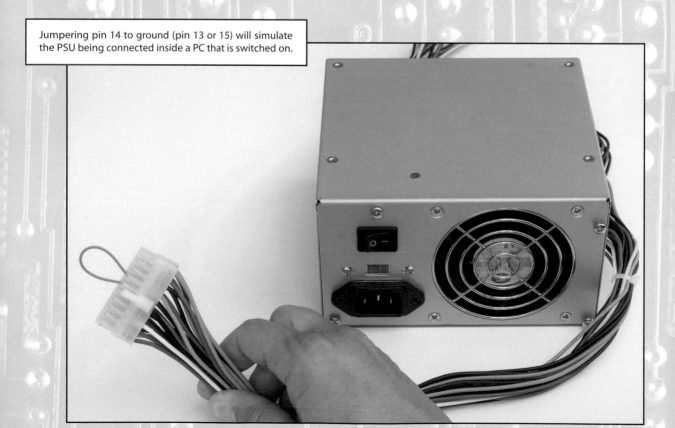

Fitting a 40-pin 80-wire hard drive data ribbon to IDE connector 0 (colored blue) on the motherboard. Above it is IDE connector 1 (white), and to the right is the floppy drive connector head (black).

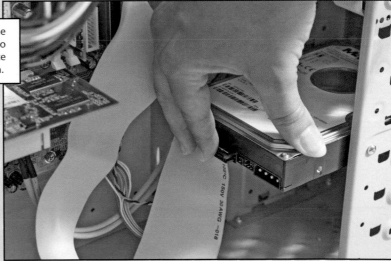

The hard disk drive has been secured into the drive bay with screws. Use gentle pressure to connect the data ribbon to the hard drive. Note the red strip leading to pin 1 of the data ribbon.

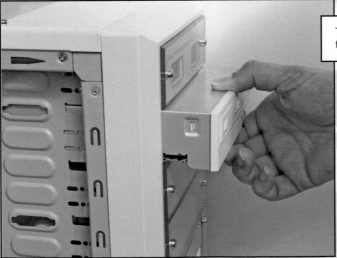

The optical drive is inserted through the front of the case and secured with screws.

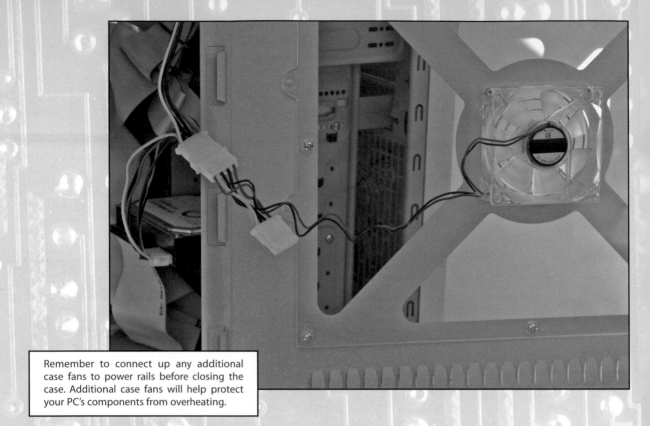

Remember to connect up any additional case fans to power rails before closing the case. Additional case fans will help protect your PC's components from overheating.

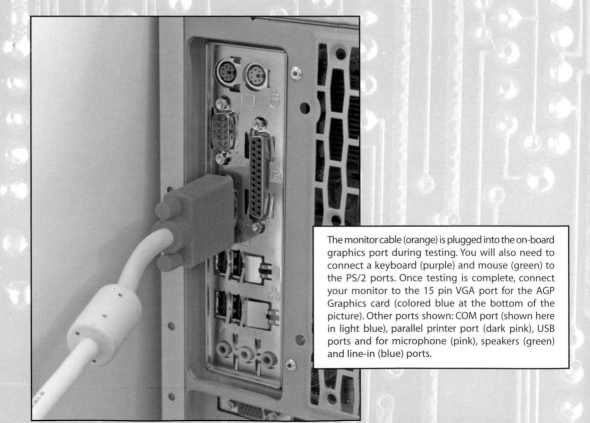

The monitor cable (orange) is plugged into the on-board graphics port during testing. You will also need to connect a keyboard (purple) and mouse (green) to the PS/2 ports. Once testing is complete, connect your monitor to the 15 pin VGA port for the AGP Graphics card (colored blue at the bottom of the picture). Other ports shown: COM port (shown here in light blue), parallel printer port (dark pink), USB ports and for microphone (pink), speakers (green) and line-in (blue) ports.

Fitting the Basic Parts

The excitement is rising! By the end of this chapter, you will have a PC that will contain almost all of the vital parts needed to make a PC. Over the course of this chapter, you will:

➤ Fit the motherboard

➤ Wire the motherboard into the PSU and case

➤ Fit the CPU

➤ Fit the CPU cooler

➤ Add RAM

➤ Fit a video adaptor

➤ Configure the motherboard

Sounds like a lot to do, but it's not really. Assuming that you have all the parts ready and your workspace is clear, then expect this to take no more than two to three hours, and possibly a lot less.

So, let's get on with building your custom PC!

Getting Ready to Get Started!

Get your tools ready before you begin (see Figure 14-1). In fact, you don't need much at all to carry out this step (an indication of how simple it's going to be!). You need:

➤ A Phillips screwdriver (No. 2)

➤ An ESD wrist strap

The only other thing that we suggest you might need is a good flashlight. It can be dark working inside a PC and a little light can help a great deal, especially in the wiring up stages. A little light to drive away the shadows can make all the difference.

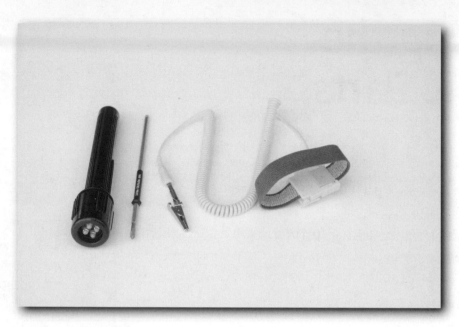

FIGURE 14-1: Tools for the job.

You have the tools and you have the parts, so it's time to get going. Before you begin, here are a few suggestions:

1. Make sure that you have all the parts. For this chapter, you'll need:

   ▪ Case

   ▪ PSU (already fitted)

   ▪ Motherboard and motherboard fitting screws (supplied with the case usually)

   ▪ CPU and CPU cooler

   ▪ RAM

   ▪ Video adaptor (optional — you might be using an integrated on-board solution)

   ▪ Monitor and keyboard for testing

2. Set aside quiet time to build. That means no phone calls, no knocks at the door, no having to break off in the middle to go out. You want undisturbed time to get on with building your PC.

3. No beer, no wine . . . goes without saying. Coffee is fine (and may be essential!); just keep it well away from the parts!

OK, you're now ready to begin. The phone is off the hook, and the coffee pot is on. Time to get started!

Motherboard

By now, you have your case with the PSU fitted (from the previous chapter). The next part that requires fitting is the motherboard. To do this, we suggest that you take the case and lay it down flat, with the side opening facing upward. Working like this is infinitely easier than trying to fit the motherboard with the case sitting upright (you'll figure out why when you get around to doing it!).

Tip Put a cloth (or use your dust cloth) under the case to avoid scratching your case or your work surface.

Motherboard Mountings

The first thing you need to do is fit the motherboard mounting to the case chassis. These mountings are more than likely going to be small brass bolts with a hex head and a threaded hole in the top for a screw to go through (see Figure 14-2).

FIGURE 14-2: Brass motherboard mount.

Tip Remove any screws already fitted into the posts. Do this now in case you forget later!

The basic idea is that the brass fittings are screwed into the threaded holes in the chassis, the board is laid on top, and the screws are passed through holes in the motherboard and screwed into the brass fittings.

The first thing to notice is that you probably have more screw holes in the chassis than you have mountings (see Figure 14-3). This is because different boards have holes for screws in different spots, so you're not going to need all of them.

FIGURE 14-3: Lots of motherboard mounting points in a single case!

Some cases have the different holes marked, but don't rely on those markings as being an accurate guide. We've found this information to be inaccurate more than once!

The best way to make sure you put the mountings in the right spot is to take a look at the board and see where the screw holes are placed in that.

Note Some PC cases might have default motherboard mountings already built into the chassis. In this case, use these mountings as opposed to fitting mounts (although even with mounts you will need to screw in some additional mounting points).

The easiest way to orient the board is to look at the PCI slots and match these up to the card slots on the case, as shown in Figure 14-4.

Figure **14-4: Correctly oriented board.**

An even easier way to make sure you put the mountings in the right spot is to carefully hold the board inside the case and see which motherboard holes match up with which case holes (see Figure 14-5).

FIGURE **14-5**: Motherboard holes matching up with
mounting points.

 Tip

Do this one hole at a time if that's easier for you. Just take care when handling the motherboard.

When you've spotted the right chassis holes to use, screw the motherboard mounting screws into each of these holes.

Just because these screws have a hex head is not an invite to do them up too tight. In fact, because they are made of brass or aluminum they are really quite soft and can quite easily snap off, leaving a hard-to-remove thread in a chassis hole right where the motherboard needs a fitting!

 Tip

To remove a broken motherboard mount, it's usually possible to get that the thread from the other side of the case. Grasp the thread with needle-nosed pliers and rotate it to work it free.

As with most fittings, hand tight is tight enough.

After they are all fitted, lay the motherboard inside the case and check it out. Make sure that you have a mounting post behind each of the screw holes on the board. Nothing is more guaranteed to break a board than fitting it to an uneven surface. If you put a mounting in the wrong spot, just remove the one that's in the wrong place and reposition it.

To Use Washers or Not to Use Washers?

Next, we come to a controversial aspect of PC building. Remember a few chapters ago when we looked at the motherboard fittings that you saw that there were three parts to the motherboard mounting system:

- The mounting screws
- Screws designed to go into these to hold the board in place
- Little red fiber washers

It's those little red washers that are controversial. Do you need them or can you forget them?

The arguments go something like this.

Those in the "pro" fiber washer camp say that if you didn't need these they wouldn't be supplied. They also point to the fact that having a fiber washer between the motherboard fittings and the board itself acts as a cushion and prevents damage to the board through overtightening of the screws holding it in place.

From the "anti" fiber washer camp, the word is that in the first place these fiber washers are really tricky to fit and you're actually increasing the chances of motherboard damage through all the additional messing around that you need to do to get them into place. Those in this camp also point out that the screws don't need to be done up tight in the first place so a fiber cushion to prevent damage isn't needed. Finally, they point to the fact that most major PC manufacturers don't bother fitting these washers anyway, and if it's good enough for them, it's good enough for everyone else.

We agree with the "anti" camp. These fiber washers are extremely tricky to fit because you have to place one on the top of each of the mounting posts and then place the board on top without knocking any of them off. If one falls off you have to start again because you can't fit the board onto an uneven surface. This means additional unnecessary handling of the motherboard. In fact, if you go ahead and decide to use them when building your PC, this is likely to be the most complicated and frustrating part of the build, and expect to have to remove and replace the motherboard a number of times before you get it right.

Add to this that it's quite true that most PC makers haven't bothered with these for years and that as long as you don't overtighten the screws they're not needed anyway. So, for the purposes of this book, we're going to say forget the little fiber washers.

Fitting the Motherboard

Now it's time to fit the motherboard. In the previous section, you've already fitted the mounting posts and made sure that there's one for each mounting hole in the motherboard and that you have fitted them all into the right spot. It's now time to fit the board, as described in the following steps.

Caution From this point on, it is important that you take the steps necessary to protect components from ESD. Wear an antistatic wrist strap at all times when handling components!

1. The first problem you are likely to have is keeping all the wiring in the case away from the board. The best thing to do with the wiring is bring all the wires coming from the PSU out over the edge of the case and keep it out of your way. (This way you don't needing three hands or an assistant.) The case wiring is usually small enough and thin enough that you can tuck it out of the way in the case so that it won't bother you when fitting the motherboard.

2. The next thing to do is to pop out the generic connector plate supplied on the case (see Figure 14-6). Replace this one with the proper one supplied with the motherboard.

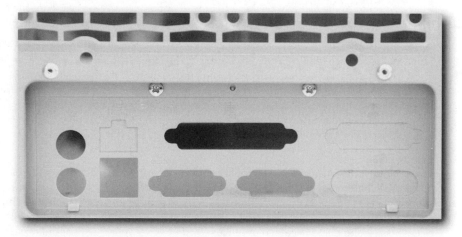

FIGURE 14-6: Generic connector plate on PC case. Note the screws holding the plate in place.

You will generally find that the generic plate is either held in place with screws and needs undoing or (more likely) it is the push-out kind which you have to break out by bending the metal. To break out the generic plate, bend the plate back and forth until it pops out.

3. After the plate has popped out, replace it with the plate that was supplied with the motherboard. Fitting this is easy:

- Take the plate and look at the marks stamped on it. These face outwards. See Figure 14-7.

- From the inside of the case, orient the plate with the plate hole. See Figure 14-8.

- Push the plate into place. Generally, this is a friction fit, and it will stay in place well after fitting.

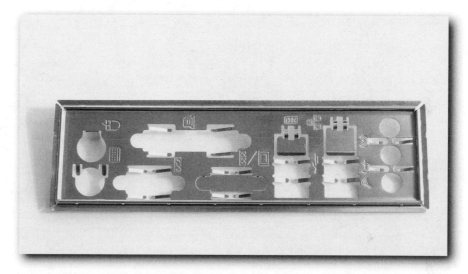

FIGURE 14-7: Orienting the connector plate the right way.

FIGURE 14-8: Lining the plate up with the case.

4. With the PSU and case wiring out of the way and the back plate fitted, lay the board on the mounting posts and begin by using one screw to fit the board in place (see Figure 14-9). It doesn't matter which one, just choose an easy one. Don't do this one up all the way—all you need for now is a few turns.

FIGURE 14-9: First motherboard screw in place.

Note

It is important to note that once the motherboard is properly fitted it will have no contact with the chassis other than through the mounting posts.

5. After you have one screw in place, add the rest, but again, only do them up a few turns.

6. When you have all the screws in place, tighten them up. Do this slowly and don't use too much pressure—hand tight will suffice for these screws, there's no need to overtighten the screws. The fitted motherboard is shown in Figure 14-10.

As you are working look for any signs of board distortion that might indicate that you've either missed a mounting post or that something is wrong. If things look like they are going wrong, backtrack and check out for problems.

FIGURE 14-10: Motherboard fitted.

Caution Never try to force a motherboard flat by using screws or brute force. If it doesn't lie flat in the first place, something is wrong.

Once you are satisfied that everything is fitted into place properly, you're ready to move on to the next step, fitting the CPU.

CPU

People who are new to building PCs are often daunted by the idea of fitting the CPU. Often, the sheer number of pins on the base of the CPU leads beginners to think that these pins must be fitted separately. Nothing could be further from the truth.

If you are one of those people who feels a bit nervous about fitting the CPU, you can rest assured that by the time you've finished this chapter you will almost certainly be wondering what it was you were worried about!

Note Newer Pentium 4 CPUs don't use a ZIF socket. Instead they use a LGA775 socket. These CPUs don't have pins at the bottom, but instead they have little metal pads. Fitting these CPUs is much easier. You open up the CPU socket cover, pop the CPU into the socket, and close the cover on it.

Given the widespread popularity of ZIF compared to the manufacturer-specific LGA775, we will cover only ZIF in detail.

Opening the ZIF Socket

Fitting a CPU is easy because of the ZIF socket that it fits into on the motherboard. ZIF stands for Zero Insertion Force, and that's exactly what you need when fitting a CPU. The hundreds of pins on the base of the CPU are designed to slip effortlessly into the ZIF socket (see Figure 14-11).

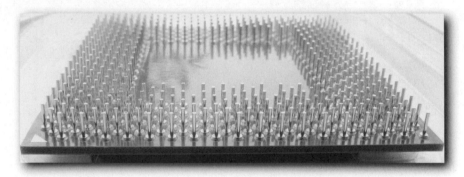

FIGURE 14-11: CPU pins.

For the moment leave the CPU in its box — it's a lot safer there than anywhere else! Let's take a closer look at the ZIF socket on the motherboard (see Figure 14-12).

FIGURE 14-12: ZIF socket.

1. The first thing we want you to notice is the little lever next to the ZIF socket (see Figure 14-13). This lever can be metal or plastic. This lever is held in place by tucking it under a small plastic clip (see Figure 14-14).

FIGURE 14-13: Open/close lever.

FIGURE 14-14: Close-up of clip.

2. To fit the CPU, you first need to lift this lever up. Grasp the lever and gently swing it out to the side and away from the plastic clip, and then swing it to the upright position. This opens the ZIF socket and makes it ready to receive the CPU (see Figure 14-15).

FIGURE **14-15: ZIF socket in the open position.**

Orienting the CPU

Take a look at the ZIF socket or the pins at the base of the CPU. At first glance, it will look like all the pins are lined up symmetrically and give you the impression that the CPU will fit into the ZIF socket in any one of four possible ways (with the straight sides of the CPU lined up with the sides of the socket). This isn't true, and there's a tell-tale both on the CPU and on the holes in the socket.

Note The pin configurations will be different for different types of CPUs.

If you look closely at the holes in the socket, you will notice that one corner of the socket looks different from the other three. The configuration of holes will be different on one or two of the corners than it will be for the others. See Figure 14-16.

Now take a close look at the CPU, paying attention to the pins at the corners. If you look closely, you'll find that the pins are different at one or two corners. See Figure 14-17.

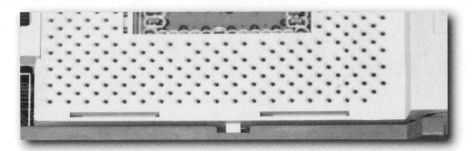

FIGURE 14-16: Socket is different at the corners on the right-hand side of the socket.

FIGURE 14-17: Pin configuration matches socket.

Now, flip the CPU over. You'll notice that there is a marker that conveniently marks the bottom-right corner of the CPU. See Figure 14-18.

FIGURE 14-18: Corner marker.

So, to fit the CPU you need to line up this arrow with the bottom-right corner of the ZIF socket (with the lever at the bottom) to line up the odd configuration of pins.

Fitting the CPU

The great thing about ZIF sockets is that absolutely no force is needed to fit the CPU. In fact, if you have it lined up the right way and the ZIF socket lever is up, the CPU will just drop into the socket with ease.

1. Pick the CPU up by the sides (usually the packaging it comes in is designed for you to do this), gripping it by the edge of the CPU, not touching any pins or components on the surface.

2. Now all you need to do is line up the CPU properly, and the pins will slide into place with the holes. You can just let it go. (See Figure 14-19.) There will never be the need to press on it with your thumb or fingers at all. If it feels as if force is required, then something is wrong and you need to stop and investigate. Usually, all that is needed is for you to lift the CPU out, realign it, and try again.

FIGURE **14-19: CPU fitted.**

Be sure to properly line up the CPU with the socket before fitting it. Try not to drag the CPU across the surface of the socket because the pins are very delicate and prone to bending or breakage.

Closing the ZIF Socket

All that's left to do is close the ZIF socket.

1. Gently grasp the lever and pull it down. The clip designed to hold it in place generally will be tapered so that the lever will easily slot into place.

2. With the lever down (closed), the pins on the CPU are gripped and the CPU is held firmly in place. See Figure 14-20.

FIGURE **14-20: ZIF socket closed and holding CPU firmly in place.**

Never try to remove a CPU from a ZIF socket when it's closed because you are almost guaranteed to damage either the CPU or the socket, or possibly even both.

That's all there is to it! The CPU is now fitted to the motherboard, and you can now move on to fitting the CPU heatsink and fan assembly.

CPU Cooler/Fan Assembly

The next step of the build is to fit the CPU cooler/fan assembly to the CPU on the motherboard (see Figure 14-21). If you do this right after fitting the CPU, it eliminates the chance that you will forget to fit it later and fire up the system without proper thermal protection. Fitting the cooler/fan assembly now will eliminate the problems.

FIGURE **14-21: Heatsink and cooler fan assembly.**

Applying Thermal Grease

Many of the heatsink assemblies supplied with CPUs already have a small patch of thermal grease stuck onto the bottom on the heatsink (see Figure 14-22). This means that you don't have to worry. All you have to do is fit the heatsink over the CPU, and you are ready to go. There's no need to mess about with any additional thermal grease.

Caution

Never add additional thermal grease on the top of any thermal grease already stuck to the heatsink. If you want to use different grease, you will have to remove the existing grease first by carefully scraping it off with the plastic spreader.

Don't be too harsh. You don't want to damage the smooth surface of the heatsink.

FIGURE 14-22: Ready-applied thermal grease.

Another vital component in the CPU cooling system is the thermal grease that creates a conduit for the heat to pass from the CPU to the heatsink. Air is a very good thermal insulator, and if you were to fit a heatsink onto a CPU without thermal grease, the thin layer of air trapped between the two would act as an insulator and trap heat at the CPU, causing a dangerous temperature build-up that would damage the CPU. Thermal grease eliminates this and provides an excellent medium for heat to move from the CPU to the heatsink.

Thermal grease comes supplied in little tubes (see Figure 14-23). All you need to do is apply a little grease to the base of the heatsink and spread this into the thin layer using a piece of cardboard. Generally, a plastic spreader is supplied to do this job. You only want a thin layer (paper thin, no more), but it does need to be free from air bubbles, which can cause pockets of heat to build up.

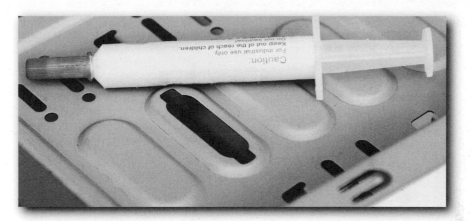

FIGURE 14-23: Thermal grease.

One question many people ask is how much of an area of the bottom of the heatsink they need to cover with thermal grease. You certainly don't want to go covering the whole thing — this is both wasteful and messy. You only need to apply thermal grease to the areas of the heatsink that are going to be in contact with the CPU.

Along with the plastic spreader, many thermal grease tubes will come with paper templates for a variety of CPUs that help you get the grease on in the right spot. You apply the template to the base of the cooler, add the thermal grease, and spread it. This way, not only do you get it in precisely the right spot, but you also get a paper thin layer onto the cooler, which is precisely what you are looking for.

 Never smear thermal grease on with your fingertips or touch the grease with your fingers. Not only is it nasty stuff, but no matter how clean your hands are it will be contaminated with oils. Also, you'll get far too much on the cooler! If you happen to touch the grease accidentally, wipe it off with a clean cloth and start again.

Fitting the CPU Cooler/Fan Assembly

The CPU heatsink and cooler assembly fit over the top of the CPU and clip either to the surround of the ZIF socket or to a plastic frame fitted to the motherboard (see Figure 14-24).

Different coolers fit onto the board in different ways, and the best way to guarantee that you get this step right is to read the instructions. What follows is general guidance on fitting the cooler to the CPU. For specifics, consult the documentation that accompanied your cooler.

FIGURE 14-24: Heatsink clips.

Spring-Loaded Cooler Assemblies

Coolers are generally fitted over the CPU by means of a spring-loaded assembly that holds the cooler tight over the CPU (see Figure 14-25). This tight fit is essential in order to create a proper fit that will allow the heat to pass from the CPU to the heatsink so that it can be safely dissipated.

Use the following steps to fit your cooler over the CPU:

1. The trick with these coolers is that you have to fit one side first (generally the side without a thumb catch on it), as shown in Figure 14-26. To do this, you might have to angle the heatsink in such a way that it allows you better access to the clips.

2. And of course, you have to fit the next side (see Figure 14-27). The heatsink that we have for our AMD processor needs to be pressed into place with a straight-edged screwdriver. You fit this into the slot on the plastic thumb catch and press downward and outward slowly but carefully.

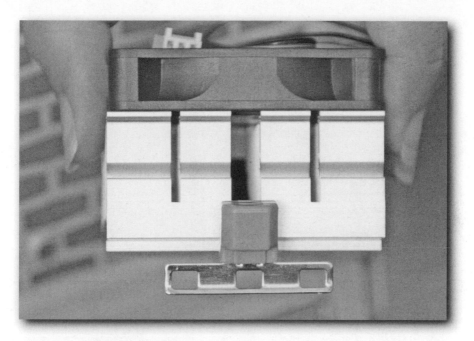

FIGURE 14-25: Spring-loaded catches.

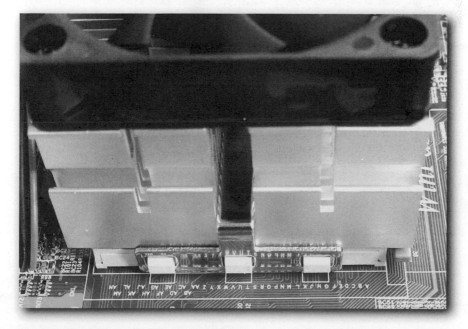

FIGURE 14-26: Fitting the catches on one side.

FIGURE 14-27: Fitting the second catch using a straight-edged screwdriver.

3. Press gently and smoothly but firmly and the catches will come together and fit.

4. Sometimes there's a locking mechanism to tighten up the spring and keep it in place, while other times there isn't. This depends on the cooler assembly you have. If necessary, tighten your locking mechanism.

Note Be careful when fitting the heatsink. Sometimes, quite a bit of pressure is needed to get the spring clips into place, and you need to take special care not to damage the motherboard or knock off any components.

Connecting the Fan to the Motherboard

Finally, that fan on the cooler needs power. The fan draws its power and supplies information on how fast it turns via a thin 3-wire cable (4-pin for LGA 775 CPU coolers) that connects to the motherboard via a 3-pin connector head. Spotting this on the motherboard can be tricky, but there are only normally two connectors like it—the CPU fan connector and a case fan connector.

To tell the difference, you need to look closely at the writing on the motherboard to spot the right connector. (See Figure 14-28.) Fit the CPU cooler fan to the header marked "CPU Fan" or something similar, or take a look through the instructions that accompany your board.

FIGURE 14-28: Markings on the board for the CPU fan header.

Generally, your instructions will have diagrams of the board showing all the connectors. This makes the right header much easier to find and is much better than squinting at microscopic text!

The connector and header are both keyed, so there's no chance of fitting them the wrong way. See Figure 14-29.

With that done, the fitting of the CPU and cooler is done and it's time to move on to the next item on the list—wiring the board.

Tip   You might want to take a small break at this point, get a cup of coffee, and find that flashlight we mentioned earlier!

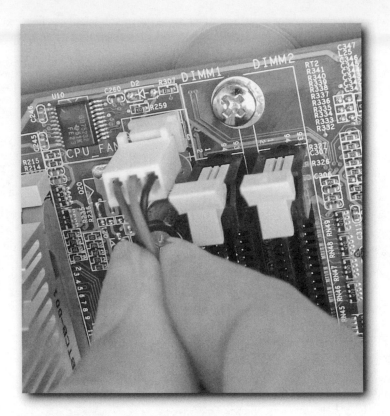

FIGURE 14-29: CPU cooler fan header and connector.

Wiring the Motherboard

Your motherboard should now be sitting in the midst of a lot of wiring. There are two sources of these wires:

- Case wiring
- PSU wiring

Tip   A flashlight is definitely going to come in handy for this stage of the build!

Case Wiring

Wiring up the case to the motherboard can be tricky, not because it's in any way difficult but because it can be tricky to match the right connector to the right header on the motherboard.

The positions of all the headers, along with the connectors from the case, all vary, so the information here should be considered generic. The best way to find out what goes where is to consult the manual that came with your motherboard. This will show you where all the connector headers are.

Note Most of the connector headers and connectors themselves aren't keyed, and there is a chance of fitting them incorrectly. Despite this, there is little or no risk of damage. If you connect something the wrong way (say, a hard disk drive LED light or the power LED), then the LED simply won't work. After the testing phase, all you have to do is reverse the connector, and it will then work!

Connectors that may need fitting include:

- Power switch
- Power LED
- HDD LED
- Reset button
- Case speaker
- Case fan
- USB/FireWire connectors
- Audio connectors

Figures 14-30 and 14-31 show the case wiring before and after being fitted.

PSU Wiring

With the case wiring out of the way, you're now ready to connect the PSU to the motherboard.

This is a simple job because you have only two connectors:

- The 20-pin (or 24-pin) motherboard power connector.
- The 4-pin auxiliary power connector, which supplies extra power to the motherboard to cater for modern AMD and Intel CPUs.

Both of these connectors are keyed, and there's no risk of plugging a connector into the wrong socket.

FIGURE 14-30: Case wiring.

FIGURE 14-31: Case wiring fitted.

Note If you are unsure about the location of the power connector on your motherboard, check your motherboard documentation.

Motherboard Power Connector

This is the 20-pin (or 24-pin) connector that supplies power to the motherboard. Fitting it is easy:

1. Untwist the wires and get them tidy before you begin. This is a big bunch so things will go better if you start off tidy!

2. Line up the clip with the clip holder on the connector on the motherboard.

3. Gently push the connector into place. Begin with gentle pressure but you are probably going to need to increase it slightly because this can be quite tight.

4. Push it on until the clip goes over the retainer. Then stop.

Your power connector is now properly fitted (see Figure 14-32).

That's all there is to it!

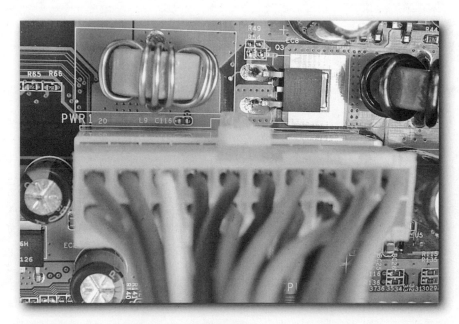

FIGURE 14-32: PSU wiring fitted to motherboard.

Auxiliary Power Connector

Fitting the 4-pin auxiliary power connector is similar to fitting the 20-pin connector for the motherboard power. The main difference, however, is that this connector is smaller and less pressure is needed to fit it.

1. Line up the clip with the clip holder on the connector on the motherboard.

2. Gently push the connector into place. Begin with gentle pressure, but you are probably going to need to increase this slightly again because it can be quite tight.

3. Push it on until the clip goes over the retainer.

RAM

The next stage in the build is to add RAM modules. How many you add depends on:

- How many slots or banks you have on the motherboard
- How many modules you bought

Fitting RAM modules is easy. But first, a few safety precautions:

- Use ESD protection. Antistatic wrist strap can prevent module damage!
- Keep all RAM modules in their ESD bags until needed. Minimal handling is the key to prevent damage to the components.

To add the RAM modules:

1. Spot the RAM banks (see Figure 14-33). Usually at the top or right-hand side of the motherboard when fitted into a tower-style case.

FIGURE 14-33: RAM banks.

2. Look for the clips at either end of the bank slot. Using your thumbs (or index fingers if you have big thumbs!) push these back and away from the slot. (See Figure 14-34.) This should be simple to do and little pressure will be required.

FIGURE **14-34: Pushing back the RAM holding clips.**

3. Grasp the RAM module with your index fingers/thumbs at either end, avoiding all the chips and circuitry built onto it, and take the RAM module to the bank slot. Notice a notch in the connector edge — that needs to match up with the notch in the bank slot; if it doesn't, spin the module around.

4. Gently work the module into the slot and with your thumbs/index fingers; push the module evenly and by the edge only into the slot (see Figure 14-35). As you push you will notice that the clips on either side of the slot will close around the module automatically. At this point, you can help the module on its way by slowly closing these clips around the module. No real force is needed to do this — if you find you need to add a lot of force, things are wrong! Remove the module carefully and start again.

FIGURE **14-35: RAM module fitted.**

Once the module is in place and seated properly and the clips are closed, it's fitted (see Figure 14-36). Your work is finished! Unless, of course, you have two modules, in which case you need to repeat these steps to fit the second module.

FIGURE 14-36: Close-up of clip in the closed position.

Note Your motherboard will have two or more RAM banks, but it doesn't usually matter which bank you fit the RAM module into.

Video Adaptor Card

By now your PC is starting to take shape and you've loaded a lot of the components into the PC chassis. Well done for getting this far, and feel free to take another break, either take a small one for a quick coffee or break off and come back to it another time.

Note If you have chosen to make use of the integrated on-board video adaptor on the motherboard, you can skip this section.

The next component you need to add is the video adaptor card. This will be the first expansion card you need to install in the PC.

The video adaptor card will fit into either an AGP slot or a PCI Express slot, depending on your motherboard and the video adaptor you chose. This will be the first slot on the motherboard and will look different from the PCI slots in it.

Installing an expansion card is easy. Here are the steps you need to follow.

Removing the Cover

The first stage in fitting an expansion card is to remove the expansion slot cover from the back of the PC. There are two types of covers that you might come across:

- **Removable cover.** This is an expansion card slot cover that can be removed by undoing the screw holding it in place and then lifting out the cover (see Figure 14-37). The idea behind this is that you can replace the cover if you ever decide to remove the card. This is a feature nowadays only seen on expensive cases.

- **Snap-out cover.** This is a cover that is partially cut out of the case, and to remove it you need to bend it to break the metal joints. This type of cover is not replaceable and is commonly found on cheaper PC cases.

Remove the cover covering the AGP slot (this might not be the top slot in the case — check to see which one to remove!). If you have removable covers, keep the cover and the screw in case you need it later. If your case has snap-out covers, carefully remove the cover by slowly bending it back and forth in the slot until it snaps off, taking care not to damage any components on the motherboard.

Fitting the Video Adaptor Card

You're now ready to fit the card.

1. Pull the card from its box and out of the protective ESD bag.

2. Then carefully hold the card by the metal rail and the edge of the circuit board (being careful not to touch the components on the card), take the card to the PC, and place the edge of the rail to the exposed slot cover on the case and line up the connector edge with the AGP or PCI Express slot.

3. When you have them lined up put your thumbs against the spine of the card and gently push the card into the slot (see Figure 14-38).

FIGURE 14-37: Removing a slot cover.

Tip

The reason that you use your thumbs against the back of the card and not your fingertips is that it is far less likely that your thumbs will slip off the card and hit anything important on it.

The card should slot easily into the connector with only a little bit of pressure. If you feel a lot of resistance check to make sure that the card is properly aligned with the slot and try again.

The card is properly seated when it has been pushed all the way into the slot, the top edge is horizontal with the motherboard, and the tab on the metal end plate with the hole that the screw goes through to attach it to the case is flush with the chassis.

If the card seems to be crooked in the slot or won't go in straight, don't force it; simply remove it and try again.

FIGURE **14-38: Fitting the AGP card.**

Note Some video adaptor cards need additional power to operate. It's not uncommon for some of the higher-end AGP video adaptor cards to need a power feed from a drive rail to work. Don't worry if you don't have a spare. Most cards that need them come with a splitter that you can place in between a hard drive/CD/DVD drive and the power connector to tap off some power.

PCI Express video adaptors might also need a power supply, usually in the form of a 6-pin connector (again, don't worry about this as most cards will be supplied with a converter for a drive rail power supply).

When the card is seated properly, fit the screw and do this up hand tight plus an eighth turn. The card is now correctly fitted (see Figure 14-39).

Caution Never use this screw as a means to seat the card. Seat the card properly before fitting the screw or you might damage the card or even the motherboard.

FIGURE **14-39:** Video adaptor card fitted!

Summary

Well done for getting this far in the book. All your hard work reading and buying components has started to pay off and you're making good progress on the building.

You've done a lot of work in this chapter, some of it easy, some of it fiddly, and you've fitted many of the components to the PC chassis. You've also wired up the PSU and the case to the motherboard. Your pile of parts should by now start to resemble a PC.

You now nearly have a complete PC! Congratulations!

In the next chapter, we'll move on to adding storage to the PC.

Adding Storage

I n this chapter, we're going to add storage to the PC in the form of a hard drive, a CD-ROM drive, and a floppy drive. These three devices will be the final required components of the PC. After this chapter, you will be ready to plug the system into the electrical supply and fire it up. Then you can carry out basic tests to make sure it is working properly.

We will begin by adding the optional floppy disk drive and then go on to add a hard drive and CD-ROM drive.

The Floppy Drive

Chances are that you probably won't make much use of the floppy drive you're going to install into the system. Over the past decade, the use of floppy disks has declined dramatically with the increased popularity of first CD and then DVD formats. However, given the price of a floppy disk and its importance in the many diagnostic and troubleshooting routines you may need to make use of, we still recommend you spend $10 on getting a floppy drive.

Preparing to Fit the Floppy Drive

Floppy drives are connected to the PC with a 34-wire cable that joins the floppy drive to the floppy drive connector on the motherboard. This cable looks very much like the 40-wire cables that are used to connect PATA hard drives and CD/DVD drives to the PC, but it's not as wide and the connector is smaller, and therefore you won't get the cables confused.

The floppy drive is fitted to a 3-$^1/_2$ inch bay at the front of the PC. To gain access to this bay, you will need to remove both the plastic fascia on the front of the PC (see Figure 15-1) and the metal plate that lurks behind the fascia.

There are two ways that you can remove the plastic fascia from the front of the PC.

> ➤ Lever the fascia carefully by using a screwdriver. This works, but care needs to be taken not to damage the case. A small length of tape stuck on the case at the point where you are going to lever it off will prevent marking.

> ➤ Use a thin screwdriver to push the fascia from behind. To do this, you will need to take the screwdriver inside the PC and work it between the metal plate and the chassis so that you can pop the fascia off.

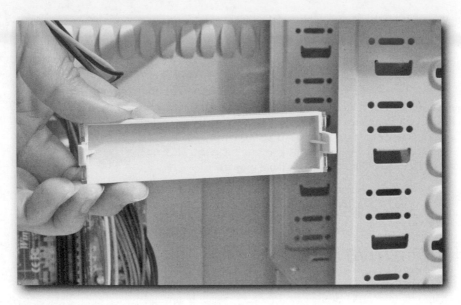

FIGURE 15-1: Plastic fascia.

Once you have this fascia off you will see the metal plate underneath (see Figure 15-2). To remove this plate, you will need to either break it off or unscrew the holding fastener (depending on the style in your case).

FIGURE 15-2: Metal plate removed from behind fascia.

Be careful when breaking off this metal plate. The edges can be very sharp and can give you a nasty cut! Stout gloves can be useful, as can covering any particularly sharp edges temporarily with tape.

The knack to breaking off this plate is to alternately push the top and bottom of it, stressing the joints at which it's attached. Work slowly and carefully, and soon one side will break free. Once this happens, you can give it a twist to get it off completely.

 Never try to saw the plate off with a hacksaw or attempt to grind it off, which will create a lot of nasty metallic dust that will damage the PC.

If there are any rough edges left after removing the plate, use pliers to carefully bend the edges back and get them out of the way. Cover with tape — remember, use decorator's tape, not insulating or duct tape, which will leave a sticky residue that will be a major dust trap.

With the plate off it's time to fit the floppy drive.

Fitting the Floppy Drive

Before you fit the floppy drive, you need to find the right screws for the job. If you were provided screws with the drive when you bought it, then this makes life easy. If you weren't, you will have been provided screws with the PC case. Find the right screws by trying a few in the floppy drive — screw them in by hand. If they fit, they will thread into the drive easily. You need a minimum of two screws to hold the drive in place, with four being recommended.

 Don't use a screwdriver when you're looking for the right screw to fit components because if you have the wrong screw, it can become jammed and damage the drive. By hand, it's much harder to force the wrong screw into a thread and damage it.

1. Take the floppy drive and fit it to the chassis through the front of the PC (push it in backward), as shown in Figure 15-3. If you look at the drive bay, you will notice that there are two screw holes on either side that will line up with the holes in the floppy drive just as the front of the drive becomes flush with the molding on the front of the system.

2. When the floppy drive is flush with the molding, you can then use one screw to hold it in place temporarily (see Figure 15-4). For now, just do the screw hand-tight. You can then add the second screw.

3. To add the remaining two screws, you will need to take the other side of the PC case off (this would be the right-hand side as you look at the case from the front). The mechanism for removing this is similar to that of removing the left-hand side. If in doubt, consult the instructions that came with your case.

Figure 15-3: Fitting the floppy drive.

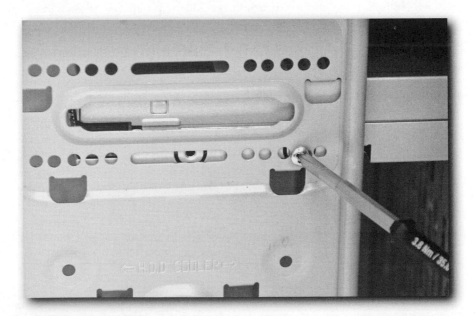

Figure 15-4: Fitting a floppy drive screw.

Getting the screws in from the other side can be easy or tricky, depending on the overall design of the case. With some cases, the screw holes are easily accessible by hand and the screws fitted normally, but some cases are designed so that it's actually quite hard to reach to fit the screws into the screw holes. If this is the case with your PC, don't be tempted to get a magnetic screwdriver to use on your system. Not only is a magnetic screwdriver a bad idea because the magnetism can damage components, but it can also be hard to control the magnetized tip to prevent it from hitting other components.

A good trick for getting screws into awkward screw holes is to fit a small blob of modeling clay onto the tip of the screwdriver and embed the screw into this (see Figure 15-5). By using the clay, you can stick the screw to the screwdriver and steer it into hard-to-reach places. Once there, thread the screw into the appropriate screw hole. This arrangement is much safer than a real magnetic screwdriver.

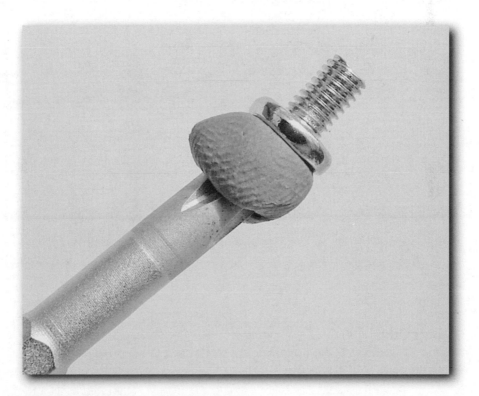

FIGURE **15-5: Improvised "magnetic" screwdriver.**

4. With all the screws in the right holes, you can then do them up tight. There's no need to overtighten them — hand-tight with an extra eighth or a quarter of a turn is fine.

Fitting Cabling

The final part of fitting the floppy drive is to fit the cabling. There are two cables:

- Power cable
- Data cable

Power Cable

The power cable will come from the PSU. It is a small 4-wire connector, much smaller than the power connectors for hard drives.

The connector is keyed, so there's no chance of fitting it incorrectly. Just push it over the pins on the floppy drive and it's done. See Figure 15-6.

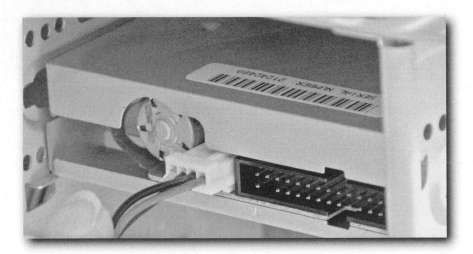

FIGURE **15-6: Fitting the power cables.**

Data Cable

The 34-wire, 34-pin data cable has two ends that look identical, but they are not. You need to fit the correct end to the device and the motherboard to make sure that everything works.

1. Take a look at the data cable and nearest to the end of the cable; look for the connector with a twist mid-ribbon. This connector must be connected to the floppy drive (see Figure 15-7).

2. Connect the other end to the 34-pin connector head on the motherboard. This connector head looks similar to the hard drive connector heads, only smaller (the connectors are different and keyed to prevent you fitting them to the wrong header or fitting them incorrectly). Both ends are keyed and can only be fitted one way. Put your fingers behind the motherboard to support it if you need to push on the connector.

FIGURE 15-7: Fitting the data cable.

Note If your floppy drive cable has three connectors, ignore the connector at the middle of the cable and just use the connectors at either end. The central connector is for attaching a second floppy drive to the system (which is never needed nowadays).

3. Push the connectors into the sockets slowly and with the minimal force required. Push them straight on and don't wriggle the connector from side to side to try to make it easier. This is likely to damage the cable or the connectors on the floppy drive or even the motherboard.

Tip Fit the cable—untwisted—between the motherboard and the floppy drive. A twisted cable is both untidy and hard to tie back when the job is done.

With that, the floppy drive is now fitted to the system and you are ready to move on to fitting the hard drive.

Note For now feel free to leave both sides off your PC case while you work.

The Hard Drive

The hard drive is the PC's main storage system, and every PC needs to have at least one fitted. For the purposes of this book, we will fit one hard drive to the system.

The hard drive can be fitted either directly to a 3-$\frac{1}{2}$ inch bay or to a 5-$\frac{1}{4}$ inch by using a 3-$\frac{1}{2}$ to 5-$\frac{1}{4}$ inch drive bay converter. There are a number of types of converters, but they all work in the same way by allowing you to screw rails to the side of the drive (attaching them to the screw holes on the sides of the hard drive), which make it wider and allow it to be fitted to the bigger bay.

There is little in the way of benefits associated with fitting a hard drive to a bigger bay (other than it gives you choice and flexibility over where it's fitted), so to make life simple and minimize on confusion, we will be fitting the drive to a 3-$\frac{1}{2}$ inch bay.

Preparing the Bay

Unlike when we just fitted the floppy drive, there's no need to remove the plastic fascia or pop out the metal plate from the drive bay to fit a hard drive. Hard drives are fitted from the inside and don't require any kind of external access.

Preparing the Hard Drive

The first thing to do when fitting a hard drive is to remove it from the protective packaging and carefully take it out of the ESD bag in which it should have been shipped to you. By keeping it in the bag until the last minute, you are affording it the best possible protection from static discharge.

When you have the drive out of the packaging, carefully hold it by both sides with the back of the drive (where the connectors are) facing toward you. You will notice that on the back you have power and data connectors, and between these two you will find a set of jumpers. *Jumpers* are simply small bridges that connect two connectors together and act as switches to change configuration settings.

These jumpers are there to allow you to control whether the hard drive is a master or slave. However, with a modern PC you don't need to worry about this. All you need to do is make sure that the drive is jumpered to set it to "Cable Select" or "CSel." This allows the master and slave settings to be controlled by the position of the drive on the cable — master (or main drive on that particular cable) goes on the end of the cable, slave (or secondary drive on the cable) in the middle. With "Cable Select" or "CSel" selected, the drive will recognize its position on the cable and adjust accordingly. See Figure 15-8.

Fitting the Drive

With the jumpers set, it's now time to fit the drive. This process is unscientific and simply involves taking the drive and pushing it into a free 3-$\frac{1}{2}$ inch bay. This is done from inside the PC rather than from the front, as was the case with the floppy drive. See Figure 15-9.

Handle the drive by the sides only. Take special care not to handle it by any connectors or circuit boards that may be exposed because this increases the risk of EAD damage to the hard drive.

FIGURE 15-8: Configuring the jumpers for cable select.

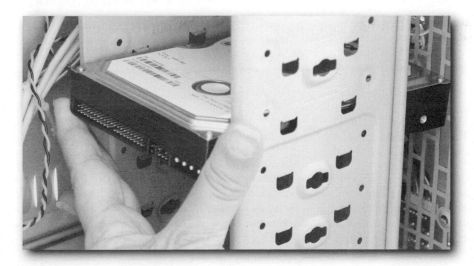

FIGURE 15-9: Fitting the drive.

1. Fit the drive so that the connectors face toward the inside of the PC. It might be tricky to get the drive into the bay, so use the screw holes in the bay and the screw holes in the drive as a guide — line these up first as it makes fitting the drive much easier.

2. Most hard drives are supplied with the screws you need to fit them. Go ahead and get out these screws. As with floppy drives, it's important to first start the screws off in the threads by hand (the threads on hard drives are cut in very soft alloy and are easily sheared by overzealous use of the screwdriver or trying to do up a cross-threaded screw).

A good way to get screws into their holes properly is to take the nose of the screw up to the thread and turn it a couple of turns anticlockwise (in effect undoing it rather than doing it up) before starting to do it up. This cleans the thread tips and allows the screw to get a better and cleaner bite on the thread.

3. There are three screw holes in each side of a hard drive, but you only need to fit two screws in each side. (In fact, the drive bays in most cases will only allow you to use two each side.) Do these up the standard hand-tight plus a quarter or eighth of a turn and no more.

Once again, you might need to use the modeling clay on the tip of the screwdriver technique to get the screw to the appropriate screw hole on the drive.

Fitting the Drive Cabling

The next job is to fit the cabling for the hard drive. Just as with floppy drives, you have two cables to connect:

- Data cable
- Power cable

Data Cable

The *data cable* is a ribbon-style cable with three connectors on it, one at each end and one in the middle. The cables connectors are color-coded (refer to Chapter 10 for details), but an easy way to tell which end of the cable connects where is to look at the connectors. The two connectors closest to each other fit the drives, whereas the one on the end farthest from the middle one connects to the motherboard. See Figure 15-10.

On the motherboard, you will find two connectors, which will be marked IDE 0 and IDE 1. Both should be printed on the motherboard, but if you find that hard to read, then consult the motherboard's manual. As a general rule, however, the IDE 0 connector is the one on the right of the bank of two.

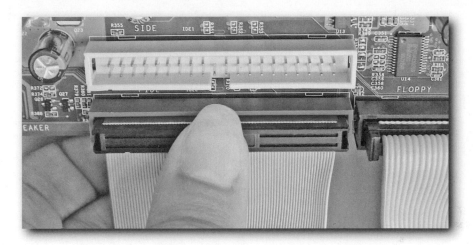

FIGURE 15-10: Fitting the data ribbon to the IDE connector on the motherboard.

1. Fit the connector farthest away from the middle connector to the motherboard IDE 0 connector, and then fit the end connector to the hard drive. See Figure 15-11.

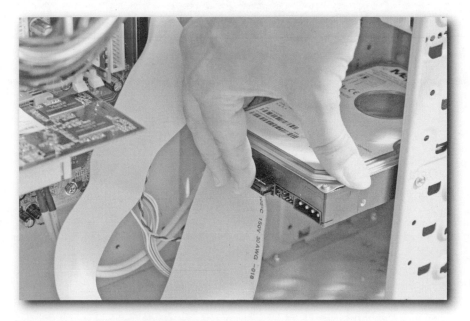

FIGURE 15-11: Fitting the data ribbon to the hard drive.

2. Use gentle pressure to push the connector into the socket—don't wriggle the connector because this can damage pins or the cable connector.

Both are keyed, and it's impossible to connect the connector incorrectly to either the drive or the motherboard.

Hard Drive Power Cable

Finally, connect up the power cable. This is a 4-wire connector that fits into the socket on the hard drive. The pins on this are quite large, so there's very little chance of damaging it.

The connector is keyed. If you hold the connector so that you can look at it head on, you'll see that the curve is at the top. Hard drive connectors are bulky, and you might need to use a fair bit of force on it to slide it in (this is why you need to fix the drive firmly in place before attaching the cables).

Push the connector into the power socket on the drive to fit it (see Figure 15-12).

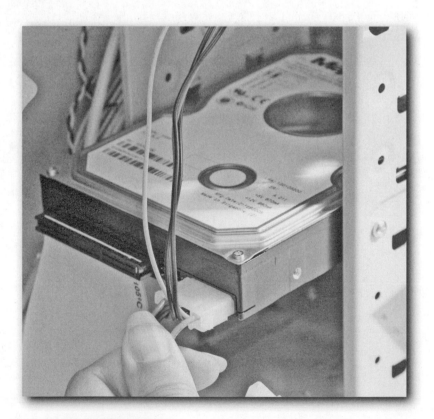

FIGURE 15-12: Fitted power cable.

A Word on SATA Drives

Your motherboard may come with support for SATA, or Serial ATA, hard drives. These differ from PATA drives in respect to both data and power cabling (although some SATA drives have both a SATA and a standard hard drive power connector on them). You should only connect one of these and never both! Also, because they are serial, you can only have one drive per cable. The connectors are smaller and much easier to fit than the ones outlined here (they are also keyed, so there's no chance of getting it wrong).

Tip   Hard drive power cables can become tightly wedged in the socket and need *a lot* of pull to get them free. If you find you have a stuck power connector, grasp the connector firmly and pull. Start off gently, but increase the force until you start to feel the connector give way. Don't try yanking the connector out by the cable—that could easily rip out the wires and break the power rail.

With the correct fitting of the power connector, you've now completed the hardware installation of the hard drive.

Fitting a second hard drive is the same as fitting the first—as long as you can find a space for it on a cable (either as a master or a slave) and configure it to cable select, you won't get any problems at all.

The CD-ROM Drive

The process of fitting a CD-ROM drive is a hybrid of fitting a floppy drive and fitting a hard drive. You might think the first thing to do when fitting a CD drive is to remove it from the protective packaging. But before you do that, you should prepare the drive bay.

Preparing the Bay

To fit a CD or DVD drive, you will need one free 5-¼ inch drive bay, and you need to give it front access. This means popping off the plastic fascia and the metal plate that you will encounter behind that. Follow the steps in the section "The Floppy Drive," earlier in this chapter to carry out this operation.

Preparing the CD Drive

With the drive bay prepared, you can now remove the CD drive from its protective packaging.

A CD or DVD drive is not as delicate an implement as a hard drive. These drives rarely have any exposed circuitry, and they are far more resilient against ESD damage. The more likely way to cause damage is by dropping it!

Take a look at the back of the drive (where the connectors are) facing toward you. You will notice that there is an arrangement similar to a hard drive. You have power and data connectors, and between these two connectors is a set of jumpers. Recall that jumpers are simply small bridges that connect two connectors together and act as a switch to change configuration settings.

Again, these jumpers are there to enable you to control whether the optical drive is a master or slave. As with the hard drive, jumper the drive to "Cable Select" or "CSel" if these are present on the drive. This allows the master and slave settings to be controlled by the position of the drive on the cable. The master goes on the end of the cable, and the slave goes in the middle. With "Cable Select" or "CSel" selected, the drive will recognize its position on the cable and adjust accordingly. See Figure 15-13.

FIGURE 15-13: Setting the jumpers.

If this option is not available, then how you jumper it depends on how you are going to fit the drive. If you attach it to the end of a new cable, jumper it as "Master" or "M." If you are going to fit it onto the second connector on the existing data ribbon, jumper it to "Slave" or "S."

Fitting the Drive

Fitting the drive is similar to the process of fitting a floppy drive.

1. Start by pushing the drive through the open 5-¼ inch drive bay into the drive, as shown in Figure 15-14. Make sure that the connectors are inside the drive!

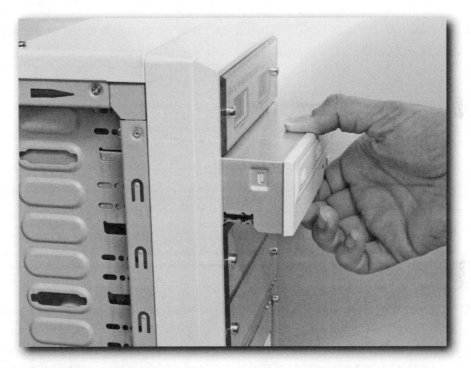

FIGURE 15-14: Fitting the drive.

2. A CD or DVD drive has four threaded screw holes on each side, and you need to fit at least two on each side. Use the screws supplied or find the appropriate ones from the set supplied by the motherboard.

3. Push the drive into the bay until the screw holes line up with the holes in the bay, and then fit one screw to hold the drive in place while you add another three (so that you have at least two each side).

4. Tighten up these screws hand-tight plus a quarter or eighth of a turn and no more.

Fitting the Drive Cabling

The final job is to fit the cabling for the optical drive. This process is identical to that of fitting the cabling on a PATA hard drive and consists of two cables:

- Data cable
- Power cable

Refer back to the section "The Hard Drive" earlier in this chapter for details on this process.

One main difference is if you decide to fit the optical drive onto a different cable. To do this, you will have to connect the second data cable ribbon to the connector marked IDE 1 on the motherboard.

Fitting the power cable involves finding a spare power rail and hooking it up to the drive.

After the fitting of the power connector, you've now completed the hardware installation of the optical drive, as shown in Figure 15-15.

FIGURE **15-15:** Optical drive complete with power and data cable fitted.

Now all that remains for you to do is to refit the sides on your PC case (refitting is just the reverse of removal), and you're done on the inside for now!

Summary

In this chapter, we've looked at how to fit three types of storage to your PC:

- Floppy drive
- Hard drive
- Optical drive (CD or DVD)

This now completes the process of adding storage to the PC. You might later decide that you want an additional hard drive or an extra optical drive, but if you follow the information here (and in earlier chapters about hard drives and optical drives), this will be a simple job.

With the drive all installed, you're now ready to connect the PC to the electrical supply and bring life to your creation!

Starting and Testing Your PC

part

Fire Up and Burn In

The most exciting moment of building a PC is now upon you! You have assembled your PC, and it is ready to go! There are only a few things left to do:

➤ Carry out some preliminary checks

➤ Hook up a monitor

➤ Attach a keyboard and fit a mouse

➤ Connect the PC to a spare electrical outlet

➤ Fire it up and see if it works!

➤ Give it a good test! This first run test is usually called a "burn-in."

Pre-Startup Checks

Before you fire up the system, you need to do a few things and run a few checks to make sure that everything will run smoothly.

At this stage, both excitement and tension will be high, so it's important to work methodically through these steps so that you don't miss anything. It would be a real shame to break something at this late stage!

Eyeball the Inside of the Case

First, have a good look inside the case. You want to look for:

➤ Tools left in the case

➤ Spare parts

➤ Loose screws or components

➤ Wiring spilling out of the case

➤ Anything else that looks out of place (for example, if you installed two RAM modules, are both still installed?)

These are just basic checks, and they are handy to follow not only when building a PC but also when you have been upgrading or carrying out repairs on a PC.

Check the Voltage Slider

Remember that voltage slider that's on the back of your power supply unit (PSU)? (Not all power supplies will have this, so you need to check. If you're unsure, refer to the manual that came with your PSU.) Make sure that the slider is set to the right voltage setting for your country. If the slider is in the wrong position, slide it across until it displays the correct voltage (see Figure 16-1). In the United States this needs to be set to 115 volts.

FIGURE 16-1: Voltage slider.

 This is a vital step—check, check, and check again, and make sure that it's right! A wrong move here can seriously wreck things for you.

 You might find it difficult to slide the voltage selector by hand. If you do, use the tip of a screwdriver to move it.

Button Up the Case

If you are using an AGP or PCI Express video adaptor card to provide video support, the video connector hooks up to the video adaptor connector on the video adaptor card. If you are using on-board video support, the video adaptor connector will be on the motherboard.

Fit this connector carefully, making sure to tighten any screws used to keep the connector in place on the socket. Again, remember that there's no need to overtighten the thumbscrews — hand-tight is tight enough! See Figure 16-2.

FIGURE **16-2: Hooking up the monitor. Here the monitor is connected to the on-board video adaptor port.**

Tip

Never stress this connector by pulling too much on the cable. The video cable is a hefty cable. Combined with the big connector, the cable can exert a lot of leverage on the connector, possibly damaging pins or the connector itself.

A good way to maintain slack in the video cable is to grab a loop in the palm of your hand and wrap a few rubber bands around it. The rubber band will then give if you stress the cable rather than anything important (like the connectors). This also works for smaller, thinner cables (just use thinner rubber bands).

Power Cable

Connecting the power cable is easy enough. Remember that some monitors have an integral cable (nonremovable), whereas others have a removable power cable. If the cable is removable, you will need to find a suitable cable (which should be provided with the monitor).

Tip

Safety Tip: If the cable is a removable cable, fit the cable to the monitor before connecting it to the electrical supply.

Fitting the Keyboard

The keyboard will connect in one of two ways to your system:

- PS/2 connector (A small, round connector with 6 pins used to connect a keyboard or mouse to a PC. There are two sizes, $^1/_4$ inch and $^3/_8$ inch. The smaller size is now the more common of the two, but adapters are available to convert one size to the other.)
- USB

During the testing phase, if PS/2 is available (most keyboards offer this, either directly or via a converter), use PS/2 as this eliminates possible problems you might have with the keyboard not being detected.

PS/2 connectors and sockets are generally color-coded (normally purple) with the ports on the motherboard, so fitting is easy. There's also a little keyboard-like logo that you can look for (see Figure 16-3).

It can be tricky to orient a PS/2 connector. The easiest way to fit it is to bring the connector to the socket and push gently while slowly rotating the connector until it lines up and slides into place.

FIGURE 16-3: Connecting a keyboard.

USB Tip: Fitting a device into the USB port is easy. The blade connector will only fit one way, although sometimes a little bit of force is needed with new USB ports.

Fitting the Mouse

Just as with the keyboard that you've just seen, a mouse can connect to your system in one of two possible ways:

- PS/2 connector
- USB

As with the keyboard, during the testing phase, use PS/2 if it's available, to eliminate possible problems you might have with the mouse not being detected.

Again, the PS/2 connectors and sockets are generally color-coded (usually green) with the ports on the motherboard so fitting it is easy. And again, if that's not enough there's also a little mouse logo that you can look for.

Powering Up

You're now ready to fire up your PC! You're probably very excited at this stage — you've put in a lot of work into planning the system, acquiring all the components, and then building it. Also, don't underestimate the mental work you've done. It's been a learning process, and at some stages the learning curve will have been quite steep.

Give yourself a pat on the back for getting this far!

Before You Power Up

OK, with that out of the way, here's an important point to bear in mind as we move on. Very soon now, you're going to plug your PC into the electrical supply and fire it up. There's a very good chance that it will work just fine. However, there's also a chance that it won't. We'll come to this in a moment, but for now we just want to get across to you that problems do happen.

If, when you come to switching on and nothing happens (or you see error messages) don't worry about it. There are a number of things that can be at the root of the problem, and we'll look at these. Even if you've followed the instructions to the letter and done everything right, you might be unlucky enough to suffer component failure (it does happen).

At this stage the motto is:

Don't Panic!

Turning on Your PC

OK, plug the power cable into the PSU on the PC and connect the other end to the electrical supply (see Figure 16-4). Make sure that the switch on the back of the PSU is set to the on position (if present), and then press the on button on the front of the PC.

FIGURE **16-4: Connecting the power cable.**

Watching for Signs of Life

After you press the on button, what you should see happening is this (roughly in this order):

1. **Your PC should hum into life.** The sound you are hearing is the sound of the PSU, hard drives, optical drives, CPU, and case fans all whirring into action.

2. **The LEDs should light up.** The power on LED should light up, along with the hard drive light (which might be marked HDD).

3. **The monitor should crackle into life.** If you are using a CRT monitor, you should hear this crackle into life (the noise is static on the monitor). You should also notice the LED on the monitor change color. Flat-panel monitors will just quietly start up.

4. **On-screen information displays.** With the display working, you should begin to see information being displayed on-screen. The exact nature of this information will vary, depending on the parts you have installed, but you should see the following:

- BIOS information.
  This includes name, version number, and so on

- Video adaptor information (depends, not always displayed)
  Name, amount of RAM installed, and so on

- CPU information
  Type, speed, and so on

- RAM installed
  How much? Which banks?

- Drives present
  Hard drives and optical drives, including model numbers and data capacities.

Sometimes, all this important information is concealed behind a startup logo or splash screen. Generally, this screen is a good sign, because any errors will mean that the screen won't be displayed or it will be replaced by the error.

There is also usually an on-screen message for you to press to show the startup information instead of the logo screen.

After all this, you will see an error regarding boot drive or boot device not being present. This is perfectly normal because at this stage you only have a blank hard drive in the system.

Things That Can Go Wrong

Hopefully, your system started up and you got as far as seeing the error message about the boot drive or device not being present.

If so, well done and congratulations! You're ready to move on to the next stage of the build.

If not, read on for troubleshooting tips. Don't worry too much at this stage if you have problems. The most likely cause of problems is something incorrectly fitted — there are a lot of parts in a PC, and many can be tricky to fit right.

Follow these troubleshooting steps, and you will find the cause of the problem. Feel free to jump to the section that best describes the trouble you are having.

Sometimes, you might find that you solve the problem without really knowing what it was — you press cables into the connectors or recheck all cards fitted, and then the system works fine even though nothing seemed out of place. Chances are that something just wasn't pressed in right and rechecking it fixed it.

Remember, if you have to go investigating a problem inside a case, take ESD precautions.

Little or No Life Signs from the PC

The most common problem is that of there being either no life signs present at all or some life signs but nothing on-screen. These can be troubling, but fortunately, most of these problems are easy to solve.

Checks

The first thing to do when you experience this problem is to perform each of the following checks:

- Is the power cable plugged in at both ends? Believe it or not, this is an easy step to forget, and it is the most likely cause of a lifeless PC.

- Is the monitor connected and turned on?

- Is the switch on the PSU on? Another common error!

- Have you selected the correct voltage? If you set this to 220 volts in a 110 volt area, swap it, no harm should be done. However, if you set this to 110 volts in a 220 volt area, chances are the PSU or other components are damaged.

- Check the power cable. Try with a known good cable if you have a spare.

After working through these steps, try starting up your PC once more. If you still don't seems to be having any luck, run through these steps one more time. If after double-checking you still can't start your PC, you need to start checking inside.

Disconnect the power cable from the PSU, remove the case sides and try the following:

- Check that the motherboard power connector is firmly attached. Remove it and refit it to make sure.

- Check that the power on connector from the case switch to the motherboard is correctly fitted. Check the motherboard's instructions, and make sure it's fitted in the right place.

- Check that the video adaptor card is fitted correctly.

Now, go ahead and button up the case. Connect back to the power and try again. If everything starts up as planned, you're in great shape. If not, you may have a serious problem, as described in the following section.

Possible Serious Faults

If after performing all of the previous checks your PC still doesn't start up properly, look for the following errors:

- **Dead PSU.** If there are no signs of life at all (no drive spinning or anything), then a dead PSU is likely. If possible check as outlined in Chapter 11, "Checking and Testing Components," or return it for a replacement.

- **Video problems.** If there are signs of life from the system, then video adaptor problems are likely. Your system may make a number of beeps to indicate a problem. Consult your motherboard manual for details as to what these beeps mean because they vary depending on the BIOS installed.

  With this problem the PC will fire up but you won't see anything on-screen. Check the video adaptor and remove and refit it. One way to test this is to move the monitor onto the on-board video connector (if present) and try again.

- **Faulty motherboard.** If there are signs of life from the PC (such as hard drives spinning) but nothing on-screen (even after checking for video problems). You may or may not have any error beeps when dealing with a faulty motherboard (consult the manual for details). Check connectors and try again.

OK, we've been looking at things that you can check if the PC is completely dead, but more likely is a PC that works but not completely. Next, we'll look at common problems that mean that the PC is working but not exactly right.

System Works But Some LEDs Don't

Often you might find that your system works just fine but that some of your LEDs don't light up. This is a common fault because some motherboard and case models don't have instructions that make it clear which way to connect the LED connector to the heads on the motherboard. Basically, LEDs need the power to flow though them in one direction and if this is reversed, nothing will happen.

Fixing this is easy:

1. Make a note of which LED is not working right.

2. Switch the system off (press and hold the on/off button or use the switch on the PSU) and disconnect it from the power supply (removing the cable to the PSU is the easiest way) and pop open the case.

3. Find the appropriate cable and check the connection. If it is fitted in a way that seems correct reverse the connector (undo it and flip it over).

4. Test again!

Noisy PC

A common problem when building your own PC is to find that it's noisy when you switch it on. It's best to investigate noises early on and see if they can be eliminated.

The first thing you need to try to find out where the noise is coming from. This is trickier than is seems, and the best way to locate the sound is to run the PC for a short time with the side of the case off, keeping tools and fingers and long hair away from the inside.

There are a number of causes that can be at the root of a noisy PC:

- **Something touching a fan.** A wire touching a fan like the CPU fan or case fan can cause a huge racket that you need to fix (not only because the noise will get on your nerves but because this is going to eventually harm the fan or wire). In this case, you'll need to reroute the cabling. Don't tie it back at this stage as you might need to undo it again later.

- **Rattling case fan.** An incorrectly mounted fan can also cause a lot of noise. Fit it properly to eliminate the noise.

- **Noisy fan.** Some fans are just plain noisy when you buy them because they are damaged. We recommended that you replace them because the noise is generally a precursor to failure.

- **Noisy PSU.** PSUs contain fans and if these fans are faulty, they can make a terrible noise. If your new PSU makes a lot of noise, it's recommended that you get a replacement because a failing fan can wreck the whole PSU.

- **Noisy hard drive.** Hard drives can be noisy devices, but there's a point at which that noise indicates a problem. A regular buzzing or whirring sound is okay, but irregular knocks, rumbles, screeches, whines, or grinding is a bad sign. Fortunately, problems with new hard drives are very rare unless the drive has been mishandled is some way, either in storage, shipping, or prior to fitting.

CPU Not Detected

It's hard to incorrectly fit a CPU into a ZIF socket, and an error relating to the CPU generally indicates a damaged CPU — either from ESD or from bent or broken pins.

To correct this, remove the CPU and check for damaged pins. You might be able to straighten out a bent pin. Otherwise, return the CPU for replacement.

RAM Not Detected

When your PC doesn't recognize the RAM, you might either get an error message telling you there are RAM problems with the system or you might just find that the PC is displaying less RAM than you thought you installed.

Problems with RAM come down to one of three issues:

- Wrong RAM installed
- Incorrectly fitted RAM
- Defective RAM module

Wrong RAM

First, check the motherboard specification against the RAM you have. Does it all match up? If possible, take a look at the label on the RAM module itself as the RAM module might have been packaged or labeled wrongly.

If you suspect you have the wrong RAM, get in touch with the vendor.

Incorrectly Fitted

Next, check to see whether each module looks as if it is seated properly in the bank on the motherboard. Are the clips done up right?

The best way to check is to remove the RAM module. Be sure to disconnect the PC from the electrical supply and take ESD precautions. Then, carefully refit the module and test again.

Defective RAM

Despite being checked by the vendor, RAM modules can still reach the customer in a defective state and cause problems.

It's easier to test RAM if you have more than one module. If you have only one module, then you're stuck with either testing it on a known good system or sending it back to the vendor.

To test RAM, follow these steps:

1. Remove one RAM module and test the system.
   Does the system work? If it does, then it's likely (although not 100% guaranteed) that the RAM module in the system is OK. If it doesn't, consider it possibly defective.

2. Remove the installed RAM module and try the second one.
   Does this work? If not, consider it defective.

3. If both seem OK by themselves, try swapping the banks they are in and trying again.

You might find that both seem okay on their own but won't work together or that both seem defective. In these cases, return both to the vendor for replacement.

Hard Drive Problems

It's also possible that your hard drives won't be detected during startup. There are a number of reasons why a hard drive wouldn't be detected during startup.

- **Is the data cable properly fitted?** Check that the data cables are fitted properly and that the hard drive is on the correct connector (at the end if you only have one). Take a flashlight to help you see if the connectors are seated properly. Is the cable correctly seated on the motherboard? Is the cable the right way around? Make sure that the wire with the red stripe on it is connected to pin 1 on the heard drive and motherboard.

- **Is the power connector properly fitted?** Undo and reconnect it.

- **Still no luck?** Visit the website of the manufacturer, and download the hard drive utilities they have available and run tests on your drives. These utilities will allow you to test the hard drive and check for improper settings. (See Appendix C, "Hardware Manufacturers," for a list of manufacturers' websites.)

If You Still Have Problems

In the unlikely event that you are still having problems, then you will need to turn to tech support or your parts vendor for replacements. If you've followed the advice in this chapter, you should have a good idea where the problem lies (for example, with the motherboard, PSU, hard drive, etc.), and you can then either get a replacement or seek assistance from the manufacturer.

Big problems are uncommon. The majority will be solved easily and quickly by following the simple troubleshooting steps. Just don't panic, take a deep breath, approach the problem methodically, and take your time.

Burn-In

By now you should have a PC that works!

Hopefully, it started without a hitch, but it's possible that some of you reading will have had problems. Many of you will have solved these problems by checking everything until you find the offending cable or device that wasn't fitted right. Some of you, though, will have experienced problems with one (or more) of the components you bought and will have had to get replacements and fit these in order to get the system up and running.

Now that the system is running you need to let it run for a while. This is to allow all the components to bed in (e.g., settle into place), and also it enables you to run the PC so that any components that might fail because of defects do so now, before you start to install software and begin using your system.

Don't be tempted to rush this stage and leap straight to installing software.

Carry out the burn-in process with the case all done up properly. This allows proper airflow through the case and also protects the components from inadvertent damage.

There is plenty of software available that is specifically designed to allow you to burn-in and stress a system, but as a rule we generally find that simply leaving the system running is a great way to burn it in. It doesn't cost you anything, and you don't have to bother installing software. Okay, you're not stressing the devices, and you're not working the hard drives much but at the same time it's a no-cost, no-fuss way to do it.

Note If you feel you want to give your system a thorough workout, then take a look at a product such as PassMark BurnInTest (www.passmark.com) or Sandra by SiSoftware (www.sisoftware.co.uk). Both of these will carry out comprehensive tests on your system, but you will need to install software on it, which takes additional time. They will also cost around $50—for software that you might only use once.

What we do is fire the system up and then enter the BIOS screen (by pressing Del or F2 key generally, there will be an on-screen prompt for this at the beginning). Then we locate the screen that displays the CPU and system temperature and leave it on that. This allows us to do two things:

- Leave the system running
- Monitor system temperature

Watch the temperature display and see what happens. If the CPU cooling system is working fine, you will find that the temperature will rise and then level out quickly. There are no hard-and-fast rules for CPU temperature as it varies between brands and models, and you are advised to visit www.amd.com or www.intel.com for details about your specific CPU.

You should leave the system running like this for at least two hours—although you should not leave the system unattended. Then shut the system down and allow it to cool down for at least half an hour before switching it on for another two-hour session. The reason for leaving it to cool between the run-in sessions is to check for component loosening as a result of the expansion and contraction due to the temperature changes as the PC is run in and switched off. Other faults, such as circuit board cracks or component manufacturing faults, can also be uncovered during the burn-in process.

This should bring to light any problems that might be lurking unseen in your system. However, problems are quite rare, and there's a very good chance that after two two-hour burn-in sessions that you PC is functional and ready for you to use.

Congratulations! You have a working PC! A PC that you designed, planned, and built yourself!

Summary

In this chapter, you've fired up your PC, hopefully ready to receive the operating system. Chances are that this has gone without a hitch, but you needn't worry if you hit a snag because chances are that the problem is due to something not being fitted right as opposed to something serious, such as a malfunctioning device.

Don't panic, and follow the simple steps. Chances are that this will lead you to something that's simple to fix, such as a badly fitted cable. However, it is possible that you have a malfunctioning device that you will need to return for replacement. This can be irritating but the troubleshooting process itself can be both educational and rewarding itself.

Even if your PC seems to be working fine, it's important to give it time to run before installing software on it—this burn-in time will give all the components time to bed in, and it might also bring to light problems with some of the components that will fail soon after their first use.

Remember, don't rush this stage—it's better for component to fail now than fail when you have installed software and are using your PC!

In the next chapter, you will see how to install Windows XP onto your newly built PC.

Final Tweaks and Installing Windows XP

You've now got a PC that's working and fully functional — but the problem is that it still can't do anything because you don't have any software installed on it.

In this chapter, we're going to remedy that by making a few tweaks to the PC and then going through the process of installing Microsoft Windows XP onto the system.

BIOS Tweaks

The *BIOS* is the program that handles the initial start up routine of your PC when you first switch it on and before any operating system that you've installed takes over. This program handles communications and the loading of initial default parameters suitable for the hardware installed on the PC.

There are a couple of tweaks that you can make to the PC's system BIOS. Some are operational, and others are performance-related.

Let's take a look at some of these now.

Switch on the PC and enter the BIOS screen. Consult your motherboard manual for instructions on how to enter the system BIOS (usually a key press such as Del or F2).

Generally, the BIOS screen shows yellow, white, and red text against a dark blue background — not the most friendly or aesthetic sets of colors to choose but nonetheless they are the ones most commonly used, so don't be worried about it!

The main BIOS title screen will contain all the top level menus for all the changes that you can make to the BIOS. You navigate from menu to menu using the cursor keys on the keyboard (the up, down, left, and right arrows) and select an option by pressing Enter.

Tip Consult your motherboard manual before making any changes. All BIOS options relating to your particular motherboard/BIOS configuration should be detailed in there.

Performance Tweaks

In particular, you should take a look at two performance options. These options have to do with the system defaults that are loaded into the BIOS and used to control key functions of the PC.

There are generally two performance options to choose from:

- Fail-safe defaults
- Optimized/performance defaults

Names vary among various BIOS setups, but as a rule you will find these two options to choose to load.

So, what's the difference?

Well, the *fail-safe default* option loads values into the BIOS that are pretty much guaranteed to work no matter what. These won't be the best defaults, but it's the way to get your PC going.

Optimized defaults are just that — the best settings to get the best performance from your motherboard, RAM, and CPU. The problem with this setting is that being performance-related you might experience problems with instabilities, and you'll need to tweak certain settings to overcome these problems.

Choosing between the settings is easy. Use the cursor keys to navigate to the setting you need, then press Enter and move to the option to "Save & Exit Setup" before pressing Enter again to confirm that you want to carry out the operation.

We recommend that initially you access the BIOS and choose the safe defaults for the BIOS. This will give you good performance without the chance of problems resulting from pushing components to their limit.

Note Of course, you might want to try to get the optimum performance from your PC and go with the optimized/performance settings straight away. No problem! Go ahead and select this and see what happens. There's a good chance that everything will work just fine. However, if you find that your machine becomes unstable, crashes, and hangs a lot then reenter the BIOS and select the fail-safe defaults to see if that solves the problems you're having.

Operational Tweaks

Finally, you need to carry out a few important operational tweaks to the BIOS.

There are a number of changes that you might want to try out and experiment with. Here are just a few ideas of changes that you can examine. We'll provide information relating to a particular type of BIOS (a Pheonix Award BIOS) here. Remember that your BIOS may be different and the layout unfamiliar, so consult your manual for precise details.

Note The details below refer to the Award BIOS. Your BIOS may vary. Consult the motherboard manual for details.

Boot Order

Your PC can boot up using information from a number of locations. The three most common are:

- Hard drive
- Optical drive
- Floppy drive

A good tip is to set the optical and floppy drive to be the first and second boot devices for your PC, especially in the early stages, because it will allow you to work faster when installing your operating system from the optical drive.

To make these changes, select Advanced BIOS Features and press Enter to go into the advanced BIOS features screen. From here, you can change the first, second, and third boot device.

While setting up the PC we recommend the following settings:

- First boot device: CDROM
- Second boot device: Floppy
- Third boot device: Hard Disk

For normal operation we recommend:

- First boot device: Hard Disk
- Second boot device: CDROM
- Third boot device: Floppy

To save the settings, select Save & Exit Setup, press Enter again, and confirm that you want to carry out this operation.

Setting the System Time

If you enter the Standard CMOS Features, you can set the time and date for the PC. This isn't a vital step, but it does help you keep track of files created on your system before you install the operating system.

Note If you are going to run Windows on your system, these settings will be changed automatically when you make changes in the Windows Date and Time utility.

You don't usually need to Save & Exit Setup to make the time and date setting permanent in the BIOS.

Other Settings and Tweaks

The BIOS contains a whole host of settings and tweaks that you can alter. We're not going to cover them all here because there are so many and they vary between BIOS makers. We suggest that after you have spent some time with your PC you sit down and read through the motherboard manual. You can then spend some time experimenting with your BIOS settings. Some examples of changes that you might like to change include:

- Enabling the hard drive S.M.A.R.T. fault detection routine.

- Don't forget to set a system password. (Don't forget this! Most motherboards have a jumper that you can change the setting on to erase the password in the event that you do forget it, so the security offered by this is limited.)

- Disable support for the floppy drive controller (if you don't have one installed).

Tip

You can make these changes at any time to your system, either before or after installing your operating system.

Here are just a few tips to help keep you out of trouble when making BIOS changes:

- Make a note of what the original values are before you change them!

- Make only one change at a time — that way if you have a problem you'll know it's because of the last thing you did and you can easily fix it.

- Keep notes of all the changes you make in case you want to roll back to earlier settings (or you can reload the defaults).

Loading the Operating System

Now we come to the step of installing the operating system on the PC. After this step, your PC will be ready for you to take over control and install applications and make changes to it as you see fit.

In this section, we are going to take you through the process of installing Microsoft Windows XP Professional onto a bare machine. This is a version of Windows XP that contains all the updates and changes up to and including Service Pack 2 (known as SP2).

The steps outlined here will also apply to other versions of Windows XP, including Windows XP Home and versions that don't have SP2 integrated.

Make sure that you have the operating system CD along with the product key that you need to enter during the installation process. You will find the product key on the back of the cardboard CD holder in which the CD is supplied.

Installing Windows XP

Having made the necessary alterations to the boot device order in the system BIOS, you begin the installation of Windows XP by putting the CD in the drive and rebooting the PC Just either press the On/Off button or the reset button. At this stage, you're not going to harm anything by pressing the off switch on the PC while it's in use.

Beginning the Setup Process

With no boot information on the hard drive, the system will detect the boot information on the CD and begin the boot up and installation process automatically, as shown in Figure 17-1. (This assumes you're starting with a blank hard disk. If your hard disk already contains boot information, possibly from a previous installation, you will be offered the option to boot up from the CD by pressing any key.)

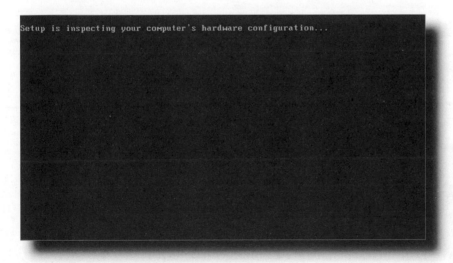

Figure **17-1: Setup process begins automatically.**

The initial stage of copying files and drivers off of the CD onto the PC will take a few minutes. Along the bottom of the screen, a status line will display as to what Windows is doing (although if this comes across as gibberish to you, don't worry, you don't need to know this stuff and there isn't going to be a test!). See Figures 17-2 through 17-4.

Press F6 if you need to install a third party SCSI or RAID driver...

FIGURE 17-2: File copy begins.

Setup is loading files (Dynamic Volume Support (dmio))...

FIGURE 17-3: Setup process keeps you informed.

1. After this file copy process has finished, you will be faced with the Welcome to Setup screen and given three options (see Figure 17-5):

   ■ Set up Windows

   ■ Repair Windows

   ■ Quit setup

FIGURE 17-4: Setup hands off to the Windows Setup Wizard.

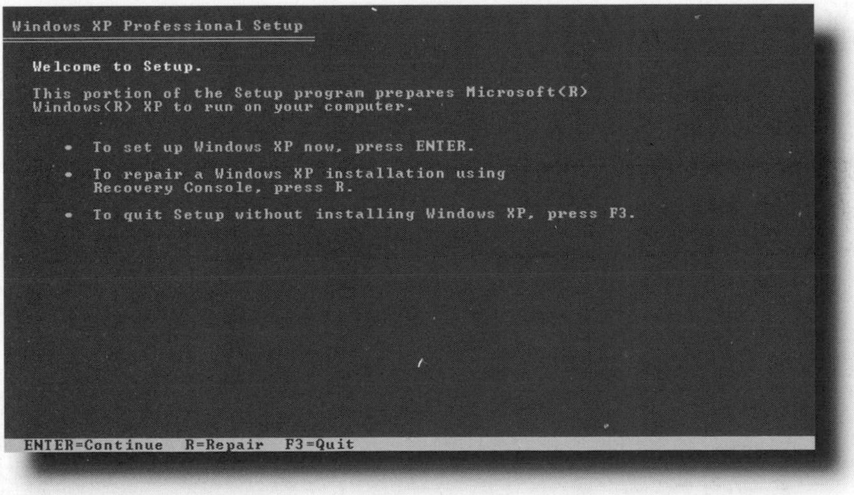

FIGURE 17-5: Setup options.

You need to choose to set up Windows on your new PC, so press Enter to continue with this.

2. Next, you will need to agree to the licensing agreement displayed (see Figure 17-6). Read this and press F8 if you agree and want to continue or press Esc if you don't agree and want to abort the setup.

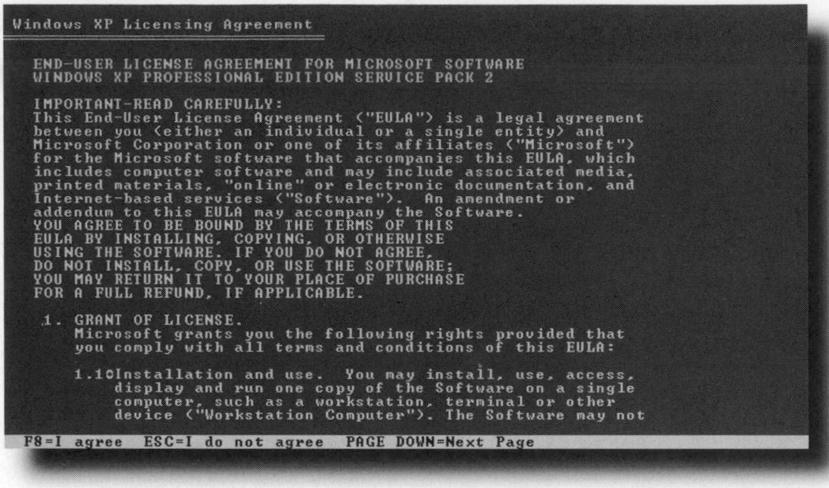

FIGURE **17-6:** Agreeing to the license agreement.

3. After this the Windows XP Setup Wizard will detect your empty hard drive. Because the hard drive will be unformatted, the next step is to choose the hard drive and partition it to give Windows XP the space needed to install the Windows operating system (see Figure 17-7). Choose the unpartitioned space displayed for Disk 0 (the first hard drive — if you only have one hard drive then this will be the only option).

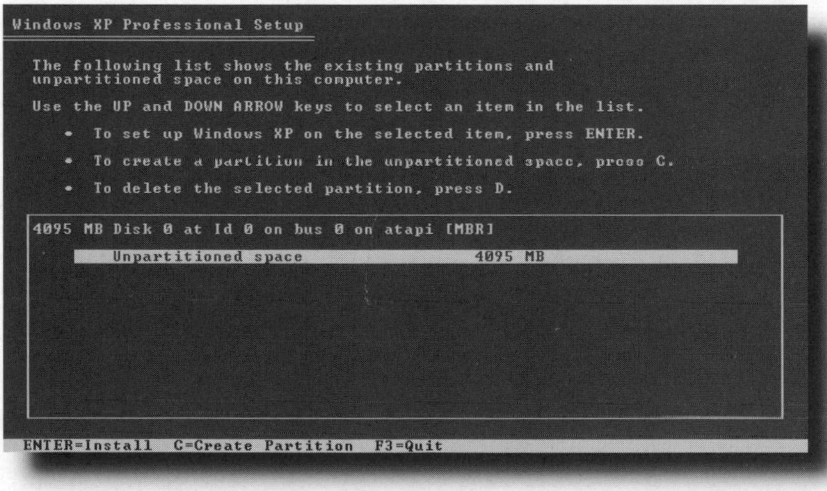

FIGURE **17-7:** Choosing where to install Windows.

To create a partition on the empty space, press C or press Enter. (In this example, we will press Enter.)

There is a difference between the two options. At this stage if you press Enter, then all the drive space will be used for the partition, whereas pressing C allows you to choose the size of this partition; for example, if you wanted to turn a single disk into two or more logical drives (see Figures 17-8 and 17-9). To simplify the process, you are going to use the whole of the drive for the partition, so you can simply press Enter.

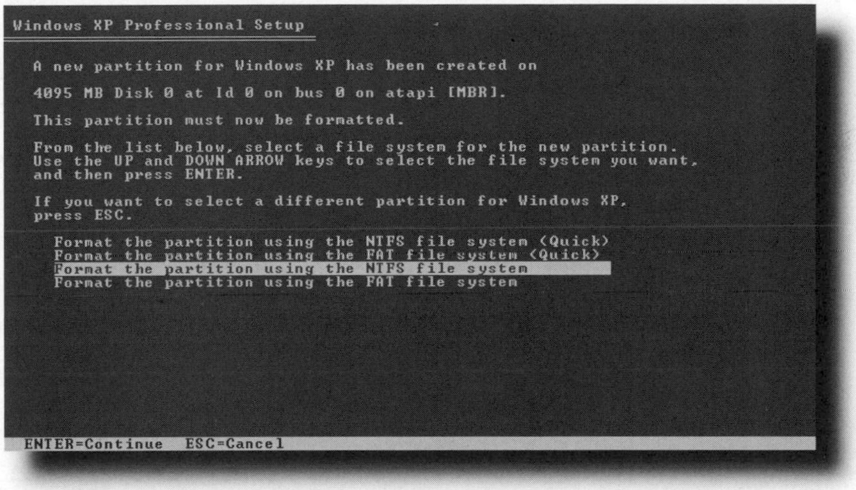

FIGURE 17-8: Option presented when pressing Enter.

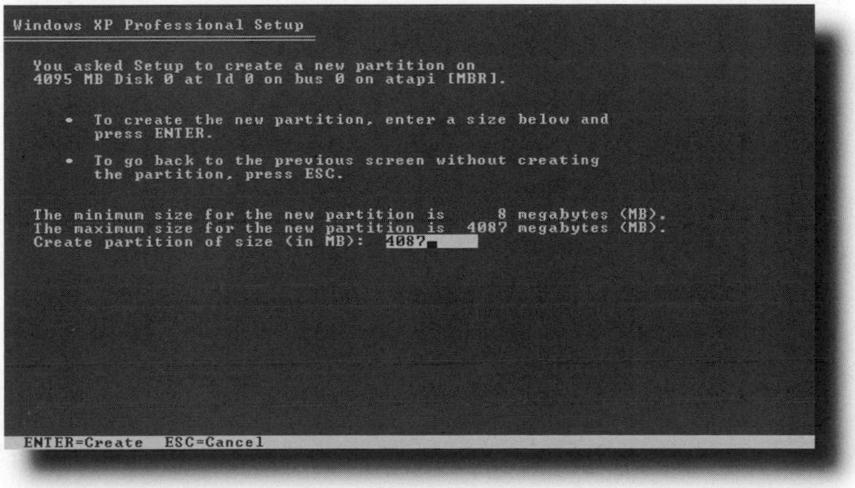

FIGURE 17-9: Options presented when pressing C.

Note

Eagle-eyed readers may have noticed that we only have a small drive listed—this is because in order to get screenshots for this book we have to install Windows XP into a virtual PC using software known as VMware Workstation that enables you to create a number of virtual PCs within one single physical PC. (For more details on virtual computing with VMware visit www.vmware.com.)

Notice how our new partition is now displayed as C: (see Figure 17-10). This will become the main system C drive on the final PC.

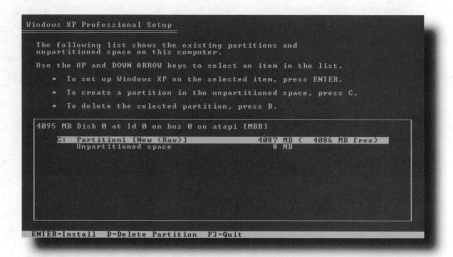

FIGURE 17-10: New partition labeled as C drive.

4. The space is currently RAW, which means that it's not been formatted—that stage comes next. Press Enter to continue or Esc to make changes.

5. Next are the formatting options (see Figure 17-11). There are four to choose from:

   ■ Quick format using the NTFS file system

   ■ Quick format using the FAT file system

   ■ Standard format using the NTFS file system

   ■ Standard format using the FAT file system

It is recommended that you choose the option to carry out a standard format using the NTFS (New Technology File System) file system. The NTFS file system offers you far greater robustness and protection from data errors than FAT (File Allocation Table), and by carrying out a full format you will be get to check the disk's data surface for errors, which is always a good idea with new drives. You are free to choose FAT as a file system for your PC, but unless you know of a specific reason why you really need it, you probably don't need it!

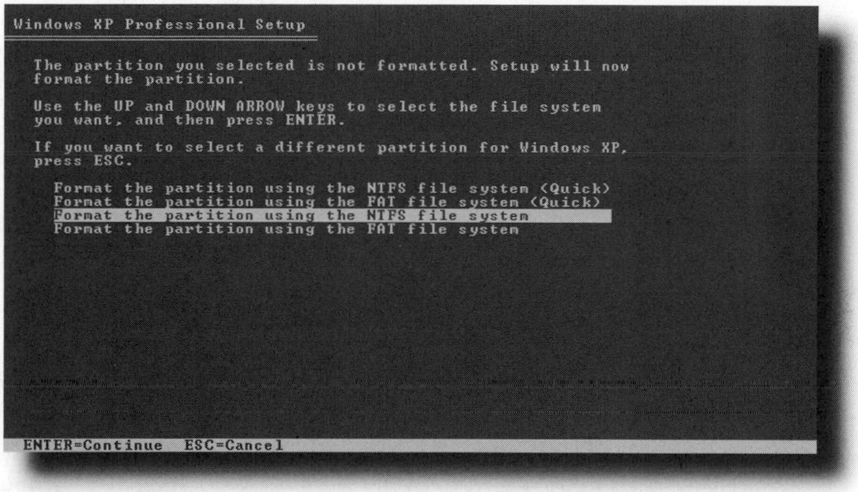

Windows XP Professional Setup

The partition you selected is not formatted. Setup will now
format the partition.

Use the UP and DOWN ARROW keys to select the file system
you want, and then press ENTER.

If you want to select a different partition for Windows XP,
press ESC.

    Format the partition using the NTFS file system (Quick)
    Format the partition using the FAT file system (Quick)
    Format the partition using the NTFS file system
    Format the partition using the FAT file system

ENTER=Continue   ESC=Cancel

FIGURE 17-11: Formatting options.

The drive will now be formatted — if you have a big drive don't be surprised if this takes some time. See Figure 17-12.

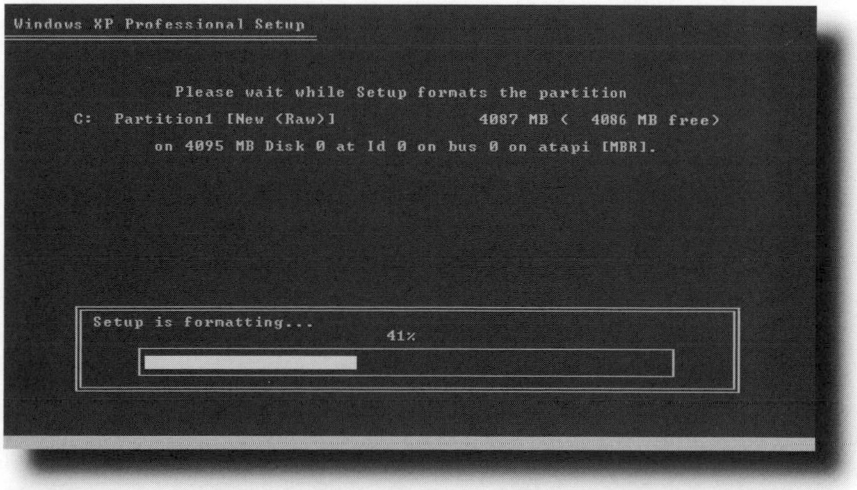

Windows XP Professional Setup

            Please wait while Setup formats the partition
    C: Partition1 [New (Raw)]   4087 MB (4086 MB free)
        on 4095 MB Disk 0 at Id 0 on bus 0 on atapi [MBR].

        Setup is formatting...
                              41%

FIGURE 17-12: Formatting in progress.

6. After this, the Setup Wizard will check for the necessary disk space in order to install Windows XP and then begin copying system files from the CD to the hard drive. See Figure 17-13.

Windows XP Professional Setup

Checking drive C:...

FIGURE 17-13: Setup checking for adequate disk space.

7. After this the Setup Wizard will create a list of files to be copied to the hard drive and then begin the copy process. See Figures 17-14 and 17-15.

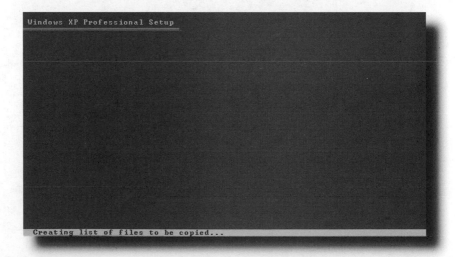

Windows XP Professional Setup

Creating list of files to be copied...

FIGURE 17-14: Creating a list of files to be copied during installation.

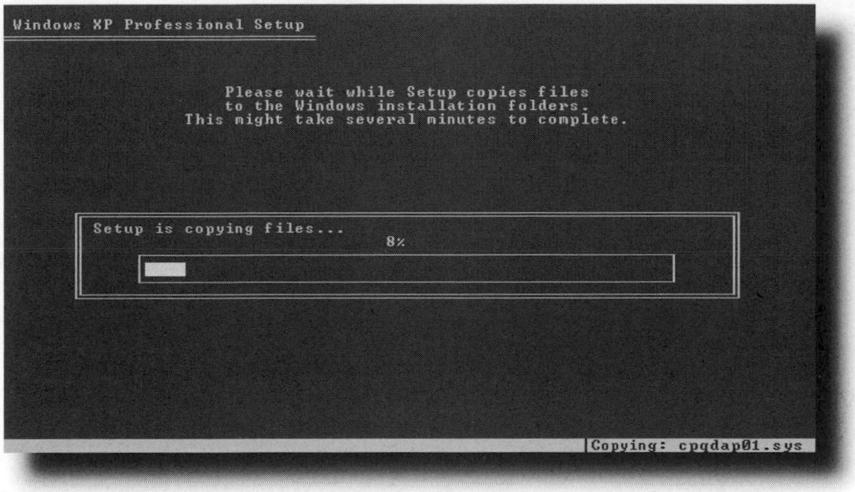

FIGURE 17-15: Copying files.

This process will take quite some time. (See Figures 17-16 and 17-17.) You might want to take a break away from the keyboard and maybe get a cup of coffee or take a short walk.

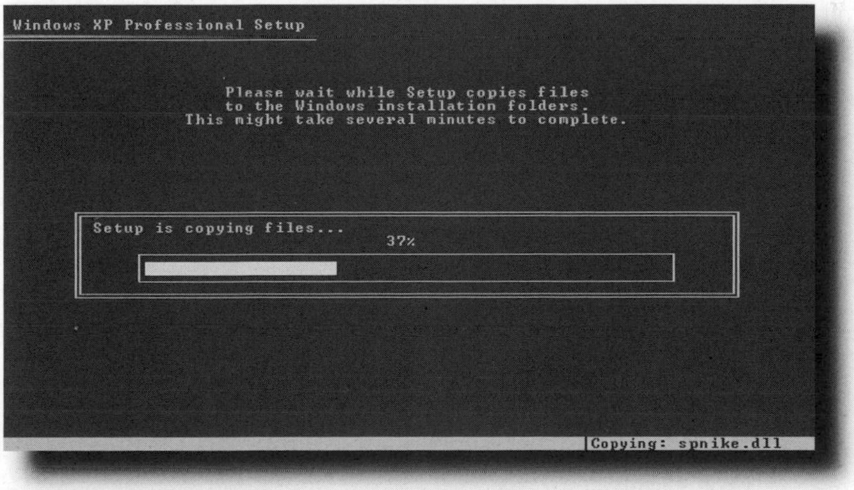

FIGURE 17-16: File copy process is a long operation.

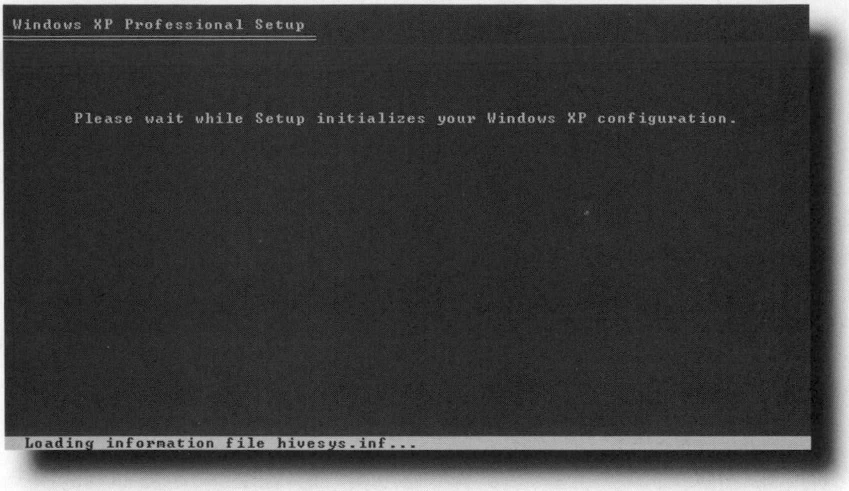

FIGURE **17-17: Initializing installation.**

After the install process, the PC will reboot and the process will continue from a graphical interface (see Figure 17-18).

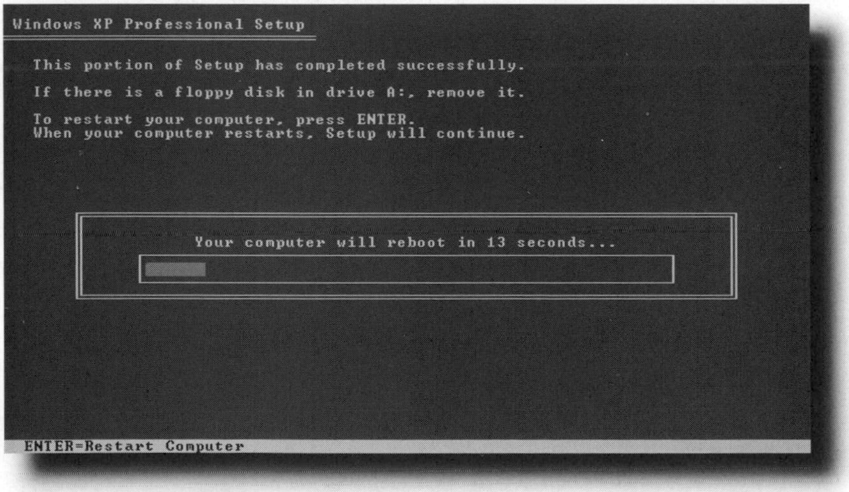

FIGURE **17-18: Automatic reboot after file copy.**

Second Stage of the Installation

Your PC should now begin to look a bit familiar to regular Windows users. The next splash screen looks a lot like the regular Windows XP startup screen (see Figure 17-19).

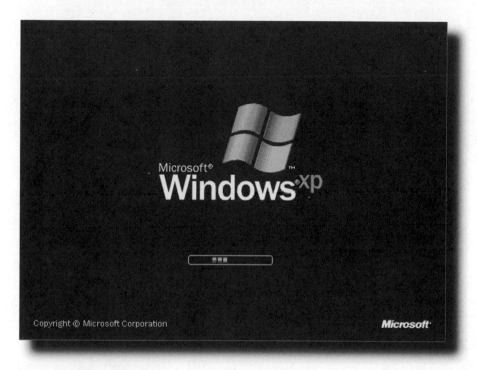

FIGURE 17-19: Splash screen.

The next stage of the installation will feature what's known as the *taster screens* (see Figure 17-20). These screens contain information about Windows XP that newcomers might be interested in. If you've never installed Windows XP on a PC before you won't have seen these screens, so you might want to watch and read.

While this is going on, Windows will do a number of things in the background such as installing drivers for devices (see Figure 17-21).

Also, at this point you should notice that you have a working pointer, as shown in Figure 17-22!

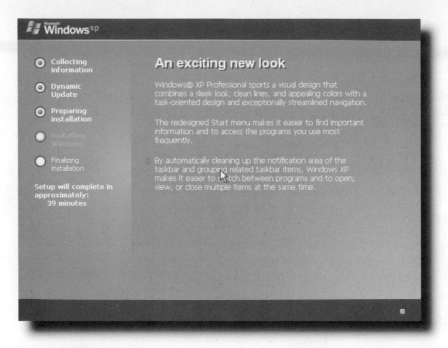

FIGURE **17-20:** Taster screen on the right—here telling you about the exciting new Windows look.

FIGURE **17-21:** Setup continues is graphical mode.

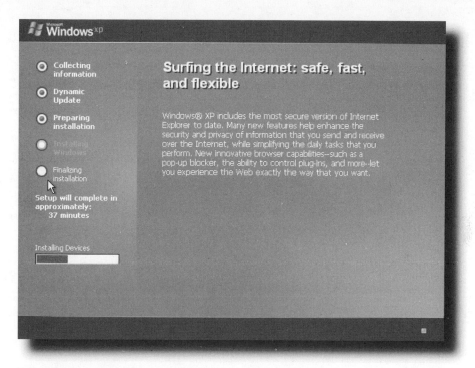

FIGURE 17-22: A working pointer will come in handy soon!

Note

At the left side of the Installation Wizard, you will be given a time estimate of how long the installation will take. If you have built a PC of reasonable specification, then this will be an over-estimate of how long the process will take!

Entering Information

Don't go too far away from the PC at this stage of the installation, though. This process does require some input on your part!

1. The first such input is to choose the regional and language options (see Figure 17-23).

   The default is to set the language to English (United States), the location to the United States, and the keyboard to the U.S. keyboard layout. If you are in the United States, great, if not, click on Customize... and Details... to change these settings. See Figures 17-24 and 17-25. Click Next to proceed with the installation.

2. In the Personalize Your Software screen, enter your name and company name (if applicable), and click Next when you are done. See Figure 17-26.

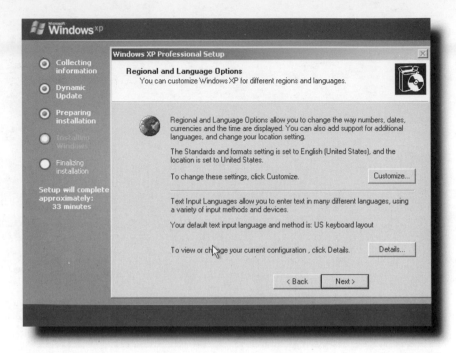

FIGURE 17-23: Regional settings.

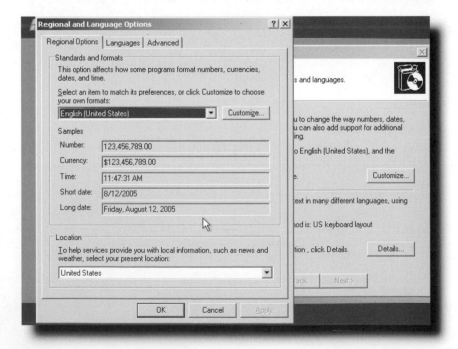

FIGURE 17-24: Customizing options.

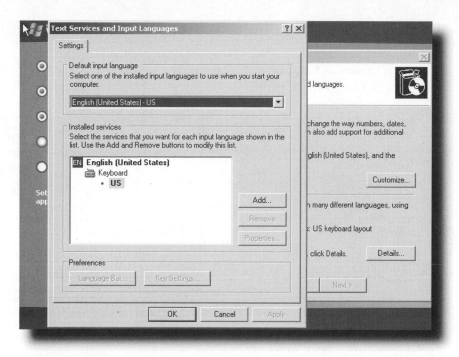

FIGURE 17-25: Keyboard language options.

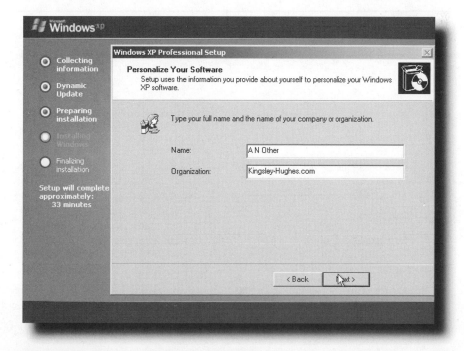

FIGURE 17-26: Enter your name and organization.

3. In the Your Product Key screen, you have the task of entering the 25-character product key into the box on the screen off the back of the cardboard wallet that your CD came in. See Figure 17-27. When you have entered your product key in the boxes, click Next. If you have entered this information incorrectly, you will have to enter it again (the setup wizard knows the difference between a legitimate product key and one that isn't).

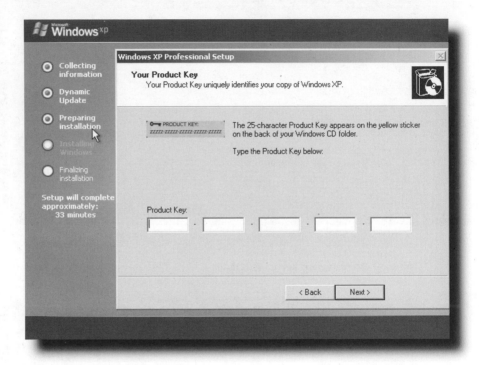

FIGURE 17-27: Product key screen.

4. If the product key information you entered is correct, the Computer Name and Password Administration screen displays (see Figure 17-28). You need to give the PC a name (one will be suggested but it's likely to be an odd one, and it's better to give the system a new and less obscure name) and enter an administrator password. This password will be the main password needed for logging into Windows XP as an administrator.

5. Click Next.

6. The Date and Time Settings screen allows you to enter the date and time and your time zone (see Figure 17-29). You can also choose to have Windows alter for daylight saving changes automatically. Click Next to move on.

The Windows Setup Wizard will now move on to installing the network, as shown in Figure 17-30. This process is automatic at first but does need some user input at the end.

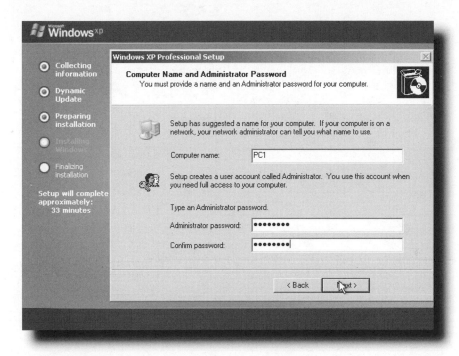

FIGURE 17-28: Computer name and administrator password options.

FIGURE 17-29: Date and time settings.

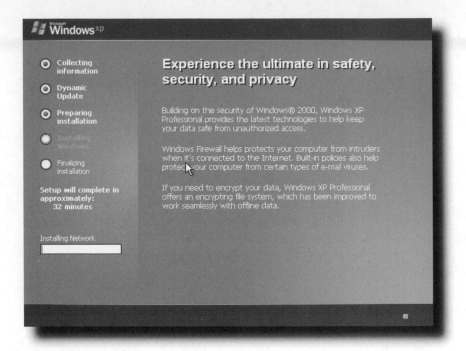

FIGURE 17-30: Installing network components.

7. You need to choose network settings and, unless you have a reason to think you need something out of the ordinary, you should choose Typical settings. (See Figure 17-31.) Click Next to continue.

8. Now, you need to specify whether your PC part of a workgroup or domain (see Figure 17-32). For home networks, choose Workgroup. If your PC is to be connected to an existing network, enter this workgroup name in the box. Click Next to continue.

The setup will now enter another portion that doesn't require user input, and it will copy the necessary files to the appropriate folders. See Figures 17-33 and 17-34.

What Makes a Good Password?

The recommendations are:

- Six to eight characters
- Combination of uppercase and lowercase letters
- Combination of letters and numbers

Whatever you choose, make it something you'll remember!

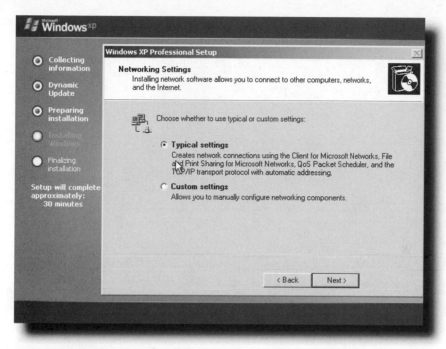

Figure 17-31 Choose installation type.

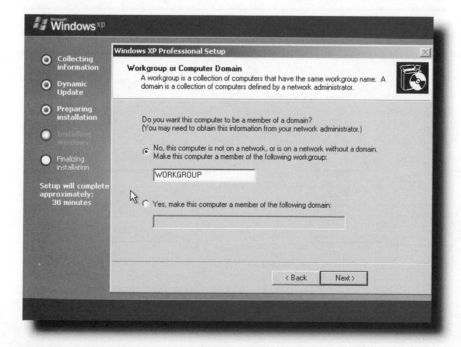

FIGURE 17-32: Workgroup or domain information.

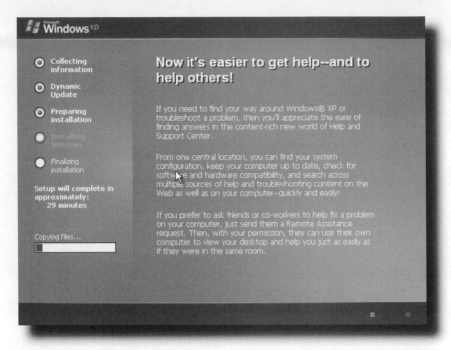

FIGURE 17-33: Another batch of copied files.

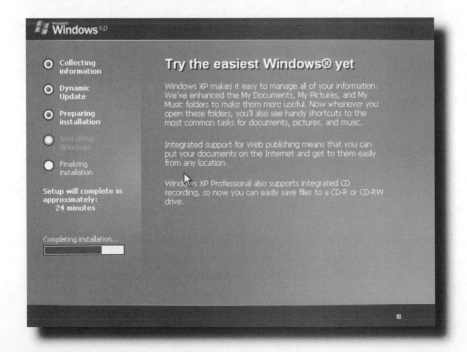

FIGURE 17-34: Completing installation.

Then the Setup Wizard will install Start Menu items, register installed components and then automatically move on to finalizing the installation. See Figures 17-35 and 17-36.

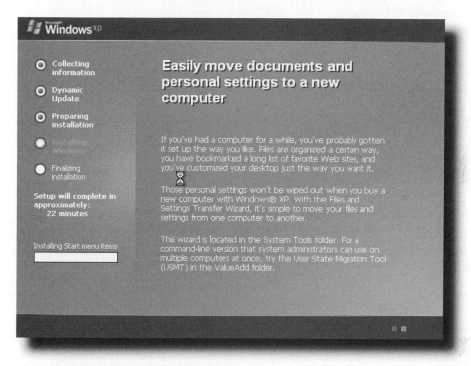

FIGURE 17-35: Installing Start Menu items.

Finalizing the Installation

After this, your computer will enter the stage where it reboots to complete the installation.

1. Upon reboot you will see a splash screen (see Figure 17-37). At this point, you might be given the option to allow Windows to improve the display and screen appearance (see Figure 17-38). Click OK to proceed.

2. If the monitor settings are acceptable, click OK again to continue. See Figure 17-39.

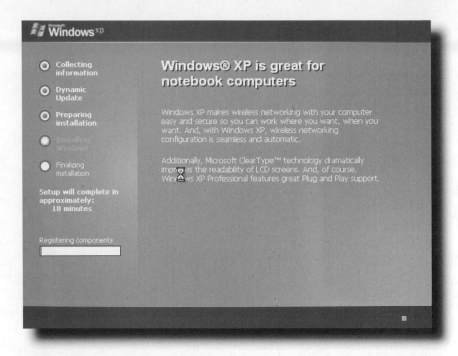

FIGURE **17-36:** Registering components.

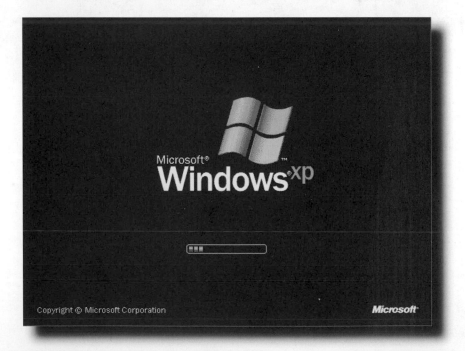

FIGURE **17-37:** Splash screen after reboot.

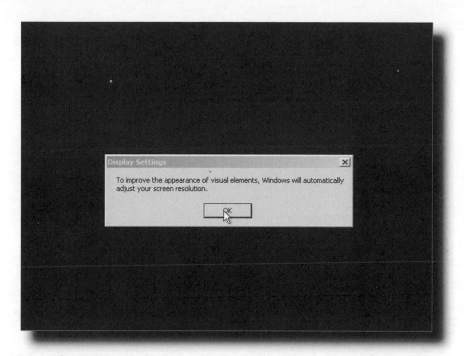

FIGURE **17-38**: Improving display.

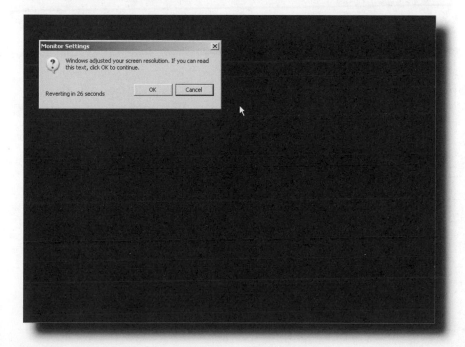

FIGURE **17-39**: Click OK to accept changes.

3. The final stage of the installation is to finish setting up Windows. On the screen, you will see a Welcome to Microsoft Windows screen (see Figure 17-40). Click Next here.

FIGURE 17-40: Welcome to Microsoft Windows.

4. The next step in the installation is the security settings screen where you can choose to turn on or off the Windows Update mechanism. It's recommended that you enable this so that your copy of Windows is always kept up-to-date automatically. (See Figure 17-41.) Click Next to continue.

5. Now the Windows Setup Wizard will check to see if you are connected to the Internet and asks for some basic information. See Figures 17-42 and 17-43.

   Enter this and click Next. Alternatively, you can choose to Skip and enter the details later.

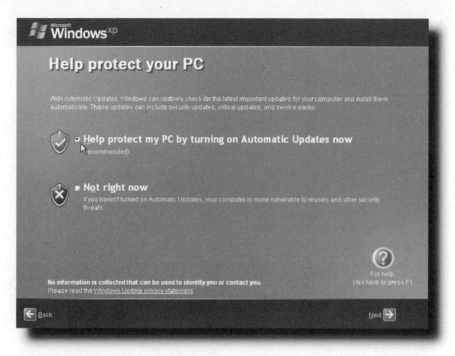

FIGURE **17-41**: Help protect your PC.

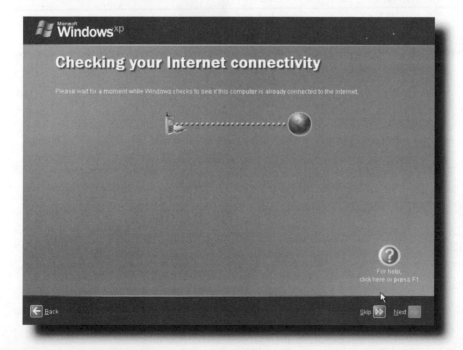

FIGURE **17-42**: Checking for internet connectivity.

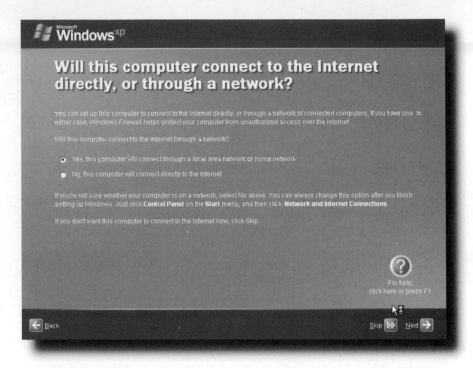

FIGURE 17-43: Configuring connection.

6. The next step is product activation. This connects to the Internet and verifies that your product key is a valid one (see Figure 17-44). Choose the option that you want. You can activate your copy of Windows at a later date — you have 30 days. Click Next.

   If you choose to activate, the next screen gives you the option to register your product (see Figure 17-45). This step is not mandatory, and you can choose not to do so if you prefer. Click Next.

7. Finally, set up the user names that will use the PC (see Figure 17-46). The administrator account that you set up earlier (by providing a password) will be the main account but won't be displayed on the login screen. (To access it, you will need to press Ctrl-Alt-Del twice to do a manual login and type *Administrator* as the user name.) These are user accounts. Click Next.

Windows will take you to a screen that confirms what's been done (see Figure 17-47). If the PC has an Internet connection and you chose to activate it, the result of this activation process will be displayed.

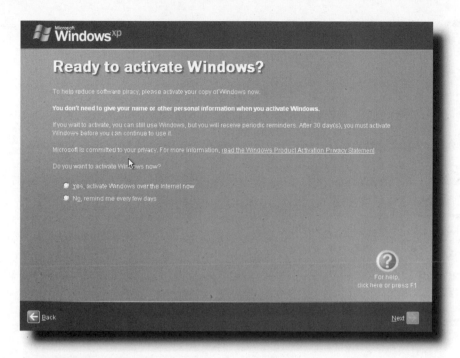

FIGURE 17-44: Windows activation.

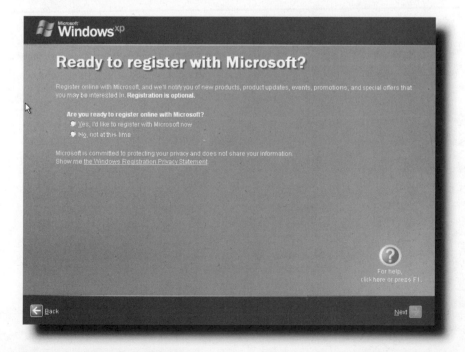

FIGURE 17-45: Registration screen.

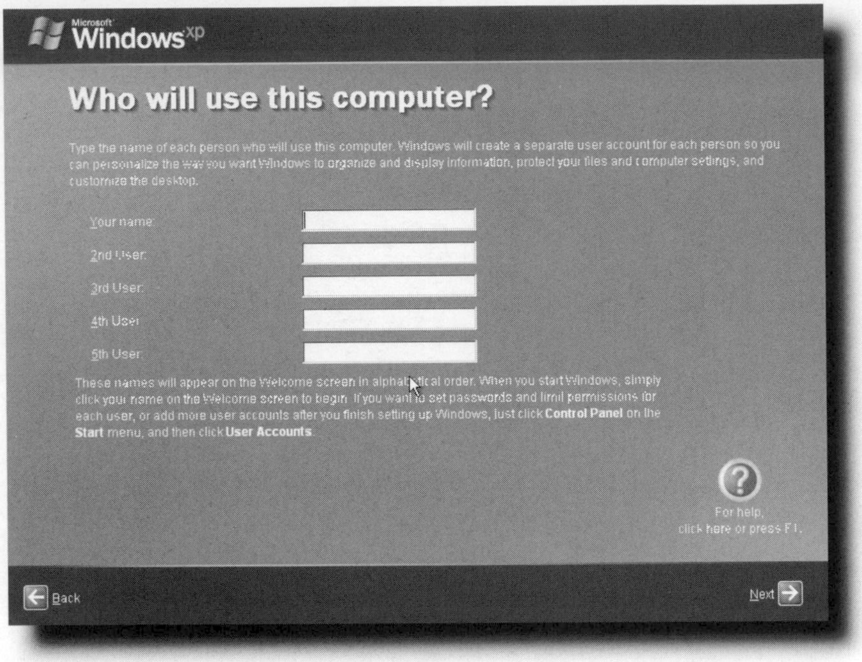

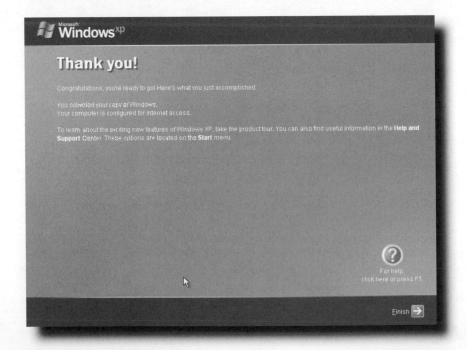

FIGURE 17-46: Setting up users.

FIGURE 17-47: Final setup screen.

And that's it! Click Finish and you're now ready to use your PC and Windows XP! See Figure 17-48.

FIGURE **17-48: Windows XP up and running.**

You can now go on and explore Windows XP. Before you go ahead and install additional applications, there are a few small things that you might want to check up on, which we will look at in the next chapter.

Note   We'd recommend that you install antivirus and firewall software onto your PC to protect it from hackers and malicious users on the web soon after installing Windows XP.

Summary

In this chapter, you looked at how to make a few basic BIOS setting tweaks and how to install Microsoft Windows XP onto your new PC. Hopefully, this process will have gone smoothly for you and you now have a fully functional PC complete with an operating system installed on it!

Well done for having made it this far. It's now time to sit down in front of your new PC and enjoy it for a little while.

In the next chapter, we look at a few final system checks that you can do before moving the PC into full use.

Check and Test, Check and Test Again!

Your PC is now running, and you've installed on it the operating system and all seems to be going well. Now it's time to carry out a few final checks on the system and finish off a few jobs that we've been putting off until the PC was working and we were confident that everything seemed to work okay on it.

We'll divide these checks and tests into two categories:

➤ Internal

➤ External

After completing these final checks and tests, your PC will then be ready for use and for you to install software on it and begin using it.

Internal Checks and Testing

It's difficult to drag yourself away from a new PC, and you're probably eager to get on and use it now, but take a few minutes to make sure that everything is okay on the inside. Shut the PC down, unplug it from the power, and pop the side off the case to give you internal access to check a few things.

Heat

Heat can build up inside a case, and the more heat you have the greater the likelihood of trouble. As we mentioned in Chapter 16, "Fire Up and Burn In," there are no hard-and-fast rules about how hot a PC should be, but the cooler it is, the better it will be and the longer it will last.

The air inside of the PC case will undoubtedly be warmer than the air temperature surrounding the PC, but if you've had the PC running for half an hour or so, this is a good opportunity to check the PC for hot spots that might need dealing with. To do this, you will need a temperature measuring device — we all come equipped with some good ones, these are called hands!

With the PC off and unplugged, run your hand along the inside of the PC case. As always, take care not to cut yourself on any sharp edges, and take proper ESD precautions, which should by now be second nature to you.

Partly because warm air rises over cooler air and partly because the CPU, PSU, and a number of other devices are near the top of the case, it's natural that the case will be hotter at the top than the bottom. But look out for areas that seem unusually hot — such as around hard drives. Generally, a component being too hot to touch after you've turned off the PC is a sign that components may need additional cooling through the fitting of extra case fans. Given that heat problems get worse the longer you use the PC and that as the PC gets used it will start to collect dust that will itself begin to exacerbate the problem by trapping more heat, you might want to consider fitting more case fans to keep the temperature down.

If you want to take more accurate temperature readings, then you'll need a thermometer. Placing a glass thermometer inside a PC is very bad news as are contact thermometers such as those found on some digital multimeters (unless the probe is insulated). The best piece thermometer for measuring in-case temperatures is a laser thermometer (see Figure 18-1). These thermometers fire a beam of invisible infrared light and take a reading of how much infrared radiation is reflected back from the target area. This is used to measure the temperature of the illuminated component. These are great because you won't need to touch anything to take a reading. The great advantage of a laser thermometer is that you can use it on a PC when it is up and running for instant on-the-spot measurements.

Cabling

This is also a good time to tidy up some of the cabling inside your PC. Tidy cabling not only makes the PC look smarter inside (which is a vain point, but if you have a clear side panel on the case, you won't want to look at a cluttered interior), but it also benefits the PC by allowing air to flow more freely through the case, aiding in the cooling process. Also, if the cables are wrapped away tidily, they will collect far less dust while the PC is in use. Also, in shifting the PC about and carrying out the initial testing, you might find that some cables have slackened, cable ties might have come off, or you forgot to tie up all the loose cables — not to worry, that's what the final checking is all about!

The best thing to keep cables under control are plastic cable ties (see Figure 18-2). Use these to wrap around the cables. Don't overtighten the tie because this can damage the cable — just tie them up loosely.

Start off by tying back the drive data ribbons. Carefully wrap them around themselves, make a small square bundle, and use plastic ties to hold this in place. Then take any loose power rails and wrap these up and tie them away safely. Do the same both with rails that are completely unused and rails that are partially used.

Finally, wrap up and tuck away any unused case cables. Finish off by tucking cable bundles out of the way and securing them in place using cable ties.

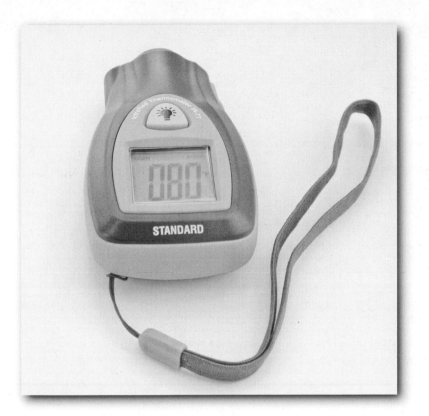

FIGURE **18-1**: Laser thermometer.

Tip

Be careful when doing this step. Make being tidy second to keeping the cables safe. Never wrap a cable up tightly or clamp it too tightly with a cable tie because this can damage the delicate wires inside the cable.

Also, never stress connectors when tidying up cabling. Always have a decent amount of cable slack so as not to break connector heads, snap off pins, or damage the connectors.

Now that all that's done, carefully cut the spare ends off of all the cable ties that you used. Do this with scissors or a pair of diagonal cutting pliers.

Odd Smells and Smoke

When you have a new PC that's filled with new components, it's not uncommon to have it give off a slight "odd" smell that people often describe as an "electrical smell." This is nothing to worry about and is caused by the protective lacquer on components being heated up.

However, always be on the lookout for strong burning smells that might indicate something overheating.

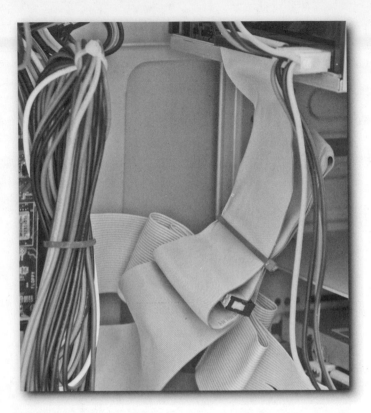

Figure 18-2: Tied-up cabling.

And while on the subject of smells, a quick word about smoke — a slight odd smell coming from a new PC is quite common and usually nothing to worry about, but smoke is an entirely different matter. If you suspect that your PC is giving off smoke, then immediately disconnect it from the power supply (don't even bother shutting down the operating system properly if there's smoke — get the system off as quickly as possible). If you investigate, usually the culprit is a damaged or faulty power supply unit, and this will need replacing to correct the problem. Another possible source of smoke is a cable caught or rubbing on fan blades. You will need to replace any damaged cabling before switching the PC back on.

Screws and Fittings

After you've tidied up the cabling inside your new PC, take a few minutes to make sure that all the screws and fittings are still done up nice and secure. The expansion and contraction caused by the heating and cooling of a PC can cause screws to loosen and work their way out, and this is especially true in new PCs.

The best thing to do is pick up your Phillips head screwdrivers and check each screw. Undo each screw half a turn or so, and then tighten them once more by following the rule of hand tight plus a quarter turn. Although you'll need to check a lot of screws, this process should take only a few minutes to go through them all. Plus, it will save you headaches later because you won't be losing your screws.

The best way to make sure that you get all the screws is to work methodically. Begin with the motherboard and go around each one. Work clockwise and toward the center of the board as this will help you keep track of which ones you've done and which you have left to check.

After checking the motherboard screws, move on to the expansion card screws, and finally check the screws for all of your drives.

Fans

Check all of your fans for security and to make sure that nothing is touching or obscuring them. Take special care to route cables away from fans. This not only improves airflow but prevents cables from getting jammed in or damaged by the fan.

If you have any additional case fans, now is the time to connect these up appropriately (see Figure 18-3).

Finally, make sure that any screws holding case fans in place are firmly done up.

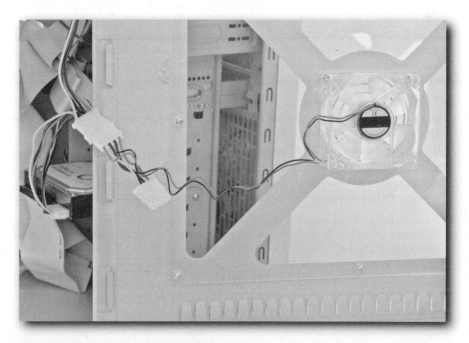

FIGURE **18-3:** Connecting up additional case fans.

Check CPU Cooler Security

CPU coolers are generally firmly attached to the CPU and the motherboard, but it's still worth giving yours a quick check.

A flashlight makes this job much easier. You are looking specifically for heatsink clips that aren't properly seated in place. These clips might give the impression of being secured, but over time (especially as a result of heating and cooling) it is possible for an improperly seated cooler to work its way loose, with disastrous consequences for the CPU.

With this last check in place, you can now button up your PC case.

External Checks

We're now going to shift our attention from the interior of the PC case and focus on the exterior of the case. In this section, you'll go through a number of quick checks before rolling your new PC out into full service.

Case Exterior

The first thing to do is to check the case exterior. If you've been taking care of the case during the build, then there shouldn't be any damage on the case or anything like that. There are, though, a few things you should check for.

- **Dirt.** Building a PC is normally quite a clean job (as opposed to upgrading PCs that have been in use for some time and that have usually filled with dirt and dust over time), but handling tools and components can sometimes mean your hands get a bit dirty. This dirt you can easily pass onto the case and your nice, clean case can start to look dirty.

  This is a good time to give the PC case a wipe down with a clean, dry cloth to remove any marks. If you come across any stubborn marks, you can target these with a small amount of kitchen cleaner on the cloth.

  Another thing that can afflict the case is sticky residue left over from any tape or labels that might have become accidentally stuck to it. Don't be tempted to use solvents on a plastic case as they can cause the plastic to melt and become gooey. Never use anything stronger than a clean cloth with a little cold water or some kitchen cleaner.

- **Fascias.** Because you added CD/DVD drives and probably a floppy drive, you've had to pull some of the plastic fascias from the front of the PC and also removed the metal plates that lie behind these. Check that the remainder of the fascias is properly fitted — you don't want to lose one! Also, as you might have noticed already, these also help to keep fingers away from sharp metal edges.

- **Robustness.** Have you put back all the screws used to hold the sides in place? If not, it's now time to do so.

Optical Drive

With the PC switched on, check that the optical drives work. Not just from the point of view of reading CDs or DVDs; check that the disc trays open and close properly and that all of the drives have been secured firmly into their bays. Investigate any rattling (especially if you have done up all the screws correctly). Don't go overtightening screws to try to remove a rattle as you might snap off a screw and be in bigger trouble. Remove the drive and investigate further.

A tray that doesn't open (accompanied by no LEDs being illuminated on the front) is usually a sign of the power cable not being attached properly, while a drive that seems physically okay but won't read a disc might indicate an improperly fitted data cable.

Floppy Drive

Check that the floppy drive works. This is a simple test—insert a disk, see if the PC can read it, then copy a small file to the disk, and then remove the disk from the PC.

That's all there is to that!

All Ports

Next, check that all of the ports on your PC work, or at least check all of the important ports. Your PC will have a serial (COM) port and a parallel port, but you might not have devices for either of these (most having been replaced by USB).

Check that all the USB ports work. The easiest way to do this is to plug a device into each one separately and see if it works. A USB flash memory stick is ideal for this, as shown in Figure 18-4. Check too that they are operating at full speed. You can do this by plugging in a USB 2.0–compliant device into each of the port, such as a USB flash memory device. You should be able to see from within your operating system if they are detected and working at full speed. For example, Windows XP will pop up a balloon display telling you if you have plugged a high-speed USB device into a non-high-speed port.

Stuck Discs

Got a stuck disc in a CD or DVD drive that won't open? Generally, there's a little-known escape hatch.

Take a close look at the front of the drive, and you should find a small hole. This is the emergency tray release mechanism. Take a straightened paperclip and poke it into this hole carefully. You should feel a little resistance. Keep pushing, and you should notice that the tray starts to slowly open. Pull the paperclip out when you get as far as you can go and keep on repeating this until you have the tray opened far enough to get the disc out.

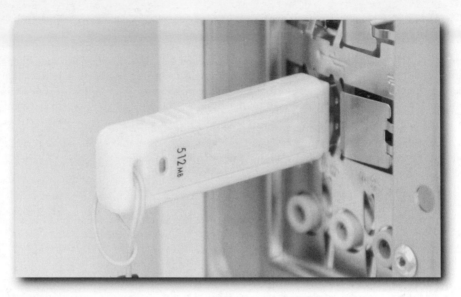

FIGURE 18-4: Checking USB ports with a USB flash memory device.

All modern motherboards support USB 1.1 and 2.0, but if yours doesn't seem to support the faster USB 2.0 standard (Windows XP will inform you of this when you connect a USB 2.0 compatible device to the PC), it's generally a driver issue — consult the manual that came with your motherboard for details on how to correctly install the drivers.

If you have FireWire ports on your machine and you have a FireWire device, check them too.

External Cabling

This is one check to put aside until you have moved your PC to where it's going to be used. Take some time to tidy up the cables coming out of the back of your PC. In fact, given the number of cables that tend to emanate from the back of a PC these days, it's always a good idea to label each cable clearly with a sticky label. This way if you do need to undo everything, you can easily put it back again with the minimal of fuss.

Another good tip for all of you that have a digital camera is to take a photograph of the back of your PC complete with all the cables fitted. This way you have a record of where everything goes (and, because the PC is new, it will be tidy!).

Congratulations Are in Order

Well, that wraps up the building phase in this book. We hope that you have enjoyed planning your PC, buying the parts, assembling it, and testing it. All that's now left for you to do is enjoy using your PC.

If you'd like to share with you your experiences of building your custom PC, please visit us on the web at www.kingsley-hughes.com/build-it and send us your build stories.

If you have documented building your PC in a blog or on a website then drop us a note — we've love to see it!

It's now over to you!

Enjoy your brand new, custom-built PC!

Summary

In this chapter, we've looked at the various elements that you should check on your new PC before rolling it out into full service. We've looked in some detail at both checks that you can carry out on the interior and exterior of the PC.

We've kept these checks to a minimum — while being comprehensive — because we know that you are eager to get on and use your brand new, custom-built PC.

In the next and final chapter, we examine your warranty options if you have problems in the future. We also show you how building your own PC gives you much more scope to get out of trouble than if you have bought a PC from one of the big vendors.

Everything You Need to Know about Warranties and Beyond

You've gotten this far in the book, and the PC that you built is hopefully up and running. Or, if you've been unlucky perhaps you've encountered a problem with a component during the building and testing phase and are looking for some help as to what to do with it. Either way, this chapter looks at what your options are when things go wrong. So, whether it's suffering a problem from day 1 or 6 months in, or maybe even 12 months from now or beyond, this chapter looks at the options that are open to you. It will also examine why, by building your own PC, you are giving yourself a much greater set of options when things do go wrong.

Note Don't let this worry you too much! Just as with cars, given the high number of PCs in circulation, people do encounter problems. But it has to be said that we encounter countless PCs every year and as a rule they are quite reliable and robust. (From a hardware point of view, most problems that people seem to encounter are actually software-related.) Many people get hundreds of thousands of hours of trouble-free service from their investment. But given the number of people who are going to build a PC based on the information provided in this book, it would be negligent of us not to include information about what to do when things go wrong!

Advantages of Building Your Own PC

One of the biggest advantages of building your own PC comes into play when you have a problem.

Let's say that, for example, you bought a new PC from a vendor and you encounter a problem with the PC at some point within the first year. Unless you took out an on-site warranty in which you can get an engineer sent out to your home or office to take a look at and repair the PC (these warranties are usually costly), then you might have to return the PC to the manufacturer for testing and repair.

You might have noticed that a PC is a very big, heavy thing that's going to cost you quite a lot of money to send via mail or courier, and you're going to be without a PC for any number of days. Add to that the fact that you have to send your PC back complete with data — something that many, especially business users, might not want to do.

The advantage of building your own PC is that each and every component in the PC is covered by a separate and independent warranty that you can take advantage of. It's far easier to return a motherboard or hard drive to the manufacturer by mail than it is to return a whole PC!

Another advantage is that even a PC that costs, say, $1,500 is made up of parts that themselves cost far less. If your main PC is put out of action by a defective hard drive or dead video adaptor, then you might choose to buy a replacement part for the PC before you try to get a warranty replacement. That way you get your PC up and running swiftly (and because you bought and assembled all the parts yourself, you'll already be familiar with handling and fitting the components), and you can keep the replacement part as a backup or use it as a basis for an upgrade or new PC.

The same goes for problems that occur when your components are no longer covered by warranty. You can get out of trouble and get your system working by buying a replacement part to swap out the defective component. You might instead decide to use some of the working components as a basis for upgrading the system. Quite often, a dead PC is just the stimulus that people need to upgrade or build a new PC!

Don't Throw Away Any of These Things!

When you buy any item we recommend that you keep the following items in case of future problems:

- **Sales receipt.** This is vitally important because without this as proof of purchase and proof of when you bought the item, many vendors or manufacturers won't deal with you (or at least give you a harder time).

- **Outer packaging.** If the item you bought was sent through the mail or by courier then keep any boxes for at least a few weeks in case you need to return the item (or at least until you complete building the PC).

- **Documentation.** This will tell you what to do in the event of a problem. Initially it's a good idea to keep all the part's documentation with the actual part, but after you've installed it into the PC and the PC is working you might want to move it into a "Your PC" folder or use some other method of filing it away where it's safe but easy to get at in the event of trouble. This might be something that you keep and add to (if you upgrade the system, say) over the life of the PC.

- **Packaging.** This is handy to return the item in. Otherwise, you'll have to find alternative packaging.

Before Things Go Wrong

Your life will be so much easier if, before things start to go wrong, you start making plans for the possibility that things might go wrong. You don't need to make a Herculean effort — a few simple steps can help you if trouble does come your way.

- **Keep packaging for a few weeks.** I know that some people like to keep their place tidy but we'd recommend that you put up with keeping the packaging of products for at least 30 days after purchase (or 30 days from installing or starting to use the product or component if possible). This way, you will have everything that you need to send back or take back any defective parts you might encounter.

- **Fill out and send off any registration cards or documents.** This way the manufacturer knows about you (they might want to take that opportunity to send you junk mail too, so look out for any boxes to check to tell them that you don't want any junk), not only if you have to get in touch with them because of a problem but also if they want to get in touch with you because of a product recall or important safety information.

100% Reliability Is an Illusion . . . 99.5% Is Not!

Because a PC is made up of so many different parts (parts that you are now very familiar with), and those parts themselves hide a greater level of unseen complexity, there is, unfortunately, a good chance that something will eventually go wrong. No matter how high the quality of the parts you have used, how much they cost, or how well you looked after them, it's impossible for any manufacturer to guarantee that every component will reach the end user in good condition. Even if the manufacturer takes the utmost care of the components, there's no telling how badly they might have been handled in transit or by the vendor you bought them from.

Things can and sometimes do go wrong.

If all the parts that make up your PC are in good working order now, that might not be so in the following weeks, months, or years. Given enough time, even the best components will fail.

What to Do When Things Go Wrong

Okay, you have a problem. What do you do?

How you progress depends primarily on how old the defective parts are. We'll look at a number of scenarios:

- Products that are dead or defective when you open the package

- Products that fail within this first days or weeks

- Products that fail within the first year

DOA

DOA is an abbreviation that stands for "dead on arrival," and this is what components that are dead or defective at the point of purchase are usually called.

DOA components cover a few possible scenarios:

- Components damaged in transit or damaged before sale. Basically, you open the package or parcel and find that the component is obviously smashed.

- Components that don't work once connected up. The device looks OK but just doesn't work.

In either of these situations, you need to return the component.

Returning a Product to a Store

When dealing with DOA components, the quickest and easiest way to get a replacement is to take the parts back to the store where you bought them from. You can ask either for a replacement or for your money back.

When you return a product, make sure you return all of it, including the packaging, any cables or power supplies and any manuals, CDs and instruction booklets.

Be clear about what your problem is and how you came to the conclusion that the item is defective. Also, remember to take your sales receipt along with you! Most stores will be more than happy to keep a customer happy and gladly exchange the products for you or arrange a refund.

Returning a Product Bought by Mail Order

If you bought the DOA component via mail order, then the first thing you need to do is to contact the vendor and let them know what's wrong and ask for advice on how you should return the product. Never return a product without first getting in touch with the vendor. Most simply won't accept returns unless accompanied by a valid returns code. Also, by getting in touch with the vendor in advance, you can discuss what you would like to have happen after they receive the DOA component or product.

Ways to contact the mail order company include

- Email (or web contact form)
- Telephone
- Snail mail (takes a long time and isn't recommended)

Tip

One of the best ways is using email (available on their website usually). That way, not only do you get everything down in writing but you also get a response in writing. In addition, you get the contact name of the person at the company who will be handling your problem.

When you get in touch with a mail order company make sure that you give them the following information:

- Your name
- Address
- Order number
- Defective item in question
- Brief description of how the item is defective

When you get in touch with a mail order company by email or web contact form, then allow them two working days to respond (many will respond earlier). If you don't get a response, then you can either send another message or escalate to the phone.

When you do return the product, make sure you return everything, including the invoice (keep a copy), your complete contact information, and a brief description of the problem with the item. If you were given a returns number, include this both on the note inside the package and also write it clearly on the outside of the package.

Take special care when packaging the item. You don't want to take any chances that the item is going to get even more damaged in transit. The best packaging to return a product in is the packaging it was sent to you in — that way the vendor can't say that you didn't take enough care of it in transit!

Think carefully about whether to insure the package in transit. If the package gets lost of further damaged in transit, the vendor might not take responsibility for it and you could be out of pocket.

Products or Components That Fail within Days or Weeks

Generally, you can deal with products that fail within a few days or weeks in much the same way as you would deal with an item that was found to be DOA. Most vendors and stores are more than happy to exchange products that become faulty soon after purchase. Most vendors have a good relationship with their suppliers and can exchange a defective product for a good one and return it up the supply chain back to the manufacturer. Get in touch with the vendor and see if they will help you.

Most products come with at least a year's warranty (and some with longer warranties — check your documentation!), and given the fierce competition between manufacturers most nowadays offer customers good warranty terms in order to keep an existing customer.

Note

Occasionally, you might come across a vendor or supplier who, after selling you a product a few days go, just won't want to know about any problems afterwards. If you come across a company like this, we'd recommend that you not deal with that company again. There are plenty of good vendors out there, especially in this age of e-commerce, and there's no reason to have to continue dealing with a poor quality vendor.

But what do you do?

Check your documentation; there should be information on what to do if something goes wrong. Sometimes it's an email address, sometimes a telephone number, and sometimes a website. Other manufacturers might offer you a variety of ways to get in touch with them. You are looking for a tech support contact — even if you know that the component or product is dead you will probably have to go through tech support and allow them to offer you hints and suggestions before they will probably accept that the product is actually defective and replace it.

One key thing to remember is to be patient during this process and remain helpful, courteous, and cheerful at all times, even though you might not actually feel that way!

Again, if possible, favor using email as a contact medium over other methods because of the written record it offers and because you will get a contact name of the person working with you.

When you get in touch with a manufacturer, make sure you give them the following information:

- Your name and complete contact information
- Defective item in question
- Details of where you bought the item
- Date of purchase
- Brief description of how the item is defective

Products or Components That Fail within a Year

If your product or component fails after the first few weeks, you are definitely in the hands of the manufacturer for warranty support. Very few vendors will offer assistance for products older than a couple of months.

Look through your documentation or look for the manufacturer's website by using a search engine and then contact them for details on how to get a replacement. There are some companies that don't really want you to get in touch!

Same contact guidelines apply:

- Your name and complete contact information
- Defective item in question
- Details of where you bought the item
- Date of purchase
- Brief description of how the item is defective

Note Check out the "Warranties Q&A" section for information on options that might be open to you beyond the first 12 months.

Warranties Q&A

What follows is a quick Q&A that relates to problems and warranties that should answer most of your questions.

1. Are problems common?

No. Given the complexity of the PC and the components that it contains, a PC is a surprisingly robust and reliable bit of kit, and you should get hundreds of thousands of hours of use out of the components.

2. What are the legal definitions of a "warranty"?

This varies — check locally and seek advice if in doubt.

3. Do I have to return a defective product in the original packaging?

No. Remember, you are returning a defective product, not defective packaging. However, it's a good idea to keep packaging until you have finished building the PC just in case you do encounter a DOA component because if you use the original packaging to return the product, no one can quibble about possible damage in transit due to using the incorrect packaging.

Note If, however, you are returning a product because you ordered the wrong item, then you will need the original packaging in order to have any chance of a refund.

4. What if I break something?

Technically, you are not entitled to an exchange product if the damage is the result of negligence or misuse on your part.

However, if you took reasonable care when handling and using the product, then most vendors or manufacturers will honor the warranty unless you deliberately tampered with the item or misused it.

5. What if I bought the wrong item?

In the event that you bought the wrong product, most vendors will be happy to help, although some might ask you to pay a restocking fee for the extra workload and inconvenience. For mail order products, you will be expected to cover both the costs of returning the wrong item and delivery costs of the replacement item.

6. Do I need to keep a receipt?

As a rule, yes, although many online vendors will accept an order number as proof of purchase. Most manufacturers will require proof of purchase if you go to them for help.

7. Do I have to have filled in and returned a warranty card in order to get any technical assistance?

No.

8. Doesn't a vendor have to give me a one-year warranty?

No. A 12-month warranty is usually offered by the manufacturer, although many good vendors will assist you in the event you have a problem within the first few weeks.

9. Are the extended warranties offered by stores any good?

As a rule, no. The cost is high and the service offered is generally poor.

10. Can warranties last longer than 12 months?

Indeed they can. For example, the exchange period of a hard drive can last for many years. In the case of a dead hard drive, it's always a good idea to check with the manufacturer's website to see if the product is covered under an exchange warranty.

11. I don't have a sales receipt! What can I do?

Don't give up! There's still hope! Many stores keep a copy of the sales receipt and will be able to check their own records if you can remember the date you bought the product.

If you ordered via the Internet, check your email, because you should have a confirmation email of your order.

Another benefit of online ordering is that many online vendors keep your order history—you could always print out the appropriate page and present that as proof of purchase.

With some products (hard drives being a good example), you don't need any proof of purchase. The drive will have on it the manufacturing date, and the makers will offer a fixed warranty period on drives.

12. If my hard drive breaks, will the maker recover my data?

No. Always, always, always make backups of your data.

13. Are there warranty issues with buying goods from a different country?

There can be. Many manufacturers only warrant goods in the country in which they were sold. If, for example, you live in Europe and you bought a product via mail order from the United States, then European tech support may not honor your warranty. With many devices they can tell where the product was sold—from the serial number, for example.

It's always better to buy goods from your own country. Quite often freight costs, import taxes, and general hassles of returning things and warranty problems quickly make any savings vanish and can in fact cost you much more in the long run.

14. Are second-hand parts covered by warranty?

Not usually. Be wary of anyone that offers you much in the way of any kind of warranty on second-hand parts.

15. What kind of warranties come with software?

Software warranties are quite complex. Usually there is a separate warranty for the actual physical discs that you receive (which can be anything from 30 days to a year) and a support period. Some software makers limit you to a fixed number of free support calls, while others offer unlimited support.

Check your software documentation for more details.

Summary

In this, the final chapter in this book, we've looked at what you should do if or when things go wrong with your PC.

We hope that you won't need this information, but that if you do, that you find it useful and that you get your system up and running quickly.

All the best with your new PC! May it give you years of trouble-free service!

Appendices

part

IV

Useful Websites

This appendix lists websites that you might find useful to visit before, during, and after you build your PC. We have categorized these websites according to their primary content, but many will have information that covers a number of categories.

Remember that anything you download can contain viruses, worms, Trojans, and other malicious applications, so make sure that you scan all downloads with an up-to-date virus scanner.

in this appendix

☑ Discover useful PC-related websites

☑ Hardware links

☑ Software links

☑ General links

Table A-1 Useful Hardware-Related Sites

Name	URL
Ace's Hardware	www.aceshardware.com
Anandtech Hardware Reviews	www.anandtech.com
BitLabz	www.bitlabz.com
Designtechnica.com	www.designtechnica.com
EXTREME Overclocking — tweaking PC hardware to the max	www.extremeoverclocking.com
ExtremeTech	www.extremetech.com
Hardware Fusion	www.hardwarefusion.net
Hardware Secrets — uncomplicating the complicated hardware secrets	www.hardwaresecrets.com
HotHardware — the hottest PC hardware tested and burned in	www.hothardware.com
InsaneTek	www.insanetek.com
IT Reviews	www.itreviews.co.uk
Legit Reviews	www.legitreviews.com
LOSTCIRCUITS	www.lostcircuits.com
Motherboards.org — motherboard reviews, news, guides, and tools	www.motherboards.org
PC Magazine	www.pcmag.com
PCStats.com	www.pcstats.com
StorageReview	www.storagereview.com
Tech Report	www.tech-report.com
TechSpot — the PC enthusiast information resource	www.techspot.com
Techware Labs	www.techwarelabs.com
The PC Doctor	www.pcdoctor-guide.com
Tom's Hardware Guide	www.tomshardware.com
ZDNet — technology reviews and buying advice	http://reviews-zdnet.com.com

Table A-2   Useful Software Sites

Name	URL
Acronis (backup and hard drive utilities)	www.acronis.com
Ad-Aware (spyware/adware scanner)	www.lavasoftusa.com/software/adaware
Adobe Reader for PDF	www.adobe.com/products/acrobat/readstep2.html
AVG Anti Virus (free)	www.grisoft.com
CDBurnerXP Pro	www.cdburnerxp.se
Crimson Editor (free text/HTML editor)	www.crimsoneditor.com
DiskInternals (deleted-file recovery tool)	www.diskinternals.com
Executive Software (defragmentation and undelete utilities)	www.executive.com
Firefox browser (free)	www.mozilla.org/products/firefoxwww.firefox.org
IMsecure — instant messaging privacy tool (free and commercial)	www.imsecure.com
McAfee — antivirus software and intrusion prevention solutions	www.nai.com
Microsoft AntiSpyware	www.microsoft.com/athome/security/spyware/software
Mozilla browser (free)	www.mozilla.org
Nero — CD-burning utility	www.nero.com
Open Office (free office suite compatible with all other major office suites)	www.openoffice.org
Opera browser	www.opera.com
Panda Software (free online virus scan)	www.pandasoftware.com/activescan
Paragon (backup and hard drive utilities)	www.paragon.ag
PGP (encryption)	www.pgp.com
Reports (ISP reviews and free bandwidth tests)	www.dslreports.com
ShieldsUp (free firewall test)	www.grc.com
SiSoftware utilities	www.sisoftware.net
Sophos antivirus	www.sophos.com
Spybot Search and Destroy adware/spyware scanner	www.safer-networking.org

Continued

Table A-2 *(continued)*

Name	URL
Symantec (antivirus/anti-spam/backup/utilities)	www.symantec.com
Sysinternals freeware tools and utilities	www.sysinternals.com
Trend Micro (free online virus scan)	http://housecall.trendmicro.com
UltraEdit text editor	www.ultraedit.com
WinAce (compression utility)	www.winace.com
WinZip (compression utility)	winzip.com
Zonelabs firewall software (free and commercial)	www.zonelabs.com

Table A-3   General Support and Information Sites

Name	URL
BootDisks	www.bootdisk.com
Computer Hope	www.computerhope.com
Darik's Boot and Nuke (disk-wiping utility)	http://dban.sourceforge.net
DriverGuide.com (hardware drivers)	www.driverguide.com
Help-Site.com Computer Manuals	http://help-site.com
Kingsley-Hughes.com (authors' website)	www.kingsley-hughes.com
Microsoft	http://support.microsoft.com
PC Doctor	www.pcdoctor-guide.com
PC Hell	www.pchell.com
PC Help	www.helpwithpcs.com
PC Pitstop (free PC diagnostics and tuneups)	www.pcpitstop.com
PC Sympathy	www.pcsympathy.com
Practically Networked	www.practicallynetworked.com
Software Tips and Tricks	www.softwaretipsandtricks.com
TechIMO	www.techimo.com
Tek-Tips	www.tek-tips.com
The Elder Geek	www.theeldergeek.com

Name	URL
Troubleshooting Windows XP	www.kellys-korner-xp.com
USBMan (USB help and information)	www.usbman.com
Windows IT Library	www.windowsitlibrary.com

Table A-4   Software Download Sites

Name	URL
Download.com	www.download.com
Free Download Center	www.freedownloadscenter.com
IT Pro Downloads	http://itprodownloads.com
Microsoft Download Center	www.microsoft.com/downloads
Rocketdownload.com	www.rocketdownload.com
TopShareware.com	www.topshareware.com
Tucows	www.tucows.com
WinPlanet	www.winplanet.com
ZDNet Downloads	http://downloads-zdnet.com.com

Checklist

This appendix provides a checklist of tools, parts, and software that you will need when embarking on a build-it-yourself PC project. Some items are optional and are marked as such.

Table B-1   Tool Checklist

	✓
Screwdriver, Phillips, size 0	❏
Screwdriver, Phillips, size 1	❏
Screwdriver, Phillips, size 2	❏
Screwdriver, straight edge, size 2	❏
Screwdriver, straight edge, size 4	❏
Screwdriver, straight edge, size 6	❏
ESD wrist strap	❏
Flashlight (preferably plastic body, LED)	❏
Magnifier (optional)	❏
Multitool (optional but really handy!)	❏
Needle-nosed pliers (optional)	❏
Diagonal cutters (optional)	❏
Tweezers (optional)	❏
Multimeter (optional)	❏
Spare ESD bags	❏
Pen/pencil and paper	❏
Adhesive labels (optional)	❏
Plastic cable ties (optional but worthwhile investing in for a professional finish)	❏
Small first aid kit (optional but can be handy for small cuts)	❏

Table B-2   Hardware Checklist

	✓
PC case	❏
Power supply unit (PSU)	❏
Motherboard	❏
CPU	❏
CPU cooler	❏

	✓
RAM	❏
Hard drive(s)	❏
Video adaptor/graphics card (optional if motherboard has one on-board)	❏
Sound card (optional if motherboard has one on-board)	❏
Floppy disk drive (optional)	❏
Optical drive (CD/DVD/recordable CD/recordable DVD)	❏
Hard drive data cables (one per hard drive or optical drive)	❏
Floppy drive data cable (if fitting floppy disk drive)	❏
Drive rails (needed if fitting hard drive to 5 1/4-inch bay)	❏
Keyboard	❏
Mouse	❏
Monitor	❏
Power cables	❏
Modem (optional)	❏
Network adaptor (optional, sometimes integrated into the motherboard)	❏
Speakers (optional)	❏
Microphone (optional)	❏
Printer (optional)	❏

Table B-3   Software Checklist

	✓
Boot disk	❏
Burn-in software (optional)	❏
Hardware drivers	❏
Operating system	❏

Hardware Manufacturers

What follows is a listing of hardware manufacturers for a variety of PC components. We've chosen the biggest manufacturers here to give you the widest choice possible in hardware for your PC. This list isn't definitive, so if you can't find what you want here or want to look further afield, fire up your favorite search engine and spend a few hours on some web-based research.

Parts and specifications change regularly, so take your time and work through the listings to find the right items for you and your new PC.

Table C-1 Hardware Vendors

CPU

AMD	www.amd.com
Intel	www.intel.com

Performance Cooling Fans

Akasa	www.akasa.com.tw
Coolermaster	www.coolermaster.com
Thermaltake	www.thermaltake.com
Zalman	www.zalmantech.com

Motherboard

Abit	www.abit-usa.com
ASUS	www.asus.com
Gigabyte	www.giga-byte.com
Intel	www.intel.com
Microstar/MSI	www.msicomputer.com
PCChips	www.pcchips.com.tw
Tyan	www.tyan.com

RAM

Corsair	www.corsairmicro.com
Crucial	www.crucial.com
Kingston	www.kingston.com
OCZ	www.ocztechnology.com
PNY	www.pny.com

Hard Drive

Maxtor	www.maxtor.com
Western Digital	www.wdc.com
Seagate	www.seagate.com

Video Adaptors/Graphics Card Chipsets

ATI	www.ati.com
Nvidia	www.nvidia.com

Optical Drives

Iomega	www.iomega.com
LaCie	www.lacie.com
LG	www.lge.com
LiteOn	www.liteon.com
Plextor	www.plextor.com
Sony	www.sony.com
TDK	www.tdk.com

Glossary

Glossary

Term	Definition
Access time	The search performance of a hard drive or other storage device, usually measured in milliseconds. In simple terms this is how long the device takes to find a file.
ACPI	Advanced Configuration and Power Interface. This is a standard that defines power management of desktops, laptops, and servers.
AGP	Accelerated Graphics Port. This is a card expansion slot on the motherboard designed specifically for video adaptors. It offers far superior performance to PCI-based video adaptor technology.
ATA	Advanced Technology Attachment. The official name given to the IDE hard drive interface.
ATAPI	Advanced Technology Attachment Packet Interface. An interface that allows devices such as CD drives, DVD drives, hard drives, and tape storage to be connected to a PC.
ATX	ATX is the most common style, or form factor, of motherboard used today. It differs from its predecessors by changing the orientation of the board in the case (the long side goes from side to side at the rear of the case) and also by having all the I/O connectors (such as keyboard, mouse, USB, etc.) built onto the motherboard.
Baby AT	This is the oldest of the motherboard styles or form factors available. This motherboard is designed to fit into a case with the long side back to front and the I/O connectors (such as keyboard, mouse, USB, etc.) are attached onto a bracket that is fitted into an adaptor card slot at the rear of the case.
Bandwidth	This is the rate at which information can be sent along a data channel. The greater the bandwidth the more data can be sent per unit time.
Banks	RAM module slots on the motherboard.
Bezel	The decorative surround that fits around CD and DVD drives.
Binary	A number system in which there are only zeros and ones. This is at the core of computing, since all computer data is ultimately a series of zeros and ones (of on and off pulses of electricity) and can, therefore, be represented by binary numbers.
Bit	Binary digit. This is a single digit number in base 2 (binary), in other words, either a 1 or a 0.
BIOS	Basic input/output system. This is software that exists on the CMOS chip on the motherboard. It contains all the code needed to control items such as the keyboard, hard drive, communications ports and basic graphics display and also carries out the function of loading the operating system.

Term	Definition
Boot disk/disc	A floppy disk or CD that contains all the files necessary to start a PC.
bps	Bits per second. A bit is a single digit number in base 2, in other words, either a 1 or a 0. Bps is a measure of how fast data can be moved.
BTX	Balanced Technology Extended. A new replacement for the ATX form factor motherboard and case. Optimized for better airflow and quieter PCs.
Buffer	An area of computer RAM reserved for temporary storage of data that is waiting to be transferred to another device.
Bus	A set of hardware lines (wires) that are used to transfer data. Buses are used to connect the CPU to RAM, hard drives, and input/output devices.
Byte	8 bits, which can make up a single character of alphanumeric data.
Cache	High-performance RAM used to speed up data transfer between hard drive and RAM or RAM and CPU.
CD	Compact disc. See CD-ROM.
CD-R	Compact disc-recordable. A compact disc that can be written to using a CD-R-compatible drive.
CD-ROM	Compact disc read-only memory. A CD-ROM is an optical disc capable of holding 650–700 MB of data.
CD-RW	Compact disc read/write. A compact disc that can be written to and erased hundreds of times with a CD-RW-capable drive.
Chip	Generic name given to an integrated circuit.
Chipset	A term used to describe the architecture on an integrated circuit. While many items have a chipset, this term is commonly applied to motherboards, video adaptors, and modems.
Clock cycles	The rate at which instructions are processed by the CPU. The smaller the interval, the faster the CPU can process instructions and the faster the perceived speed.
CMOS	Complementary metal oxide semiconductor. A technology used in making transistors. These transistors are very efficient and require little power to use. In a PC, CMOS memory is used to store the date and time and other basic system settings.
COM port	Communications port, typically a serial port.
Connector header	Two or more pins on a motherboard onto which a connector can be fitted.
CPU	Central processing unit. The brain of a PC.
Crash	Unexpected error.

Continued

Glossary *(continued)*

Term	Definition
Daisy chain	A term used to describe the ability to link devices together in a chain using cables. Some USB and FireWire devices have the capability.
Data cable	A ribbon style cable with three connectors on it, one at each end and one in the middle. Used to connect PATA hard drives and CD/DVD drives to an IDE connector.
DDR	Double data rate. An advanced version of SDRAM memory.
DIMM	Dual inline memory module. Computer RAM type.
Diskette	Another name for a floppy disk or any disk-based cartridge system.
DMA	Direct Memory Access. A technology to speed up data transfer between the computer peripherals (such as hard drives) and the RAM by circumventing CPU time limits.
Drive rail	Rails used to fit 3 1/2-inch hard drives into a 5 1/4-inch drive bay.
Driver	Software used to control hardware.
DSL/ADSL	Digital Subscriber Line/Asymmetric DSL. A method for transferring data over a regular phone line at faster than modem speeds.
DVD	Digital versatile disc. A high-capacity optical disc that looks like a CD but can hold 4.7 GB of data.
Dual channel	A memory technology that allows RAM modules in to banks to be used simultaneously.
DVD+R	Digital versatile disc recordable. DVD+R discs look like regular DVDs but can be used to record data. A single-sided, single-layer DVD+R disc can store 4.7 GB of data, while double-layer discs can store 8.5 GB and double-sided DVD-Rs can store 9.4 GB. The DVD+R is a recording format and is not quite as common as the DVD-R format, but it is still supported by most current DVD players and DVD-ROM drives.
DVD±R	Drives that can read both DVD+R and DVD-R discs are often referred to as DVD±R drives.
DVD-R	Digital versatile disc recordable. DVD-R discs look like regular DVDs but can be used to record data. A single-sided, single-layer DVD-R discs can store 4.7 GB of data, while double-layer discs can store 8.5 GB and double-sided DVD-Rs can store 9.4 GB. The DVD-R is a recording format and is more prevalent that the DVD+R format.

Term	Definition
DVD-RAM	Digital versatile disc random access memory. DVD-RAMs are writable DVDs that can also be erased and rewritten like the DVD-RW and DVD+RW formats. However, DVD-RAM discs can only be used when placed in an enclosing cartridge, which means that they don't fit into most standard DVD players or DVD-ROM drives.
DVD+RW	Digital versatile disc rewritable. A DVD+RW is like a DVD+R but can be erased and rewritten to. A DVD+RW disc must be erased before new data to be added. DVD+RW discs can hold 4.7 GB of data and are not available in double-sided or double-layer versions.
DVD-RW	Digital versatile disc rewritable. A DVD-RW is like a DVD-R but can be erased and rewritten. A DVD-RW disc must be erased before new data to be added. DVD+RW discs can hold 4.7 GB of data and are not available in double-sided or double-layer versions.
DVI	Digital Video Interface. A video connection standard that support both analog and digital displays.
ECC	Error checking and correction. See Parity.
Ethernet	The most common type of connection computers use in a local area network (LAN).
Ethernet card	An expansion card added to a PC that allows it to connect to an Ethernet-based network.
Expansion slot	A slot on a motherboard that accepts expansion cards (such as internal modems or video adaptors). The two most common types are PCI and AGP.
Fan	A component that drives cooler air over the heatsink to carry away the heat.
FAT32	File allocation table 32-bit. A table stored on a hard drive that keeps track of all your files and allows the PC locate them.
FireWire	Also known as an IEEE 1394 port. A high-speed interface developed by Apple Computer in the mid-1990s, which can be used to connect devices such as digital video cameras, hard drives, audio interfaces, and MP3 players to a computer. A FireWire port comes in speeds of 400 Mbps and 800 Mbps.
Firmware	Program code loaded onto a device used to control how the device works. This code can be updated when new versions are released. Examples of devices that have firmware include CD/DVD drives, digital cameras, and MP3 players.
Flash memory	Electrically erasable programmable read-only memory. Flash memory can be used to store BIOS information but nowadays it has found its way into digital cameras and USB storage devices.

Continued

Glossary *(continued)*

Term	Definition
Form factor	The physical layout of a motherboard with respect to the relative position of the expansion slots, the number of slots, the size of the motherboard, and the orientation of the motherboard inside the PC case.
Format	The process of testing and preparing a disk to accept data.
Freeware	Free software.
Frontside bus	Also known as the FSB or system bus. This connects the CPU to the RAM and other motherboard components, such as PCI cards and AGP cards. The speed of the FSB can be measured in MHz or GHz and is typically a ratio of the CPU speed.
GHz	1,000,000,000 cycles per second. It is used as a measure of the data processing speed of electronic devices.
Gigabyte	A measure of data equal to 1,073,741,824 bytes.
GPU	Graphics processing unit. This is a CPU used on video adaptors to speed up display of complex graphics.
Hard disk	Another name for a hard drive.
Hard drive	The name given to the disk-based storage system used in a PC. This is where data is stored permanently (as opposed to RAM which is temporary).
Heatsink	A machined block of copper or aluminum that carries the heat away from a component such as a CPU.
Hot swap	The name given to the ability to be able to disconnect and reconnect devices on a PC when the system is switched on.
Hub	A hardware device that is used to network multiple computers together.
IDE	Integrated Device Electronics. This is the most widely used hard drive interface currently on the market. "Integrated" means that the drive controller is integrated onto the drive itself.
IDE controller interface	Motherboard-based hardware that interfaces an IDE device with the PC.
ISA	Industry Standard Architecture. Architecture (now obsolete) used to connect expansion cards to the motherboard.
Jumper	A small metal connector that acts as an on/off switch. This is often used to change hardware configurations. Jumpers are now most commonly found on hard drives and CD/DVD drives.
Jumper header	Two or more pins onto which a jumper can be attached.
Kbps	Kilobits per second. A measure of data transfer rates.

Term	Definition
Keyed connector	A special connector that can only be fitted into the appropriate socket one way thanks to the use of a slot. Most connectors on a PC are keyed to prevent improper fitting of components.
Kilobyte	A measure of data equal to 1,024 bytes.
Latency	The amount of time it takes to move a packet of data. Generally measured in milliseconds (ms).
LCD	Liquid Crystal Display.
Legacy device	An old and obsolete device.
LightScribe	A direct-disc labeling technology. Using special CD/DVD drives and special discs you can label discs as easily as burning them.
Master boot record (MBR)	A small program that is executed when a computer starts up. This is used to begin the boot-up process.
Mbps	Megabits per second. A measure of data transfer rates.
Media	Media is a name given to a data storage device such as a hard drive, floppy disk, CD, or DVD or flash memory.
Megabyte	A measure of data equal to 1,048,576 bytes.
MHz	1,000,000 cycles per second. It is used as a measure of the data processing speed of electronic devices.
Micro ATX	A variation on the ATX form factor. A Micro ATX motherboard is smaller and has fewer expansion slots.
Modem	*Modulator/dem*odulator. A device that allows data to be sent over a phone line.
Motherboard	The main circuit board inside a PC.
NTFS	New Technology File System. Developed originally by Microsoft for Windows NT, it is the most common file system for Windows XP. Effectively replaces FAT32 in most Windows NT, Windows 2000, and Windows XP computers.
OEM	Original equipment manufacturer. A company that produces hardware or software to be marketed under another company's brand name.
On-board sound	A motherboard that comes with sound capability. A system with *on-board sound* capability doesn't need any additional cards or attachments in order to output sound (apart from speakers).
On-board video	Support for a monitor that's been built directly onto the motherboard. adapter

Continued

Glossary (continued)

Term	Definition
Optical drive	Any drive that uses an optical system to read data. Optical drives include CD-ROM, CD-RW, DVD-ROM, DVD±RW, and Blu-ray drives.
Overclocking	A procedure in which the speed of a device is increased beyond what it was marketed as. CPUs and video adaptors are the more commonly overclocked devices. Overclocking has downsides because it can result in damage or premature failure of the device.
Parallel port	A 25-pin interface found on the back of a PC and is used for connecting devices such as printers or scanners.
Partition	A section of hard drive to which data can be written to. A single hard drive can have multiple partitions.
Parity	Error detection added to early types of memory to reduce on data errors that could cause corruption and crashes.
PCI	Peripheral Component Interconnect. A hardware bus used to connect expansion cards to a PC.
Peripheral	An external PC device.
Pins	Two or more metal connectors on a device that allow it to be plugged into a slot.
Platters	The surfaces inside a hard drive onto which data is written.
Plug and Play	The name given to the technology that allows devices to be plugged into a PC and be recognized by the system and drivers then installed. This demands far less interaction on the part of the end user.
POST	Power-on self-test. A test carried out by a PC on vital systems at startup prior to boot up.
PSU	Power supply unit. A device that accepts line voltage and converts it to the correct electrical supply for the PC.
RAID	Redundant array of independent disks. RAID is a method of storing data on multiple hard disks where the disks are arranged so that the computer sees them all as one large disk. The big advantage of RAID is speed and reliability.
RAM	Random access memory. Memory chips attached to the motherboard that provide fast temporary storage for data.
RDRAM	Rambus Dynamic Random Access Memory. A very fast type of computer memory.
Recordable drive	Used for recording a CD (known as CD-R discs).
Removable storage	The name given to data storage media that can be disconnected from the PC.

Term	Definition
ReWritable CD drive	Used to record a CD and to erase and rerecord certain CD discs (known as CD-RW discs) numerous times.
Ribbon cable	Flat cables used to connect hard drives and floppy drives to the motherboard.
ROM	Read-only memory.
RPM	Revolutions per minute. Used to measure the rotational speed of a hard drive or optical drive.
S.M.A.R.T.	Self-Monitoring Analysis and Reporting Technology. S.M.A.R.T. monitors hard drives for any indication that the drive might be faulty or failing and then documents and analyzes this data. S.M.A.R.T. can be set to warn the user of an impending hard drive failure.
SATA	Serial Advanced Technology Attachment or Serial ATA. This is an interface used to connect ATA hard drives to a computer's motherboard. It is faster and more efficient than ATA.
SCSI	Small Computer System Interface which is pronounced "scuzzy." This is an interface that can be used to connect devices such as hard drives and scanners to a PC.
SDRAM	Synchronous Dynamic Random Access Memory. A type of computer memory.
Seek time	The amount of time taken by a device to find the correct position for the data on storage media so that it can be read.
Serial port	The serial port is a 9-pin connection on PCs that is used to connect peripherals such as mice and modems.
Shareware	Software distributed that has a time-limited trial, after which a license must be bought.
SIMM	Single in-line memory module. An older type of computer memory.
Sleep mode	A power-saving mode that a PC can enter when not used.
Slots	Generic name given to an expansion slot on a motherboard.
Socket	The generic term for the ZIF socket into which the CPU is fitted.
Substrate	The material that makes up the circuit board (the board that's usually colored green, onto which components are soldered).
Subwoofer	A low-frequency speaker that adds low bass to the overall sound.
TFT	Thin film transistor. Transistors used in high-quality flat panel liquid crystal displays (LCDs).

Continued

Glossary *(continued)*

Term	Definition
Trackball	A type of mouse where a ball is moved by a finger or thumb as opposed to the whole mouse needing to be moved.
Trojan	A program that conceals malicious code such as a virus or worm.
Ultra DMA	Technology that allows for the fast transfer of data between a hard drive and memory.
Uninterruptible power supply (UPS)	A battery backup system that provides power for a PC in the event of power interruption.
USB	Universal Serial Bus. A commonly used computer port that allows 127 devices to be connected to a port and has transfer speeds ranging from 12 Mbps for USB 1.1 and 480 Mbps for USB 2.0.
VGA	Video Graphics Array. The standard monitor or display interface used by PCs.
Video adapter	An expansion card that lets you hook up a monitor to your system.
Virtual memory	Hard drive space used as an extension to RAM when additional memory is needed.
Virus	A malicious program written to propagate from one PC to another. Most viruses cause damage to the PC.
Volume	Another name for a partition.
Wi-Fi	Wireless networking technology. Short for Wireless Fidelity. A set of standards for wireless computer networking based on the 802.11 standards. Common variants of the standard are 802.11a, 802.11b, and 802.11g. Each describes a version of the standard with different speed and range characteristics.
Work area	The place you're going to be working in, such as your living room or garage.
Work space	The area you are going to be moving about in when working in the work area.
Worm	A name given to malicious code that is transmitted by email from one PC to another.
Writable drive	A drive that allows you to take data from your PC and write or burn it to a CD or a DVD.
ZIF (Zero Insertion Force)	The socket into which a CPU is fitted. No force is required to fit the CPU, hence the name.
Zip	The name of the most commonly used compressed file format.

Index

Continued

How to take it to the Extreme.

If you enjoyed this book, there are many others like it for you. From *Podcasting* to *Hacking Firefox*, ExtremeTech books can fulfill your urge to hack, tweak and modify, providing the tech tips and tricks readers need to get the most out of their hi-tech lives.